THE
SPA BOOK

THE SPA BOOK

A GUIDED, PERSONAL TOUR OF HEALTH RESORTS AND BEAUTY SPAS FOR MEN AND WOMEN

Judy Babcock & Judy Kennedy

Crown Publishers, Inc.
New York

The quotation which appears on page 114 is from *I Have Abandoned My Search for Truth, and Am Now Looking for a Good Fantasy*, published by Woodbridge Press Publishing Company, © 1980 by Ashleigh Brilliant. Used by permission.

Published by Crown Publishers, Inc., One Park Avenue, New York, New York 10016 and simultaneously in Canada by General Publishing Company Limited

Manufactured in the United States of America

Library of Congress Cataloging in Publication Data
Babcock, Judy.
   The spa book.

   Includes index.
   1. Health resorts, watering-places, etc.—United States—Directories. 2. Health resorts, watering-places, etc.—Mexico—Directories. I. Kennedy, Judy. II. Title. III. Title: Beauty spas.
RA805.B32 1983   613'.122'02573   82-18249

ISBN: 0-517-549506
10 9 8 7 6 5 4 3 2 1

First Edition

For Frank
and
for Mark and Amy

Special thanks to Marcie Legg, Judy Hartwich, Carmen Norona, Penny Wortham, Shay Sayer, Marlene Hasler and Faith Annette Sand

Contents

CONTENTS

THE NORTHEAST 189

MEXICO 235

CANADA 255

THE WEST INDIES 267

GLOSSARY AND INDEX 271

Introduction

There are times when life is just not moving with its usual grace, vigor and direction; when all the things you normally do as a matter of course seem harder than usual, and people around you start to make oblique (and totally unreasonable) comments about how cranky you are lately.

If only you could find some energy or achieve some simple peace of mind! What you really need is a fresh new experience, some time and a place apart to pull body and mind back into shape. What you really need is a spa.

Although the variety of programs and facilities is staggering, a spa is basically any place that offers an organized program of nutrition, exercise and beauty services.

The old image most people have of a spa as a fat farm for middle-aged dowagers couldn't be more wrong. An extraordinary range of people now regularly attend spas: men, women, the young and the old, couples and families, struggling professionals, the very rich and not so rich, the fit, the unfit, and busy overcommitted people as well as those with too much time on their hands.

In response, spas are beginning to move into the mainstream of the American lifestyle. The traditional focus of most spas has shifted from pampering and beautifying their guests to helping them become more fit, more healthy and more tolerant of stress.

What kind of spa is right for you? What is it going to cost? How far will you have to travel? What should you pack to wear at a spa? Will you feel out of place going alone? Will you meet interesting people or will it be full of boring, out of shape and self-involved types? What exactly happens during a massage? Will you be regimented or can you plan your own program? Can you bring a lover or spouse? And once home again, how can you continue to benefit from what you've learned?

By visiting twenty-six spas from Maine to California and from Canada to Mexico, and from extensive research into thirty-eight more, we've been able to present here a varied and representative selection of spas. We've tried to describe exactly what each has to offer by way of programs, philosophies and facilities, and in the process we've attempted to answer most of the questions a prospective spa-goer might have.

Although our intention was always to write a positive book, we also felt an obligation to be honest; if the food was adequate but not too creative, we have said so. If the exercise rooms are crowded, we mention that too.

We wrote this book in order to share our enthusiasm for the spa experience. Both of us live busy professional and personal lives that involve the pressures of increasing responsibility, travel and deadlines. We have managed stress, in part, by incorporating the spa experience into our lives.

It's our hope that this book will help incorporate spa-going into your life also; if we have had a part in making that happen, we're delighted.

Spa Savvy

CHOOSING THE BEST SPA FOR YOU

Because there are many different approaches taken by the wide range of spas and health resorts in North America, before you choose a spa it is important to decide why you are going to one at all. If you are going to a spa to get away and solve a problem—like how you are going to tell your mother you are getting a divorce—you might choose one known, as the Golden Door is, for its serenity and meditative ambiance. If there is a big event coming up in your life and a quick drastic change for the better is required, you might choose the ascetic regimen of the Ashram. If you want a quiet rejuvenating weekend with your favorite person, perhaps La Costa or the Greenbrier is best. Figure out what it is you want, then find the spa that can provide you with it.

It's also a good idea to reflect on your general temperament and lifestyle. If you are independent, love a challenge and have fought to make major decisions in your life, you probably won't be delighted when an overzealous exercise instructor barely out of high school arrives at your room to see that your powder blue jogging suit is fully zipped and you are ready for the mountain hike. Nor would you be pleased if someone called your room and chided you for having skipped an exercise class. On the other hand, if at the moment you are tired of taking responsibility and want someone to nudge and encourage you to fitness, organizing your time and caloric intake, you don't want a spa in which few activities are organized and instructors take little interest in whether you participate or not.

There are more than eighty establishments calling themselves spas or fitness resorts in North America. How can you be

3

sure that a place is legitimate and will be able to deliver services that will provide you with new energy and better health?

First, send for information. Comb magazines and newspapers for stories on spas in which you're interested. When you are narrowing down the choices, call and talk to the director. Check to see that the food plan is supervised by a registered dietician. Ask to have sample menus sent to you.

Ask about the credentials of the exercise staff and how many classes are offered. There should be enough variety that each hour provides a new choice of class or instructor. Also, if you can, find out how the instructors look—search brochures and ask friends—a fat exercise teacher is probably doing something wrong.

Carefully read the information in brochures about accommodations. If you can't stand to be out of touch with your office or to be without the evening news on TV, find a place where telephones and televisions are accepted as normal. Also note that some spa accommodations are rustic (one brochure says "we hope to get electricity in all the cabins next year"); if you can't deal with this, do yourself a favor and try a more luxurious spa.

All this is not to say you shouldn't try something new. Just because your vacations have been camping trips for the last ten years doesn't mean you wouldn't love being pampered in an elegant setting. Or just because you love your urban life doesn't mean you wouldn't be delighted with a rustic Mexican spa surrounded by steaming jungle pools.

There are ways to tell if a spa is well managed. The best indication is happy former guests; but there are other signs. Are the brochures attractive and specific? Does someone usually answer the phone? Do you consistently get the same answers from staff if you call more than once?

You will find that any reputable spa is eager to make its program work for you, and a fair amount of adjustment to your needs is possible. If you have special dietary needs (if you are a vegetarian or a diabetic, for example), this can usually be accommodated if the staff knows in advance. If you have a bad back or some minor physical limitation, let the staff know and they will help you work around it in your exercise program. Many spas plan for this by asking guests to fill out a health questionnaire before they come or soon after arrival. Some spas even give complete physicals. Most of the staff members at spas are there because they like what they are doing, and they want you to have a good experience.

What can a spa do for you that you can't do at home for several hundred dollars less? Because so much of how we live and take care of our bodies reflects how we feel about ourselves, it is critical to leave the noise, our usual expectations and old habits, and go to a quiet, separate place where supportive people can help us learn new habits. The combination of vigorous exercise, a careful diet and a beautiful setting can work magic, and help you feel not only terrific at the end of a stay but committed to making life changes that will keep you feeling that way.

THE OPPOSITE SEX

More spas are opening that offer "separate but equal" men's and women's facilities. In fact, at some coed spas men make up 30 to 40 percent of the guest list. (As of this writing, there are no "men only" residential spas.) Many spas that previously catered only to women now offer men's weeks and couples' weeks. Special programs are planned to meet male fitness needs: weight training, Nautilus equipment, jumping rope, jogging and other activities of traditional interest to men are mixed with stretch classes, water fitness, yoga and beauty services, which men approach cautiously but end up loving as much as women guests.

Couples' weeks usually have special exercise classes planned to teach couples how to exercise together, how to learn relaxation techniques and even how to give each other a relaxing massage.

MASSAGE WITHOUT FEAR

A lot of Americans, particularly women, have never had a massage, and, like anything new, the idea can make you uneasy. One neophyte spa-goer approached an old hand and asked sotto voce if it was absolutely necessary to remove all her clothes. The answer is, fortunately or unfortunately, yes. But that, happily, is about the only thing that isn't flexible about the procedure. The idea to keep in mind is that you need to tell a masseuse before she starts what you want in a massage—for example, a deep muscle massage or a light relaxing one—and then together you will be happy with the result. If you are the

5

modest type or if you are simply nervous with a new experience, tell your masseuse, and she will drape you with a towel so that you are not exposed as she works. And too, don't be shy; if you are sore in a particular area, tell her so that special attention can be paid to that area. If you're ticklish or especially tender anywhere, or have a chronic back problem, anything that might affect how she works, tell her.

Then relax! If you have really been active in the exercise program, this shouldn't be difficult, but if you're easily spooked or nervous, it helps to breathe regularly and deeply. It also helps if you know what is going to happen. When you have your little premassage chat with your masseuse, ask her what order she will be working in so that there won't be any surprises.

Some women are embarrassed because they are overweight. Don't give this a thought. Your masseuse has certainly seen bodies of all types and is not judgmental.

You may be asked to make a choice of oils or massage creams. Natural products are always preferable to mineral oil–based products because the body can absorb them more easily. Avocado, lemon and sesame oil are common offerings. At the end of some massages, the masseuse uses a commercial vibrator, which feels a little like the Magic Fingers option featured in old-fashioned motel beds.

When you sign up for your massage, ask what choices you have for location. Some spas send the masseuse to your room for the treatment, some use a bathhouse or special massage room area and some even offer outdoor massages in a secluded private area. At least one spa offers massages outdoors in a very crowded, rather public area around the swimming pool. If showing your charms in this way does not appeal to you, request to be treated indoors. The point is: ask first, then go look at the location.

CLOTHES AND OTHER ACCOUTREMENTS

As a rule, the more expensive the spa, the less you will need to take with you. Very posh places, such as the Golden Door, the Greenhouse, Palm-Aire and Turnberry, provide everything you could possibly need, including a warm-up suit, robe, slippers, shorts and T-shirts (some even provide swimsuits, leotards and evening wear). Shampoo, soaps, conditioners, razors and an assortment of lotions are often provided by the large superspas also.

At the more medium-priced spas such as the Palms, Rancho La Puerta and Canyon Ranch, clothes are not provided, but there are small shops where you can buy anything you may need during your stay, including exercise clothes bearing the spa logo.

In any case, the first time you visit a spa, it's a good idea to take along a modest assortment of your own clothes until you get the feel of the place. The spa's togs might not fit well or might not be as flattering as you'd like (they range from the sublime to the ridiculous), or you might simply get bored with wearing the spa-issue shorts or warm-ups since you'll be wearing them every day.

As is obvious from reading newspaper ads, exercise clothes are a hot fashion item at the moment, so if you own the very latest and snazziest leg warmers or velour warm-ups, by all means bring them. Just because the spa provides clothes doesn't mean you're not welcome to wear your own.

The most important item of clothing women will need at most spas is the coverup or wraparound skirt to slip over leotards or shorts before going in to lunch or lounge areas. In some spas—particularly the resorts—guests are expected to wear sportswear, slacks and sweaters for meals. Other real necessities are a sun visor or sun hat, plus a scarf in which to wrap your head after scalp treatments.

Spas that provide clothes deliver clean ones every day or two; if you bring your own, washing facilities are usually available.

LIVING ON A SPA DIET

One of the reasons people go to a spa is to trim down and tone up. Most spa diets are planned to help you do this comfortably and healthfully.

This doesn't mean that you have to suffer through deprivation or agony, however. If you find, after being on the spa diet for a few days, that you are shaky or irritable, talk to the dietician and arrange to raise your caloric intake, or ask to have a low-calorie snack at midmorning and midafternoon if none is offered in the program.

One thing you shouldn't do is take food to a spa. In fact, if you are afraid you'll sneak out and binge on lasagna, choose a spa that is self-contained, away from such urban temptations. After a few days you will get accustomed to small amounts of healthy foods and will be glad you were virtuous.

PACKING AN ATTITUDE

"Women in our society never get a chance to be irresponsible" one spa-goer said recently. And it's true. With an engrossing job, plus a family and a network of friends to keep up, many women are just trying to keep all the appointments they've made, attend all necessary meetings and sort all the socks the family requires. Small wonder there's little time for making oneself over into an energy-charged sex object. European and American women seem to differ in this regard. No matter how busy, a European woman will take time out for a facial every few weeks or will plan an annual visit to a therapeutic spa in Germany or France.

Men also need time out to recharge without the phone ringing in their ears, and escaping to a spa is one of the few socially acceptable ways to do it.

We've found a week or two at a spa can get your attention focused on your body's needs in a way that can "last" for several months. Once body tone is achieved, it takes exercise three times a week, plus a few altered eating habits, to keep it.

The critical attitude to pack is a sense of humor. Doll-sized food portions, weird exercise positions and mountain hikes more suitable for goats than humans can all be endured if you can laugh at them. Your newfound friends and fellow guests will help.

THE WEST
COAST

Featured Spas

La Costa

Whoever proposed the theory that "less is more" had never been to La Costa. This California superresort has more of everything—land, facilities, guests, activities, even whirlpool baths—than any other spa in the country. But don't expect tranquillity and serenity.

La Costa, located just inland from the ocean forty-five minutes from San Diego and two hours from Los Angeles, will remind you of an enormous country club for the very privileged. Expensively but casually dressed guests stroll by in tennis or golf clothes. Everyone looks rich, tan and quite comfortable with life's amenities. The parking areas bloom with Mercedes and Cadillacs. Power and money underlie the casual sophistication of the guests. These are people who expect a greal deal out of life, and at La Costa they get it.

La Costa was built in 1968 as the last word in West Coast resort extravagance. The spa itself is only a part of the huge resort complex, which includes guest lodges, the hotel, fine dining rooms, a conference center, a remarkably beautiful twenty-seven-hole golf course, twenty-five tennis courts, a saddle club with almost thirty miles of riding trails, a beach club, movie houses and boutiques. The spa building has separate programs and facilities for men and women.

If you are smitten with the place, you may also buy a luxurious condominium, townhouse or plot of land, as many celebrities have. That person you see bouncing by in jogging shorts who looks like Ed McMahon may just *be* the media's most familiar sidekick.

ACCOMMODATIONS

Guest rooms are large and well decorated in the lavish La Costa style. They include enormous baths—almost a mini-spa with large bath and shower area and what seems like miles of counter space. Color televisions and large round tables (handy for room-service meals) complete the accommodations.

FACILITIES

La Costa is not the place to go if you need a quiet spot to retreat and think: sybaritic yes, secluded absolutely not.

There is a slick, cheerfully social ambiance clearly notice-able in the modern wood-and-glass spa building, the bustling hotel lobby and the busy dining rooms. Because all of these are in the same complex, you need to supply your own discipline. No one gets you up in the morning and urges you to exercise. But for the motivated, the facilities are probably the most grand and glorious in the country. There is nothing modest about La Costa.

The spa building looks a lot like the drawings of Roman baths last seen in your high school Latin book. A light-filled atrium, open to the sky and surrounded by glass walls, contains hot and cold whirlpool baths. Women sit casually in the baths in the altogether, soothing muscles worked thoroughly during exer-cise classes.

If seclusion while you soak is your preference, duck into the individual private mineral whirlpool baths. As you enter the area you can pick what types of oils or minerals you would like to have added to the water. A timer is set, and the attendant (after drawing your bath) exits quietly.

The spa building also houses rock steam rooms, outdoor exercise pools, solariums, private facial rooms, massage cubi-cles and a large and very complete beauty salon.

PROGRAM

The spa plan includes a medical evaluation, a meeting with the spa dietician, a skin analysis, unlimited golf and tennis privileges and daily use of the sauna, whirlpool, Roman pool, outdoor pools, lounges, shower rooms and other facilities in the spa building.

In addition, a daily body massage, facial and makeup class are provided. Each week you are also entitled to a manicure, pedicure, shampoo and set and herbal wrap.

When you begin your stay, a spa counselor sits down with you and discusses what you would like to do with your time there, scheduling each day's activities around your needs and interests. Usually that means exercise classes alternated with beauty treatments.

Once scheduled, you are led to the locker room. Here you undress and are outfitted in a shapeless short wrap that has all the charm of a hospital gown made out of an old towel. Your schedule for the day is pinned to your smock, making you dimly remember the first day of school.

All this ought to be depersonalizing, but it isn't because the staff members are as cozy and reassuring as a group of kindergarten teachers. They hug, they coo, they good-naturedly move you along and provide you with anything you may have forgotten. Many of them have been here for years, and the locker room is filled with shrieks of delight when a long-lost guest is sighted.

This is one of the interesting contradictions of La Costa. Surprisingly, the supersophisticated clientele seems to thrive on this folksy atmosphere created by the staff's hugging and cheerful banter. Accommodation is the password.

You forgot your bathing suit? No problem, try this one. No jogging suit? Here, try a blue La Costa outfit. Shampoos, body gels, razors and other amenities are available wherever you need them, allowing you the freedom to wander around the whole spa area without carrying a thing, or *wearing* a thing either, if you so choose. For a resort with many conservative guests in their middle years, this is another contradiction. Enter the pool area for pool exercise class and be greeted by an array of bare bodies of all ages and dimensions being massaged by the pool or merely getting evenly tanned. Not everyone goes au naturel, but it is certainly accepted with bored nonchalance.

A typical day begins with breakfast in your room at 7:30 A.M. At 8:30 a walk around the grounds is led by a pert instructor. At 9:00 stretch-and-flex class slowly but surely wakes up your muscles so that they will be ready for more vigorous stuff. Each forty-minute class leads into the next, and so Costa Curves at 9:40 is a little more strenuous, working every set of muscles, including twelve to fifteen minutes of aerobics. At 10:20 you can choose Aqua-thin-ics, a pool class held outdoors using balls and rhythmic movements under water, or spot reducing, which shows you how to work on your problem areas.

At any time during the day, you will have scheduled beauty treatments that alternate with the exercise classes, so at this point you may have a facial or a massage, an herbal wrap or a loofah treatment. If you still want exercise, dance class, which is a jazz movement session set to snappy contemporary music, is offered. At 11:30 you might have a makeup class, using, of course, La Costa's special line of cosmetics.

At noon, you probably will be very interested in lunch in the dining room, by the pool or in your room. You then take a short breather before the 2:00 P.M. fitness class, which also stresses aerobics. At 2:40 you might have a different beauty treatment or join another stretch-and-flex or pool class. At 3:20 is Costa Curves, 4:00 P.M. dance and at 4:40 the day ends quietly with a soothing yoga class.

All classes except the pool class are coed. In one class the men varied from a rosy-cheeked and moustachioed grandfather type to a seven-foot-tall pro basketball player who had come to La Costa to lose weight he gained while recovering from an injury. Women guests are in all stages of fitness, but few are severely overweight.

FOOD AND DIET

The first clue that the La Costa spa plan is serious business is your visit to the doctor and the dietician. If you are lucky, you will meet the charming and fatherly Dr. Phillip Smith, who was brought here to help create and develop the La Costa philosophy from its beginnings. Although the good doctor is not above a few entertaining stories, he is not amused by the unhealthy lifestyle that most Americans live. He is convinced the "good life" is causing many lives to be shorter than necessary and he sees his role as crucial to helping people avoid major physical disabilities such as stroke and heart attack, caused by improper diet, stress and too little exercise.

At some point between the time you enter his office and leave it you become convinced that his sound, careful approach to nutrition and exercise deserves your attention. You exit clutching a personally prescribed diet based on 600, 800 or 1,000 calories, thinking, Now that I know this is important, can I *do* it?

You can. Your first spa meal confirms it. Each person selects menus a day in advance, adding up calories noted based on three selections for each item, so that you are led to the happy psychological conclusion that you actually have some control over what you're eating.

The dining room for spa guests is separate but adjacent to the main hotel dining room, and if you gaze across the two crowded areas, you would not be able to tell which guests are the virtuous disciplined spa types and which are carefree, indulgent vacationers. Ah, but the dietician can. Not only does she check every order for validity—nutritional balance and calories—but she also has "reducers radar." Some inner magnet draws her to the tables of people who have ordered (or are about to order) something verboten. Her approach is kind, firm and convincing. Wouldn't you rather feel better in the morning? Of course you would.

The meals are lovely to look at and quite flavorful, even though the portions can seem laughingly tiny. The diet is based on the "educated eye," and a goal is to teach people that portion control makes more sense than entirely giving up foods you love.

Lunch on the 800-calorie diet includes juice or soup, a salad, an entree, a vegetable and a dessert. An example: tomato soup (25), Hungarian beef goulash (146), broccoli with lemon (16) and whipped banana pudding (40). For dinner an appetizer, salad, entree, vegetable and dessert can translate into lobster cocktail (50), crisp red tomatoes with herbs (16), lamb chops Provençal (146), toasted potato shell with chives (30) and fresh pineapple slices (40).

La Costa meals are prepared with artificial sweeteners and salt substitutes. If you do not choose to have these in your food, speak to the dietician when you arrive and she'll arrange for your meals to be prepared without them.

It is also possible to have meals served in your room, which is entertaining as each meal comes in lots of little dishes with tops and covers that take time and attention away from how little you are actually eating.

HEALTH AND BEAUTY SERVICES

With each week's visit you are entitled to a daily massage or herbal wrap, facial and makeup lesson. (Massage rooms are not clearly marked, for instance, with numbers, so that you can find the masseuse assigned to you. The masseuse has to find you.) In addition, you may have a deep facial, loofah treatment or ion treatment, for which you will be billed.

The loofah treatment is a terrific way to get rid of the outer layer of "winter skin" when it's time to wear brief clothes again for the summer. The loofah room is separate from other treatment rooms and is equipped with a table with a hose arrangement dangling over it. You lie down on wet sheets and the staff person sprinkles you with a mixture of Epsom salt and large crystals of regular or table salt. As soon as you are "dusted" with this material, you are given a brisk rubdown over your entire body with a loofah sponge mitt. This feels a little scratchy but is not unpleasant. You are then wrapped up in the wet sheets and allowed to rest for a few minutes, salt crust and all. Resting in this slightly crunchy cocoon is like lying in a bed in which someone has been eating crackers.

Soon you are unwrapped, given a few scrubs with the mitt and invited to step into the Swiss shower. (After this experience you will know why the Swiss are so unexcitable and subdued; a lifetime of dealing with this would make anyone stoic.) The shower has nozzles in vertical rows on four sides of the shower stall. Very hot water sprays out with vigor for six to eight seconds; just as you're about to protest, the water changes to ice cold. When you are beginning to feel slightly blue with cold the (now welcome) hot water starts again. The water alternates like this eight to ten times until you are rescued by an attendant, who dries you off.

The whole process is invigorating, skin smoothing and guaranteed to get your attention! Your whole body feels silkier than ever before and you get the mild urge to rush up to a perfect stranger and say, "Touch me, don't I feel great?"

In this, as other services at La Costa, the attendant is helpful and reassuring, so you needn't be concerned about trying the new experience. The herbal wrap is done in a dark, quiet room with a fireplace. Hot wet sheets are spread on a table for you to lie on. They are then wrapped around you and more are added until you are completely "swaddled." The herbs used have a lovely woodsy, lemony smell, and taking deep breaths helps give a real sense of well-being.

The massages at La Costa are competently done, using mineral oil–based massage oil, and they last for thirty minutes. Regular facials, also taking thirty minutes, include a face and neck massage. The deep facial is a one-hour machine cleaning.

OTHER PLEASURES

This is an ideal spa for couples. Men can make use of the men's spa, which has a similar program of activities, or they can golf or play tennis while their partners are enjoying the women's spa. Actually either of you could mix and match a program to suit your special needs and interests by checking into the hotel as regular (not spa plan) guests and using certain spa services by paying specific fees for only the ones you use. If one of you is on the spa plan and the other isn't, you can still have meals together in the pleasant dining room overlooking the golf course.

Since you are near the ocean, you can run off to the beach if you choose, which is a short drive. But most guests stay on the resort grounds because there is such a surprising variety of things to do. In the evening, lectures on healthy living and cooking for the calorie conscious are given. There is also an effort to get guests involved in learning backgammon and bridge. Once a week a special spa cocktail party is held to acquaint spa guests with one another.

Some guests, of course, won't need introduction; frequent spa guests such as Dean Martin, Johnny Carson, Carol Burnett and Julie Andrews are fairly easy to recognize, even in terry wrappers.

WHAT TO BRING

Bring leotards, a bathing suit and a jogging outfit for the spa program. Men should bring shorts and T-shirts, bathing suits and sweat suits also. Dress in the public areas is West Coast casual. Cotton or linen resort wear in light colors is the choice of most guests. Simple dresses and slacks outfits are seen in the dining room. Most men wear open sports shirts in the dining area, although sports jackets are also worn. No tie is necessary at La Costa.

HOW TO GET THERE

Take Route 5 south from Los Angeles approximately ninety miles, then take the La Costa Road exit, turn left on Costa del Mar Road and right onto the spa grounds.

A taxi is available from San Diego (thirty miles to the south), and a limousine is available from the San Diego airport at Lindbergh field.

SUMMARY

La Costa is a good place for sophisticated, well-off people who like sports. The men's and women's spas offer every service imaginable, including strong medical support. This is a classy, commercial spa for those who have arrived.

FACT SUMMARY

NAME: La Costa

MAILING ADDRESS: Costa del Mar Road, Carlsbad, CA 92008

TELEPHONE: (619) 438-9111

TRANSPORTATION: Limo service from Lindbergh Field is available by prearrangement with La Costa; taxis also available

ACCOMMODATIONS: Condominiums; suites; spacious, deluxe hotel-style rooms

FEE: 4-day minimum—single, $225 per day for one person; double, $355 per day for two persons sharing double room

MAXIMUM NUMBER OF GUESTS: Spa, men's and women's combined, 300

MAXIMUM NUMBER OF STAFF: Spa, men's and women's combined, 200

SEASON: Year-round

AMBIANCE: Flamboyant superspa: grand-scale resort; self-contained village

GENDER AND AGE RESTRICTIONS: None in hotel; adults over 16 in spa; coed

DIET: Regular and calorie-controlled spa food; 600-to-800 calorie diet—sugar-free, salt-free

FACILITIES: 2 spas (men's and women's), 27-hole golf course, 25 tennis courts, 4 swimming pools, 5 hotel dining facilities, spa dining room, riding trails, movie houses, boutiques

PROGRAM: Self-scheduling with direction of MD, dietician and exercise counselor; aerobics, stretch, pool exercise, dance and yoga classes

SPECIAL FEATURES: Roman baths, outdoor massage, Grecian tubs, cellulite treatments, loofah treatments, herbal wraps, room service, makeup classes, evening programs and movies

LOCAL ATTRACTIONS: Beach

Carmel Country Spa

The view as you wind through the Carmel Valley in the early morning is like a scene from *Brigadoon*. The mist from the Pacific rolls over the steep foothills and creates a mosaic of sunlight on the lush, green vegetation.

At each turn in the road one expects Gene Kelly and Cyd Charisse to appear, wearing tartan and rumpled corduroy, holding hands and running through the heather (or, in this case, native California grasses) and wild flowers. Instead of stone walls, white fences run along the roadway defining the boundaries of horse farms, small guest resorts and fine private residences.

At the end of a dirt road, one passes through a massive wooden gate and there, surrounded by weathered redwood and cypress fencing, is a charming mini-spa. To your right is the main L-shaped building bending around the corner of a good-sized swimming pool. To your left guest cottages nestle among the trees. Just over your right shoulder a garden marches up the hillside. Bright, cheerful clusters of flowers are everywhere: petunias, geraniums, azaleas and bougainvillea remind one that someone cares and works hard to make it pleasant.

Everything about this place says "casual." If your favorite eccentric aunt, who wears scarlet nailpolish, hats with giant cabbage roses and colorful caftans, opened a spa for her bridge club, Carmel Country Spa would be it.

No guest is concerned about being fat, old, weak, late, uncoordinated or different. It just doesn't seem to matter. The spa has no expectations other than those of its guests. Consequently the stress and competition of life "out there" slip easily away. There is nothing pretentious about a spa that has a huge gray monster of a steam cabinet positioned at the end of the swimming pool and asks its guests to move the lounge furniture for exercise classes.

Most guests come for relaxation and weight loss, primarily

from diet, but they do participate in the exercise. The spa is 99 percent women, with a female staff. Husbands are encouraged to join their wives for weekend sun and relaxation. The guests range in age from their twenties to early sixties, with the majority falling in the fifty-to-fifty-five bracket.

This do-your-own-thing spa makes for a low-cost treat for tired housewives, middle-management women and those who just want to get away.

If your psyche needs a structured plan, Carmel Country Spa is not your kind of place. Nothing here is pursued in an aggressive or forceful manner; there are many chaise-longue nappers and chair sitters along with the enthusiastic exercise-class goers. It's a real down-to-the-basics homelike environment with a measure of unpredictability and zaniness thrown in.

ACCOMMODATIONS

The guest cabins are arranged in small groups on narrow terraces that are landscaped in a gloriously haphazard profusion of magnificent live oaks, fir, herbs, native wild flowers and pots of orchids. It's a rather bucolic setting, and one guest who shared her room with a raccoon (she inside and he in a hollow under the floor) would heartily agree.

The rooms, furnished in early Sears, Roebuck, are more than adequate in size and appearance, but a little more airing out would reduce the mustiness. A dressing-room area with a large, walk-in shower is a pleasant attraction, and the phone and large TV prevent one from feeling cut off from "real" life. One would not confuse these accommodations with the Ritz, but they're comfortable, and just a few steps from many parts of the spa.

FACILITIES

During a recent visit a blaring Spanish-speaking radio broke the quiet of the spa, and following the noise to the vegetable garden we discovered Roberto, the Mexican gardener, digging purposefully in the soil, planting tiny cucumber vines. The unusual thing about this scenario was that it was 7:45 P.M. on a weekend evening. Roberto, like the owners, staff and some guests, considers these six acres his own. The garden needed work and he was doing it with fervent dedication, even if his official workday had ended several hours before.

The tiny, rather rustic gym will soon be replaced, the staff says, by a new structure that will allow more room for exercise classes. The improvement would be welcome.

Several massage rooms are thoughtfully located away from the heavy traffic areas, and a large outdoor whirlpool is adjacent to the swimming pool. The small sauna is beyond the beauty shop. This is really a mini-spa in many ways, and a five-minute stroll would take you from one end of the facility to the other. The convenience is rather pleasant.

The main building houses the lounge, gym, beauty shop, dining room and all the public facilities. The decor is that of a Holiday Inn or Howard Johnson motel lobby: mirrors to make things seem larger, and a great feeling of plastic everything. It's not all bad, and with some of the rough edges smoothed out, Carmel Country Spa could quickly move into the ranks of a top spa for the budget-minded who love a beautiful climate and a quiet, relaxing atmosphere.

PROGRAM

If you're a very active outdoor person you may feel somewhat out of place here; exercise classes are held inside and even the "morning walks" are leisurely strolls through rather civilized terrain.

From the casual registration and orientation, to the optional exercise program, Carmel Country Spa can only be called relaxed. Snappy efficiency or clear thinking are not de rigueur here. The two female owners are fairly visible and participate alternately as guests and staff. Some guests, who have come here for years, seem more aware of the function of the spa than the owners, who seem preoccupied and pleasantly relaxed in an absentminded way much of the time.

When several of us asked about the possibility of more outside exercise classes, no one seemed to know whom they should consult about the idea, so we made our own decision and carried on—outside.

There are five fifty-minute classes a day, including two pool classes and a vigorous aerobics class. These classes are intermingled with informative health lectures, and evening sessions include belly dancing, makeup application, stress reduction and behavior modification.

Although the staff is well acquainted with nontraditional

and holistic health practices, the concept is not stressed except in periodic classes on herbology and hypnosis.

Exercise focuses on stretching and toning, with some spot exercises. The classes are small (four to six people) and should allow for personalization and individual treatment, but strangely, this rarely occurs. Everyone does the same exercises at about the same rate.

The staff encourages a full seven-day stay, but a majority of guests come for weekends or a five-day plan. About 10 percent are frequent visitors who promptly become unofficial program directors.

FOOD AND DIET

There are few calories and even fewer carbohydrates in the diet at Carmel. The average dieter chooses a 650-calorie-per-day plan, and a special protein diet is available on request. Juice fasts are available but not recommended by the staff.

The fresh, attractive meals are portion controlled and very light in sodium and cholesterol. The protein consists mainly of cheeses, chicken and fish, with some red meat. Salt, sugar and butter substitutes are used, and many of the dishes appear to be similar to the Weight Watchers diet.

The midday meal is the main meal, which is unusual for most spas but which seems very sensible. The evening meal is considerably lighter in both content and calorie count. Meal size and presentation are pleasant and far from austere.

Communal dining in the sun-filled dining room overlooking the pool is a pleasant experience, and each day a pinewood fire brightens the decor. Much socializing is done at meals, and anyone coming alone is quickly welcomed and genially accepted.

Breakfast for the serious dieter is juice, herb tea and vitamins. For others, poached eggs and whole-grain toast can be ordered without any fear of embarrassment.

At most meals, carbohydrates in small quantities mixed with two or three ounces of protein appear to satisfy most guests. The quantity of fresh vegetables and fruits adds bulk to the diet and helps eliminate "the hungries."

Three to five pounds a week is an average weight loss at Carmel, with an additional bonus of lost inches for those who have been conscientious about the exercise programs.

The meals are supervised by one of the owners, Dr. Ruth E. Ray, a physician and specialist in bariatrics (the study of obesity), although when we commented on a particularly tasty luncheon dish and asked whose recipe it was, a chorus of people spoke up saying, "mine," including one of the owners, two staff members and a guest. That's rather typical of the slightly bemused organization of Carmel Country Spa.

HEALTH AND BEAUTY SERVICES

One of the most memorable moments at Carmel Country Spa is when one is sitting in a chair and covered with a warm blanket, gazing out with half-closed eyes at a quiet pool and the soft rounded hills of Carmel Valley while undergoing a very expert, deep-cleansing facial. The quality of the beauty services from massages to salt rubs, for sloughing off dead skin, is excellent. The staff is well trained and sensitive to each person's needs; one is treated as an individual, not as a time slot on a schedule.

While beauty services are extra, they cost slightly less than one would pay for similar service in a metropolitan area. Many guests choose one or two treatments a day with heavy emphasis on massage, which is offered most evenings until 10:00 P.M.

Cellulite treatments are offered as well as salt loofah rubs for smoothing and conditioning of the skin. Makeup classes and individual makeup consultations are available daily, as are the full services of the hair, manicure and pedicure department.

The use of the sauna, whirlpool and steam cabinet are included in your room rate.

Herbal wraps are available. Remember, if you are at all claustrophobic, keep your arms outside the herbal wraps. For real relaxation, follow with a Swedish or deep muscle massage. The masseuses are young and enthusiastic. Their style of modesty may not be your own, but feel comfortable about requesting a towel or sheet to cover as much or as little as your dignity requires. It's your massage and you and the masseuse are a team for those fifty or sixty minutes. Help the masseuse find those tight or sore spots. She will appreciate your guidance as to the amount of pressure that you require for maximum value to muscle and psyche.

OTHER PLEASURES

The small gift shop is fun for a leisurely half hour at lunch-time, and the shopping is really quite good in either Carmel or Monterey, where the emphasis is on wonderful little specialty shops. The people-watching is also great fun.

Tennis and three championship golf courses are available within a fifteen-minute ride by car. For those who like walking, there's a pleasurable walk in any direction, and the Los Padres National Forest is a real treat for serious hikers.

Wine lovers will discover that the Monterey wines are now coming into their own and are being accepted as some of the finest wines in all of California. There are many places to sample wines and a few wineries nearby to visit.

For those who can afford an extra day or so, Big Sur lies just a few miles south and presents the finest coastal scenery in California. Big Sur is very popular, though, and if you plan to stay there, be sure to make reservations in advance. "Catch as catch can" means no room at all there.

WHAT TO BRING

"Casual" is the key word. Pack informal sportswear for dinner and side trips, velour or knit jogging suits for "day" wear. Leotards and tights for exercise classes are helpful; if you don't own any, shorts and T-shirts are fine. You can eat lunch wearing a leotard or bathing suit if you wear a coverup or skirt over it.

A long-sleeved jacket or sweater and warm pants for evening are a must, even in the summer.

For morning hikes in the more civilized areas, most guests wear a jogging suit over their exercise clothes. Not everyone is charmed by seeing a long line of slightly overweight ladies speed walking along a golf course on a Sunday morning in various degrees of rumpled attire.

Don't forget well-broken-in walking shoes; tennis shoes are more than adequate.

A beach towel is a good idea for sunning or a trip to the beach. Do not expect the ocean water to be warm. Beach bathers on the peninsula are primarily rubber-suit wearers and English Channel swimmers. The surf also tends to be a bit frisky for normal bathers.

Some take-home pluses are exercise tapes (ask to check the

quality of the sound before you leave); natural beauty cosmetics, vitamins and diet supplements; there is also a nice line of aloe-vera-based products.

HOW TO GET THERE

Carmel Country Spa is located 140 miles south of San Francisco, 350 miles north of Los Angeles, and 12 miles inland. If you're traveling south on Coast Highway 1, go ½ mile past Ocean Avenue (the main street) and turn left on Carmel Valley Road. Eleven and a half miles later you'll see the spa sign, and you turn left and then take your first right into the parking lot of the spa.

If you fly into the Monterey airport, the spa van will pick you up and in twenty minutes you'll be checking in. There's a $12.50 charge for this service. The Monterey airport is served by several airlines.

Car rental, taxi and limousine service are also available at the airport.

SUMMARY

This is a cozy spa; part of its charm is in its mild disorganization and naiveté, from the spa van that never starts on the first try for trips to the beach for the morning hike (sometimes requiring guests to push it), to "leftover" guests who stay on to become maintenance employees. You need have absolutely no fear of becoming regimented here. Everyone pitches in and has a great time. If you're flexible, have a sense of humor and love Carmel, this is your kind of place.

FACT SUMMARY

NAME: Carmel Country Spa

MAILING ADDRESS: 10 Country Club Way, Carmel Valley, CA 93924

TELEPHONE: (408) 659-3486

TRANSPORTATION: Spa van pick-up and drop-off at airport

ACCOMMODATIONS: Hotel-type rooms in bungalows

FEE: 3-day minimum—single, $87–$98 per day; double, $52–

$61 per person, per day; triple, $49–$51 per person, per day; patio room $15 extra per person

MAXIMUM NUMBER OF GUESTS: 80

MAXIMUM NUMBER OF STAFF: 15

SEASON: Year-round

AMBIANCE: Cozy, rustic hideaway in green valley; no frills

GENDER AND AGE RESTRICTIONS: Adults over 16; coed

DIET: Low carbohydrate/low calorie; 650 calories per day; some herbs, vegetables grown on premises; special protein diet on request

FACILITIES: Gym, swimming pool, beauty salon, massage rooms, sauna, whirlpool, gift shop

PROGRAM: Permissive, do-it-yourself programming, exercise not mandatory; no special pampering; aerobic, stretch and pool exercise, yoga, belly dancing, stress reduction, health lectures

SPECIAL FEATURES: Small classes, easygoing atmosphere

LOCAL ATTRACTIONS: Picturesque village of Carmel, 15-minute drive to Pacific Ocean

The Fountainhead

Located in the heart of the California wine country, about an hour-and-a-quarter drive north of San Francisco, the Fountainhead is the first of a proposed chain of coed spas based on the Weight Watchers program. Because of the national popularity of the Weight Watchers diet programs it seemed that this spa might be interesting and important.

ACCOMMODATIONS

The spa is located on a pleasantly landscaped six-and-one-half-acre plot adjacent to Highway 101. It is a refurbished Holiday Inn complete with typical motel accommodations: simple but spacious rooms with small bathrooms.

FACILITIES

The main building houses the dining room, spa offices, classrooms, lobby–reception area, kitchen facilities and a well-stocked gift shop featuring sundries, sportswear and an extensive collection of Weight Watchers books and magazines. To the north, across an expansive grassy area, is a wing of remodeled motel rooms that are clean and attractive but in no way luxurious. The third structure is a newly constructed contemporary wood athletic building that houses men's and women's locker rooms, which contain saunas, whirlpools and steam rooms. The locker rooms are spacious, immaculate and well staffed, but some women guests had trouble getting warm-enough temperatures in their whirlpool baths.

The large gymnasium has mirrored walls and a soft grass-green decor, but the only equipment it contains are a half-dozen exercise bikes. Apparently the staff wants the guests to be able to adapt what they learn here to their own home situation where there is rarely a complete assortment of chrome exercise machines.

The complex also includes a beauty shop, massage rooms, and a facial room for men and women.

The delightful Santa Rosa weather helps make the large heated pool the main focus of the spa. In summer the pool area is crowded with sunbathers, and in winter months the pool is covered with a plastic bubble so that it can be enjoyed year-round.

The two blacktop tennis courts get little action, but the quarter-mile track that circles the spa buildings gets quite a bit of use. The constant hum of automobile traffic from Highway 101 doesn't seem to bother the joggers, speed walkers or the sunbathers around the pool.

PROGRAM

The fitness program begins every morning with a vigorous 7:00 A.M. stretch class that tapers off and ends gently with a yoga or relaxation class, which is a nice lead-in to the rest of the day's program.

Late-morning and early-afternoon classes are more heavily attended (in late afternoon there is a mass exodus back to the rooms to watch favorite soap operas), but no class is mandatory. Many of the guests at the Fountainhead are accustomed to using only diet as a means of weight control, so there is much groaning and some sideline watching in the more active classes. This is perfectly acceptable: at the Fountainhead, no one is forced to participate.

The afternoon activities include tours of the local wineries, the enchanting Jack London State Historic Park, and other local attractions, including the Luther Burbank Gardens and a nice collection of antiques shops. These afternoon trips and tours seem to foster a good sense of community among the guests, allowing friendships to develop. For many of the guests, walking is the exercise of choice, and planned walking tours are a standard afternoon activity. One of the purposes of these trips is to incorporate the one-and-a-half to two miles of walking per day.

Afternoon and evening programs present guest lecturers who cover a wide variety of subjects, including stress-reduction techniques, low-calorie cooking, benefits of massage and nutrition à la Weight Watchers.

FOOD AND DIET

The spa serves meals that conform to the well-publicized Weight Watchers program. Three well-balanced meals, which never total more than 1,000 calories, are served daily, and an 800-calorie-per-day diet is also available. Raw vegetables and fruit juices are served midmorning and early afternoon. During the cocktail hour before dinner nonalcoholic drinks are served while guests socialize.

Dinner is served in the spa dining room. Guests wear loose caftans or comfortable sportswear, and the conversation revolves around food. Each meal has several courses and considerable time goes by between courses in order to encourage guests to slow down their eating. Artificial sugar and salt are substituted for the real things, and oddly enough, the sweet-tooth taste is encouraged daily with Weight Watchers ice cream or other artificially sweetened desserts.

Nightly, instead of the traditional chocolate mint, a small piece of sugarless gum is placed on your nightstand.

Most guests express a confidence in the Weight Watchers diet plan and either do, or say they will, practice it at home. As if to reinforce this faith, the local Weight Watchers group meets at the spa every Monday evening.

The majority of the guests at the spa are substantially above their ideal weight levels and seem to feel very comfortable there because no one is judgmental about their size or their nonparticipation in the exercise programs. As one regular spa-goer put it, "There are no twenty-one-year-old perfect bodies here like I see at the other health resorts."

Many of the seasoned spa-goers expressed a desire to return to the Fountainhead because of the friendly, supportive staff and the nonstarvation diet. The informality of the dress and the take-it-or-leave-it program are also attractive to many of the guests.

HEALTH AND BEAUTY SERVICES

For female guests who want a little pampering, a full-service beauty salon is open every afternoon, and some beauty services are available during the evening. Facials, makeup, manicures and pedicures are offered. Unfortunately, the facial utilizes a cosmetic line with a mineral-oil base, a petroleum by-product, which is not absorbed easily by the skin and which tends to sit on the surface of the skin and clog the pores.

The massage rooms are always busy. Three excellent masseuses and one masseur are kept busy from early afternoon until long after dinner. For some guests this is the first experience with body massage, and they regale dinner partners with their blissful reactions.

OTHER PLEASURES

Santa Rosa offers many diversions to the dieting visitor. Within an hour's drive there are picturesque state parks with large stands of giant redwoods, the magnificent Pacific coastline, the lush vineyards and quaint villages of the wine country and the famed California Valley of the Moon, an area of fascinating rock formations.

WHAT TO BRING

Even in the summer the early mornings and evenings call for a sweater or jacket. Leotards or tights are most comfortable for the exercise classes and a sweat shirt and pants are recommended as coverup while you are on your way to the gym and breakfast or lunch. Casual sportswear or caftans are appropriate for the evening meal. Remember tennis shoes for jogging and comfortable walking shoes for the afternoon tours. A bathing suit is essential for sunning, lap swimming and paddle classes, although one may go au naturel in the whirlpool, sauna and steam room.

HOW TO GET THERE

If you fly into San Francisco or Sonoma County airport in Santa Rosa, there are flights that connect with shuttle service to the spa by airport vans. The spa offers a courtesy pick-up service from the Santa Rosa airport if you have given the spa advance notice. The spa is just a fifteen-minute ride from the downtown Santa Rosa shopping center, and public transportation is available.

SUMMARY

The guests we encountered here liked this spa very much. It's an unassuming place with a supportive staff and a non-competitive atmosphere. No one is made to feel uncomfortable about the shape she or he is in, and guests easily make friends through the staff-arranged programs and tours.

The food plan is a sound one and focuses on teaching people how to follow it. No problem there. Our major reservation is the ambiance; aesthetic it isn't. But many people like it anyway. You may be one of them.

FACT SUMMARY

NAME: The Fountainhead

MAILING ADDRESS: 3345 Santa Rosa Avenue, Santa Rosa, CA 95401

TELEPHONE: (707) 546-8711

TRANSPORTATION: Spa vans pick up at the airport

ACCOMMODATIONS: Motel-like rooms

FEE: 4 days—single, $335; double, $275 per person (beauty services extra), 7 days—single, $750; double, $625 per person

MAXIMUM NUMBER OF GUESTS: 200

MAXIMUM NUMBER OF STAFF: 50

SEASON: Year-round

AMBIANCE: No frills

GENDER AND AGE RESTRICTIONS: Adults over 16; coed

DIET: Weight Watchers diet; 800–1,200 calories

FACILITIES: Exercise gym; separate men's and women's spas with massage rooms, facial salons, whirlpools, saunas, steam rooms; jogging track, heated pool, putting green, 2 tennis courts, dining room

PROGRAM: Very permissive; stretch and yoga classes, jogging, lectures

SPECIAL FEATURES: Weight Watchers food plan

LOCAL ATTRACTIONS: Parks, wineries, scenic coastline

The Golden Door

In a narrow valley in the heart of southern California, forty miles northeast of San Diego, lies a picturesque replica of a Japanese country inn, perfect in every detail, from its Zen rock gardens to the constant sound of water falling softly into quiet pools filled with golden carp. The silence and tranquillity are reminiscent of an ancient monastery, but don't let the surroundings mislead you; this is the powerhouse of American spas: the Golden Door.

The energy source behind this spa is Deborah Szekely, who has been involved with health resorts (first at her more casual spa to the south, Rancho La Puerta) for more than forty years. Her philosophy is that eating natural foods, knowing how to relax your mind and body and exercising properly is the only way to create a life worth living. As a result, the Golden Door has cast a long shadow over the whole American spa scene.

The Golden Door has acquired the undeserved reputation of being elitist; actually, this is a place where all guests are equal and all feel equally at home. Because everything you will need in the way of spa clothing is supplied, no one knows whether you are a wealthy heiress or a secretary who saved her lunch money for three years to pay the tab. Only on Saturday night (graduation night), with everyone coiffed, powdered and tightened, do the silk blouses and gold bracelets come out—and by then who cares!

Limited to thirty-four guests, with a staff of well over one hundred, the Golden Door pampers its guests but keeps them busy, from a close-to-dawn mountain hike to a before-sleep mini-massage in the Japanese bathhouse.

Men are not entirely excluded from the Golden Door; there are men's and couples' weeks several times a year, and whatever your gender, everyone leaves with a healthy body, a glowing complexion and a soaring psyche. A word about couples' weeks: policy dictates that a couple must be married to be accepted into the couples program, so don't plan on a romantic interlude with your latest beau here.

ACCOMMODATIONS

The rooms are a satisfying blend of Eastern and Western culture. The full-sized beds and large baths are definitely American, but the decor includes such Japanese touches as a tokonoma—a small recess where a Japanese picture is hung and a subtle fresh-flower arrangement is placed daily. Each room has a sliding glass door that opens onto a private Oriental garden guaranteed to charm; each one is different—some have waterfalls, others stone lanterns, others plantings and waves of pebbles to simulate water. Meditating comes easy in such serene settings.

In keeping with this serenity, there are no radios or televisions in the rooms, and although the staff *will* deliver a daily newspaper to your room if you make a special request, they'd prefer that you cut your ties to the busy outside world while at the Golden Door.

Many guests get so attached to a particular room that they ask to have the same room whenever they visit. As reservations are often booked nine months in advance, this is often not so easy!

FACILITIES

The grounds are a paragon of simplicity and grace. Three courtyards of guest rooms, built around pavilions and connected by raised wooden walkways, are interspersed with artful Japanese plantings.

Guest lounges and sitting rooms are filled with custom-designed rattan furniture, shoji screens and Japanese antiques. Three glass-enclosed exercise rooms offer spectacular views of the meticulously kept gardens while you work out. Near the exercise complex are two pools. One, built for lap swimming, is kept at a cooler water temperature than the other, which is used for pool classes and water volleyball.

At the heart of the compound is a bathhouse, with steam and sauna rooms, a fan-shaped whirlpool, showers, herbal wrap area and massage tables for the evening massage.

Meals are held in the large dining room, which is accented with dark wood, sliding screens and more Japanese antiques.

PROGRAM

The rumors that the regimentation of the Golden Door is akin to the training program for a decathlon are slightly exaggerated.

You'll be awakened at 6:00 A.M. for a morning hike, after which you can climb back in bed for breakfast. Your breakfast tray will contain a pale-colored, fan-shaped schedule of a recommended hourly program for the rest of the day. This, of course, is a program that has been personally tailored to your needs on the day of your arrival. There are three levels of physical fitness; yours will be determined by your present level of physical conditioning. No one is pushed to overexert, but lazing around is not encouraged either. The highly motivated exercise instructors feed constant encouragement to participants and serve as models of fitness.

The day is divided into a series of thirty-minute exercise classes, with ten-minute breaks. Classes range from stretching and dance to a very vigorous class called "Da Vinci," which includes a long period of aerobics.

A session called the Golden Door "Special Hour" changes daily and reflects the particular needs and interests of that week's guests. Some days it is a predinner walk or jog, or an exercise class featuring movements designed by Chairman Mao for Chinese factory workers (complete with Chinese instructions and martial music!). Another day it might be a specially planned mountain hike, with the staff taking a photo of the valiant hikers who make it to the top. The final class of the day is either a yoga class or a relaxation class with a take-home tape so you can practice de-stressing when you get back to the real world.

FOOD AND DIET

The food here is absolutely fresh and home grown. You can see proof of this on the weekly orchard and garden tour that winds through the orange and grapefruit trees past a glorious vegetable and herb garden where rows of every vegetable imaginable grow in lush profusion. Even eggs and honey are produced on Door property.

Low-calorie, low-sodium, low-cholesterol gourmet dishes are the basis for the variable-calorie food plans. A member of the fitness staff confers with you on arrival and helps you select your daily caloric intake, ranging from 500 to 1,300 calories per day. Meals are exquisite to taste and beautifully presented with a pervasive Japanese awareness of color and form.

Michel Stroot, who has shed several unnecessary pounds since his arrival at the Door, is the Belgian chef. He often offers a choice of entrees at a meal, and if you don't like them, you can order a substitute more to your liking.

Breakfast is always innovative, whether it is whole-grain bread with a tomato slice and cheese, a baked egg with mushroom slices and Monterey cheese, or a hearty oatmeal, fig and apple granola.

At midmorning a deliciously fragrant tomato-vegetable broth called "potassium broth," served hot in heavy mugs with a picture-perfect plate of crudités, is just enough to refresh you for the rest of the morning's exercise.

You can have lunch served at the pool, in the dining room or in your room. Lunch menus are interesting and creative, and include the options of the incomparable fresh vegetable salad in the summer, or one of Michel's special omelettes. In the afternoon, pear juice is served over ice as a quick-energy snack.

For dinner, Oysters Rockefeller, vegetable frittata, mousse au carob and fresh pear soufflé are representative of the selection available. Appetizers and desserts are served with miniature forks and spoons to help break the all-American habit of wolfing food.

No liquids are served with meals. Deborah Szekely feels that liquids drunk in the course of a meal interfere with the digestive process. At the end of each meal, hot and cold herb teas, coffee and mineral water are offered.

The Virtue-Making Diet (under 650 calories) is available on Monday and Thursday. Entirely optional, it is a terrific way to start your week or to give you a chance to lose extra weight later in the week. On this plan, six times a day, participants are served a variety of liquids, from fresh-squeezed grapefruit juice, pineapple cucumber juice and almond milk to a refreshing gazpacho. A few raw sunflower seeds mixed with raw pine nuts are thrown in for good measure. This twenty-four-hour fast is designed to cleanse your system and "clarify your thinking."

HEALTH AND BEAUTY SERVICES

Although the emphasis at the Golden Door is on the exercise program, beauty services are also available. Each guest has an "hour of beauty" with her own beautician every day. One day's beauty session might include having an avocado oil pack massaged into your scalp. There are sessions for foot and hand massage, brow waxing, manicure and pedicure. In addition, each guest is given a facial and mask every day. Skin care and makeup sessions are available throughout the week.

A massage table in every guest's closet makes it possible to have the prescheduled daily massage in the privacy of your room. For something a little different, meet your masseuse in the solarium at the top of the hill near the compound for an outdoor massage in the warmth of the sun.

Every evening at 9:30 P.M., guests walk through the grounds to the bathhouse for a steam or sauna, a communal soak in the family style of Japanese hot tubs and a relaxing massage before going to sleep. Utter bliss!

OTHER PLEASURES

Guests seldom want to leave the compound, since there are very special pleasures within its walls.

The staff are warm and approachable and any special request is filled if humanly possible. Each guest is assigned a personal exercise instructor who works with her to develop a personalized exercise routine to take home.

Once each week the staff puts on a sort of talent night full of hilarious chorus line routines and comedy sketches. The chef gives excellent cooking demonstrations once a week, in which you'll be shown how to make several of the items on the week's menus.

Each evening a special program is held on nutrition, self-image or life planning.

WHAT TO BRING

You will never have packed so lightly for a seven-day trip. The Door supplies shorts, T-shirts, jogging suits, terry robes and rubber slippers. All you need to bring for day wear are leotards and tights (two sets will do), a bathing suit or two and hiking shoes. As the evenings get cool here, it's a good idea to bring a sweater. Evening wear is also supplied in the form of a flattering navy and white cotton kimono. Guests are also welcome to wear their own caftans or sweaters and slacks to dinner for a change from the standard kimono; most women bring one special outfit for Saturday night graduation.

Men will need swim trunks, jogging or tennis shoes and casual sportswear for dinner. No tie is necessary, but a blazer will come in handy for Saturday night dress-up.

The gift shop carries an unusually good assortment of sportswear and dinner clothes, so you may find something there that is appealing.

HOW TO GET THERE

Guests usually fly into Lindbergh Field in San Diego, although those who love trains can take the train from Los Angeles to Oceanside. A Golden Door car will pick you up at either location by prearrangement.

If you plan to drive, the reservations staff will provide a very detailed map and set of directions.

SUMMARY

If you long for a quiet retreat where you can reorder your life's priorities, the Golden Door is it. On the other hand, if you want to exercise hard, push your physical limits and get in the best shape possible in the shortest time, this is also "it."

The Golden Door produces a curious combination of serenity and stamina in its guests. In addition, couples who graduate from the couples' weeks say the experience creates an almost mystical closeness between them. All these benefits derive from the combination of carefully selected staff, superb food, vigorous exercise and one of the most beautiful settings anywhere in America.

This is one of the most expensive spas in the country. It is also one of the very best.

FACT SUMMARY

NAME: The Golden Door

MAILING ADDRESS: P.O. Box 1567, Escondido, CA 92025

TELEPHONE: (619) 744-5777

TRANSPORTATION: Complimentary Spa limo will pick up at airport or train station; driving instructions provided on request

ACCOMMODATIONS: Spacious private Japanese-style guest rooms with private garden and deck; three courtyards contain guest rooms; extensive woodwork

FEE: $2,500 per week all inclusive

MAXIMUM NUMBER OF GUESTS: 34

MAXIMUM NUMBER OF STAFF: 120

SEASON: Year-round

AMBIANCE: Serene Japanese inn; very exclusive and private; superluxurious in lush secluded valley

GENDER AND AGE RESTRICTIONS: Basically for women; 9 men's weeks; 7 couples' weeks

DIET: Low-calorie gourmet, low sodium and low cholesterol; natural food (some grown in own organic gardens); liquid fast day.

FACILITIES: 2 pools, Japanese bathhouse with steam, sauna, therapy pool; 157 acres, 3 exercise rooms; tennis courts

PROGRAM: Moderate to strenuous program personalized to each guest's needs; very pampering to active physical exercise: stretch, dance and aerobic classes; yoga

SPECIAL FEATURES: Exquisite Japanese landscaping, own hypoallergenic beauty products, take-home program, cooking class, massage in own room

LOCAL ATTRACTIONS: World-famous San Diego Zoo, Sea World, beaches 20 minutes west, horse racing, harness racing

The Spa at Sonoma Mission Inn

Chances are that you will make your way to Sonoma Mission Inn by car coming north through San Francisco and across the spectacular Golden Gate Bridge, an approach that prepares you properly for the pleasures of the Spa at Sonoma Mission Inn. During the hour-and-a-quarter trip, you'll wind through countryside filled with pleasant old farmhouses, grazing livestock and the round hills that are uniquely California.

The pink stucco inn is a restored 1930s mission revival hotel and is surrounded by a seven-acre grove of sycamore. Parked in the circle in front of the inn are Rolls-Royces, Jaguars and Mercedes, but there is really nothing pretentious about the inn itself or its new spa addition.

Inside the three-story, 100-room structure you'll see classic early California architectural design: stucco white walls, high ceilings, heavy oak beams. Tufted gray sofas and chairs in an Art Deco style surround a natural stone fireplace in the two-story lobby.

The inn has four dining areas: an indoor-outdoor restaurant overlooking the pool, for leisurely lunches and continental breakfasts; a grille room; a Provençal dining room with built-in banquettes, rose table linen and white china; and the Big Three Fountain, which has the feeling of a stylized old-fashioned soda fountain and café.

The ambiance of the spa, opened in 1981, is totally different from that of the hotel; the architecture is as avant-garde and futuristic as a space station in a science-fiction movie. The contrast makes for an experience that is both comforting and stimulating at the same time.

ACCOMMODATIONS

Before you arrive in your room, a heavy crystal vase of fresh flowers is delivered, in colors that match the room decor, and moments before you check out a single white rose is brought to your door. Edward Safdie, the owner, is well known for this kind of fastidious attention to decorative detail.

The rooms are designed in neutral tones: taupe, terra-cotta, camel and clay accented by white woodwork. The semicanopied beds with padded headboards are complemented by comfortable upholstered furniture. The carefully thought-out decor includes end tables that swivel for convenience, a ceiling fan that is thermostatically controlled, a small television, a clock radio and a telephone.

A spacious dressing room, reminiscent of an earlier age, contains a large white dresser and mirror plus a large closet with a convenient, sturdy luggage rack.

The white-tiled bathrooms, entirely carpeted, contain a deep, full-sized bath and shower; a sink-to-ceiling mirror; a good-sized counter and enough light to make it all usable.

Maids in pink uniforms deliver clean linen twice daily, turn down the bed at night, replace the spa-provided clothes (robes, warm-ups and kimonos) immediately, and return your personal laundry the following day. Even a laundry bag is provided for your convenience.

Guests seeking more creature comforts than these can choose from a master suite with a separate sitting room or several smaller suites.

Smoking is not permitted in the spa, but you can smoke outdoors or in your room.

FACILITIES

The spa facilities are located in a Quonset hut, which has been expertly redesigned to blend in with the California mission design of the adjacent inn. You enter a central first-floor foyer in which a marble fountain acts as the centerpiece for the host of plants hanging from pink stucco-and-wood columns. Around the reception area are two glass-walled exercise rooms equipped with a complete line of innovative exercise machines.

Though some rooms in this building are small, mirrored walls give a feeling of adequate spaciousness. Also in the first floor is a large gymnasium, with a stereo system that amplifies the instruction for exercises. On the second floor are the whirlpool, sauna, steam and inhalator rooms; a quiet room for herbal wraps and some wonderfully soft, well-padded massage tables.

The spare ultramodern lounge, located on the second floor, is the social center—the place where guests rest, watch TV, read, chat with fellow exercisers or wait for the always-prompt facialist or masseuse. Unfortunately, the lounge is designed more for aesthetics than comfort. Since there is no place to have a rest or nap after the massage or herbal wrap, guests end up using the couches in the lounge, which are attractive but very uncomfortable.

Adjacent to the lounge is the spacious locker room, lined with personal storage lockers for your spa gear (such as the terry robe and Italian bath shoes) and which is surrounded by individual dressing rooms. You can work like an athlete here, but the amenities of a lady are always at hand: a long dressing table, a hair dryer, skin lotion and various beauty aids, including a marvelous, vanilla-scented body lotion. Next to the dressing rooms are four showers, well equipped with heat lamps, apricot-scented soap and floor-to-ceiling stacks of towels.

The attractively landscaped pool is set in the walled courtyard of the spa and is surrounded by flowers. The pool, kept at a constant 80 degrees, was designed especially for aquatic exercises and water volleyball.

PROGRAM

The normal length of a visit to Sonoma is five very full days, beginning midday Sunday and ending at lunchtime on Friday. The program focuses on four major areas: body conditioning, hydrotherapy and herbal wraps, massage and beauty care and calorie-counted cuisine.

The morning of your first day you sit down with the spa director to discuss your goals and develop a personal schedule. Together you go over the health questionnaire you submitted and decide on what calorie count you will follow.

At 5:30 in the morning your phone rings to remind you that the mountain hike starts at 6:00 sharp, and that coffee and tea are being served in the lounge. In fair weather the hike follows a two-mile course through the hills where Jack London lived during the latter part of his life. In rainy weather (possible from December through February) you'll follow the "parcourse" past the scenic homes, small shops and open fields of Sonoma.

The parcourse is a prescribed course with exercise stations. At each station a sign, complete with stick drawing, describes the exercise that you should do here, and suggests the number of times it should be done. When you finish the exercise you move on to the next station.

Breakfast runs from 7:30 to 8:30 A.M. during which time you receive an individual schedule that divides your day into sixty-minute segments. The morning is usually devoted to physical fitness. You start with a warm-up class to stretch out the kinks, then proceed to rather energetic aerobic exercises, followed by a slimnastics class for spot reducing. The hour before noon may be devoted to private nutritional counseling, a hydrotherapy treatment or whirlpool followed by steam or sauna. Noon may bring the facial, and then on to lunch at the pool area in warm weather, or on inclement days, the inn's Provençal Room.

At 2:00 P.M. you get individual instruction on one of the fitness machines or take part in a pool exercise class. The latter part of the afternoon features relaxing activities: massage, herbal wraps, hydrotherapy tub and a stretch relaxation class. Manicures, pedicures and hair care are scheduled during this time period after midweek. The exercise day ends with a one-hour massage or a yoga class that lasts from 5:00 until 6:00 P.M. A scant half hour later it's cocktail time, followed by dinner, a lecture on biofeedback, nutrition planning or skin care. There's little time to make yourself presentable for dinner after having exercised and having been massaged, steamed, oiled and sponged for most of the day. But everyone takes it in stride, and by 9:00 or 10:00 most guests excuse themselves to rest up for the next marathon day.

If you want to go horseback riding or play golf or tennis, special arrangements can be made to include them in your schedule; just mention your interest to the spa director. Additional time for walking, jogging or swimming laps can also be programmed.

The program may be tough, but it is designed specifically for you—your own health, physical condition and goals establish the parameters for the program. The body conditioning is light or vigorous depending on your personal needs and preferences, and you go at your own pace.

On Monday at Sonoma you weigh in, are measured carefully and precise calibration is made of your body fat. Friday morning you weigh out and celebrate your new dimensions.

FOOD AND DIET

The food is attractive to look at and nutrition chief Toni Christian and chef Larry Elbert make it tantalizing to taste and easy on the calories. They use only the finest natural foods, many locally grown, and serve a lot of fresh fruits, vegetables, fish and fowl, combined innovatively with whole-grain breads, delightful sauces and herb dressings.

"How could anything that looks that beautiful and tastes that delicious be low in calories?" remarked a California executive and spa veteran. No expense is spared: grilled baby quail, teriyaki swordfish, bouillabaisse and grilled chicken breasts in mustard sauce are just a few of the reasons why there is such a great demand for take-home recipes.

Monday is cleansing day and six liquids, based totally on fruits and vegetables, are provided to each guest who opts for fasting. Each concoction is made moments before it is served: an orange-strawberry juice at 7:45 A.M. and a banana-almond-pineapple blend at 10:40.

A glass of gazpacho, with a few nuts and seeds, is served at 1:00 P.M. followed by a grapefruit-lemonade drink at 4:00, and a blueberry nectarine "smoothie" (fruit whipped into ice) at 6:00, which is then followed by a portion of sleep-inducing sesame milk at 9:00. The juice fast (which includes the nut and seed amnesty gesture) is available on Thursdays, too, for the committed dieter, and frankly it's the tastiest, most sustaining liquid diet served at any spa.

The general spa menu is calculated to deliver 800 calories per day, but a maintenance diet of 1,200 calories is available, and for those on a weight-gain diet there is a 2,000-calorie menu available. Diet expert Christian monitors all diets, provides a weekly lecture on nutrition and schedules half-hour individual consultations on each guest's nutritional needs.

HEALTH AND BEAUTY SERVICES

Soft lights, fresh flowers, luxurious facilities and expert professional treatment are the mark of the Sonoma spa, and it is impossible to leave there without feeling more beautiful and glamorous. All beauty services are geared to a guest's personal needs and preferences.

An individual skin analysis is done for each guest early in the week, and daily facials are planned with the skin's particular needs in mind. The face is cleansed, toned and moisturized, and in the process guests are treated to a tender neck, shoulder, upper chest and face massage, followed by a soothing facial mask. A fine water vapor is used daily to replenish dehydrated skin, open the pores and allow the organic creams to ease away wrinkles and tension. During the fourth or fifth facial days, a

natural bio-peel, a mask consisting of natural vegetable products, is used to help eliminate dead skin cells and revitalize
texture, tone and color. By Thursday afternoon, each guest's
skin is radiant.

Massage at Sonoma is not just a beauty treatment but rather
a part of total health care. The massages whisk tensions away,
improve circulation and give you a deep feeling of relaxation.
Japanese finger massage (shiatsu) or Swedish massage are options and you have a choice of natural oils or creams—none of
which contains a drop of mineral oil.

If the massages don't grant you that last dimension of relaxation, try the forty-minute immersion in the custom-designed
hydrotherapy tubs filled with mineral water heated to body
temperature. Thirty different jets and bubblers along the sides
of the giant turquoise tubs create a sensation of effervescence
and total calm. Massage therapists direct a regulated jet on
tight muscle areas and you feel both relaxed and stimulated.

Several times during your five-day stay herbal wraps are em-
ployed to draw out the body toxins and further release muscle
tensions.

On Thursdays and Fridays your schedule will include a complete manicure and pedicure, and on Friday there is a full hour
of hair care.

OTHER PLEASURES

The spa is located in the heart of the California wine country,
and we suggest that you consider taking an extra day or two so
that you can sight-see and shop without feeling that you're
skipping important activities at the spa. You really can't do the
program and play tourist at the same time.

Sonoma, just five minutes away, is a charming village built
around a shady, old-fashioned town square, and you can spend
a very pleasant afternoon exploring the diversity of shops and
studios for artists and crafts people. The Sonoma Arts Council
(709 Davis Street, Santa Rosa, CA 95401) will be happy to send
you a map and illustrated brochure of the Sonoma County art
studios.

There are specialty food shops too, wonderful bakeries, the
Sonoma Cheese Factory, and in Boyes Hot Springs, the
Sonoma Sausage Company.

The square is also the site of one of the last old-time

drugstores with a complete and nostalgically glamorous soda fountain.

Close to the inn is the Jack London State Historic Park where the author's last home is still maintained. Another interesting historical spot is the Mission San Francisco Solano, the northernmost of the California missions. Drive any road in any direction and you'll probably chance on a winery, but the spa can counsel you on which have the best tours and wines.

The setting is really marvelous and you may want to share it with a spouse or friend. While you are at the spa, your partner could play golf, see the local vineyards or lounge at poolside. A practical variation on this theme is for a woman to do the Sunday–Friday program at the spa and have her partner meet her at the inn for a restful weekend, by which time she should feel (and look) terrific. Men's weeks are also available periodically.

WHAT TO BRING

Packing for Sonoma is easy because the spa provides most of what you'll need to wear there. Attractive gray warm-ups and robes are provided each day. There is, in fact, a terry robe everywhere you look: a fresh one is always in each locker and in each room, and if you misplace yours there are others available at strategic places throughout the spa. Soft, colorful kimonos, to be used as coverups, and wonderful Italian bath shoes are also provided. For the crisp morning hikes in cool weather the spa provides ski hats and mittens, but you might want to bring along a turtleneck shirt or pullover to wear under your warm-up if you visit during the winter months.

Bring gym socks, tennis shoes, leotards and tights for the exercise classes. A lot of anything is not necessary, since the spa does your personal laundry each day.

The suggested dress for evening is included in your arrival instruction packet. The staff says "casual," but the most prominent sign, APPROPRIATE ATTIRE, suggests that slightly more than casual is in order. "Casual" to most Californians includes velour warm-ups, but they wouldn't be appropriate for evenings here. Slacks and sweater or a blouse are a nice in-between. Casual slacks, a sport shirt and sweater are appropriate for men who stay at the inn.

If you're a hiker or a determined shopper, then you may want to bring walking shoes as well.

Rain gear is supplied by the spa so that even wet ground and skies will not save you from the 6:00 A.M. hike.

HOW TO GET THERE

If you're flying, fly to San Francisco International airport and the spa will make arrangements to pick you up and return you in time to catch your departing flight, but discuss flight schedules with the spa staff in advance of your arrival.

The Santa Rosa airport, twenty-five miles from the spa, is another possibility, as it can handle private jets, and again the spa can make arrangements for land transportation. The small Shelleville airport, just five minutes from the inn, can accommodate small planes.

The spa is located just forty-five pleasant miles north of San Francisco. You drive north on Highway 101 to the Allejo-Napa turnoff on Highway 37 where you turn right, or northeast. When you reach Highway 121 you turn left, north, and when the road starts to bend east, you come to Highway 12. Turn left again and follow that road directly to the Sonoma Plaza. At the plaza turn left and go two-and-one-half miles to the Sonoma Mission Inn gate.

From the north, come south on 101 or 1 and turn east at Highway 12, which takes you to Sonoma. From Easy Bay go north on 17 and 80 and then west on 12. From Sacramento, come southwest on 80, and then west on 12.

SUMMARY

Sonoma Mission Inn is an elegant old California inn with a sparkling new spa addition. Since it is fairly new among spas, it is still in a period of developing a consistent level of service; the management needs to work out a few kinks and we expect that they will, as care has been taken to find excellent staff, and the furnishings and equipment are the highest quality.

At Sonoma the diet, exercise program and beauty services are all custom tailored to meet your needs and wants. The spa creates your individual program and helps you follow it. The atmosphere is delightful and the food (vitally important when you're dieting) is superb.

This is the only spa in the northwestern United States. It's needed and welcome.

FACT SUMMARY

NAME: The Spa at Sonoma Mission Inn

MAILING ADDRESS: P. O. Box 1, Boyes Hot Springs, CA 95416

TELEPHONE: (707) 996-1041; toll-free (800) 862-4945

TRANSPORTATION: Complimentary spa limo pick-up at San Francisco and Santa Rosa airports

ACCOMMODATIONS: Mission Revival country inn; twin or queen beds for spa guests; suites and king-sized beds also available

FEE: $1900 for five days (Sunday P.M. through Friday A.M.)

MAXIMUM NUMBER OF GUESTS: 30

MAXIMUM NUMBER OF STAFF: 35

SEASON: Year-round

AMBIANCE: Secluded perfection in country inn located in California wine country

GENDER AND AGE RESTRICTIONS: Adults over 16; women only; some men's weeks; couples' weeks

DIET: Gourmet continental low-calorie diets of 800, 1,200 and 2,000 calories per day; many locally grown fruits and vegetables; lean meats, fowl, seafood and fish; outstanding liquid diet once a week

FACILITIES: Tennis courts, 2 swimming pools, 4 restaurants, golf and equestrian opportunities arranged, gym, exercise rooms, steam, sauna, whirlpool, herbal wraps in special inhalation room

PROGRAM: Personalized program, moderate to very strenuous; very pampering; personalized nutritional counseling and diet; expert staff; stretch, aerobic, slimnastics, yoga and pool exercise classes

SPECIAL FEATURES: Pneumatic air-resistance machines, Dynavit exercise cycles with biofeedback computers, hydrotherapy department

LOCAL ATTRACTIONS: Wine tours, hot-air balloon rides

The Palms

In Palm Springs, undoubtedly the capital of luxury and excess in this country, there is an oasis that teaches both men and women that moderation has its rewards. One of these rewards, and the chief salable product of the Palms at Palm Springs, is energy: the unbounding physical and mental stamina that helps a person approach life head-on with optimism.

If you doubt this you need only take a look at the Palms staff. Almost all on the other side of fifty, they charge through the day with enthusiasm, determination and clear-eyed intelligence. This is not to say they are grim. In fact, this resort definitely has its share of humor. The first morning we were there the resident director, Stan Brown, casually referred to the spa's ubiquitous diet muffins as hockey pucks, and the program director, Peter Warner (who both looks and acts like Bob Hope, except he's funnier) strolled by wearing a shirt that stated plainly THE CREDIBLE HULK.

They ought to know what they are doing. This management team (led by owner Sheila Cluff) cut their teeth on their first spa venture, the Oaks at Ojai, 150 miles to the north and west and developed it into a rousing success in the four years since Ms. Cluff bought it.

Spurred by this success, and by the belief that many winter visitors and Los Angeles residents would prefer the sunny Palm Springs climate over a cooler location, the group, officially organized as Fitness, Inc., looked for a good location in the desert city where the slogan is "P.S., I love you." They found a graceful former resort built around a courtyard in a modified California Monterey style, with red-tiled roof and an upper porch and balcony dripping with flowering bougainvillea. Outside the enclosed courtyard gray and brown mountains rise sharply.

Thanks to the altitude and the absence of heavy manufacturing in Palm Springs, the air is a clean, clear electric blue.

ACCOMMODATIONS

Rooms are all on the ground floor, contained in clusters around the courtyard, and the units stretch out to the edges of the grounds, which cover a space as large as a city block.

Most guest quarters have two double beds in a good-sized

room with generous double closets. The bathrooms leave a little to be desired. When we arrived, the tub could have used a good scrubbing, and the water pressure was erratic. Good, dependable water pressure is important in a spa, since most guests feel a need to shower or bathe frequently to remove oil-based scalp treatments and massage oils. To complicate matters further, when the water did make an appearance it had one temperature: cold.

Another item that was a disappointment was the poor quality of the towels, which are provided by a local linen service. They are fairly small and definitely scratchy. We recommend bringing your own.

On a happier note, the general decor of motel modern furniture in cheerful blue and green prints is certainly acceptable, and the small enclosed private patio off each room makes it possible to sunbathe au naturel, if that is your preference.

FACILITIES

The walls of the Palms compound enclose a large courtyard, which can be entered from the street only through an arched Spanish gate. The office is just inside the entrance, and there is always someone there to take a phone call, answer a question about the schedule, take a reservation for a special treatment or tell you what's happening in Palm Springs.

In the same section of the building on the first floor is a lilliputian boutique and a beauty salon.

The centerpiece of the complex is the large exercise pool, the water of which has been known to get so hot during the fierce Palm Springs summers that staff have to dump cold water and blocks of ice into it to bring the temperature down to a normal range.

Walking across the courtyard and past the pool, you arrive at the dining room, which has a cool elegant feel to it thanks to blue and white metallic wallpaper featuring fan palm images. There are tables of various sizes so that you may eat with small or large groups and a help-yourself beverage alcove that makes coffee and tea available all day.

Just behind the dining room is a large exercise room with light blue carpet and mirrored walls equipped with stationary bikes and Universal weight machines.

Upstairs, entered through the second-floor veranda, is a small classroom for lectures and crafts, and an inviting lounge with a kitchenette (for ice water, tea or coffee) and fireplace; decor is sophisticated, with modern overstuffed furniture, bright prints and rattan chairs; blue, tan and white are obviously favorite colors here, and it gives the area a calm but upbeat appearance. The upstairs level also houses the facial and massage rooms.

PROGRAM

The day starts at 7:00 A.M. with a brisk three-mile walk through the Las Palmas residential section at the base of the foothills, or for those preferring a more leisurely walk, there is a one-mile stroll (called the "nature walk") to a local park. Afterward, breakfast is served between 8:00 and 9:00 in the dining room, followed by the first class of the day, body awareness.

When Peter Warner teaches this, prepare to laugh your way through the forty-five-minute session. He is a glib, affable fellow with a classical education (Yale) and he keeps up a running commentary on the widest range of unrelated but fascinating topics from history to sociology, while leading you through exercises that work each muscle group.

His classes are accompanied by the most unusual music selections you'll encounter at any spa. He plays 1928 recordings of Bessie Smith and talks simultaneously about her life and loves at the time that the recording was made, or mimics the clever lyrics of Cole Porter songs, or sings along with Al Jolson records, belting out the refrains while never missing a movement in the exercise routine.

When one guest collapsed on the floor in a heap (it was hard to tell whether from exhaustion or the silent giggles), Peter stepped toward her and asked offhandedly if she was doing an imitation of the classical statue of *The Dying Gaul*, complimenting her on her excellent interpretation.

He closed one vigorous class by telling a story about a fierce ancient battle in which the Greeks had lost ("one of their helicopters malfunctioned," said Peter with a straight face). Then surveying our limp bodies he intoned a few lines on the subject by the historian Thucydides: "We have fought as [sic] men must and have suffered as [sic] men will."

At 10:00 A.M. guests can choose between body dynamics, which is the most rigorous class offered and is recommended only for those having good to superior levels of fitness, or a class titled "Fitness for Hands, Face and Feet." The latter includes exercises for toning the face, chin and throat; strengthening the hands and fingers and exercises for your feet based on the principles of reflexology. The instructor provided people in the class with creams and oils and recommended that we do these exercises at home in front of the TV, which would have the additional benefit of preventing one from absent-mindedly eating, since your hands would be too gooey to dip into the potato chip bag.

At 11:00 A.M. guests can choose from Sheila Can Show You How—a series of spot-reducing exercises to use at home—or a pool exercise class. Both are excellent, no matter what your level of fitness.

After lunch there is no regular class for all guests until 2:00 P.M., although for men in attendance there is a weight resistance class, held Tuesdays, Thursdays and Saturdays at 1:30. Mondays, Wednesdays and Fridays there is a staff exercise class, and guests are welcome to attend, although most guests choose to take this time for sunning by the pool. At 2:00 P.M. pool class is repeated, and a body contouring class is held that involves exercising with wrist and ankle weights or exercise wands.

At 4:00 P.M. Eleanor Brown, district manager for Fitness, Inc., gives a superb hatha-yoga class, including the classic postures, proper breathing and a relaxation period at the end.

At 5:30 guests gather to drink juice cocktails in the upper lounge called the Winners' Circle, while in a small sitting room nearby orientation is held every day for new guests. Dinner is served between 6:00 and 7:00 P.M., and at 7:30 an evening program is presented. Topics include hypnosis, how to dress for success and a survey of Palm Springs history and activities.

FOOD AND DIET

The Palms diet is based on 750 calories and includes veal, turkey, chicken and fresh fish. Eleanor Brown plans all the menus and includes surprising dishes such as turkey divan, oven fries and cheesecake within the daily calorie allotment.

Breakfast is usually a piece of fruit such as cantaloupe or grapefruit, and a crunchy diet muffin; a packet of vitamin supplements is also offered. At midmorning there is a broth break. Lunch starts with soup, sometimes followed with a chicken tostada seasoned with chili and cumin, crowded with lettuce and cheese; or a cheese-and-vegetable quiche or a fruit and cheese salad.

Dinner can include soup, a salad and an entree such as veal loaf, red snapper with tomato and vegetable sauce, or ratatouille. Each dinner ends with a dessert, such as flan, fruit or orange zabaglione. No salt, sugar or chemical additives are used in food preparation. For seasoning, something called "Dr. Jensen's powder," a natural product made from vegetable flakes, is used instead of salt and pepper. Coffee and hot or iced herb teas are available all day; try the licorice tea—it has a surprising naturally sweet taste.

HEALTH AND BEAUTY SERVICES

Beauty and health services (all available at an additional charge) include massage, cellulite treatments and facials (which you can schedule one day in advance at the registration desk in the office), and complete hair and nail services, which are available by appointment in the beauty salon.

The forty-five-minute massage treatments, offered from 9:00 A.M. to 10:00 P.M., are competently done; try different technicians until you find one just right for you.

Cosmetics used in the facials are by Vera, and a deep cleansing with a mask and beauty grains leaves your skin smooth and pink. The cellulite massage, lasting thirty minutes, is a massage focusing on hip and thigh areas. For the cellulite wrap a technician applies oil to specific areas and wraps the body in plastic. The effect is to smooth and tighten.

OTHER PLEASURES

Palm Springs offers great shopping within walking distance. Tennis and golf are available within a few blocks of the Palms. Check at the reservation desk for how to make arrangements.

Horseback riding is another activity guests enjoy, and for those who want a real bird's-eye view of Palm Springs, there is an aerial tramway to the top of Mount San Jacinto.

If you are fascinated by the famous, you can take a tour in a limousine, which winds past stars' homes.

WHAT TO BRING

Only towels are provided, so bring all you will need to take part in the spa program: a swimsuit, beach towel, jogging shoes, shorts and T-shirts, a robe or coverup, and casual dress for evening and trips to town.

HOW TO GET THERE

Fly into Los Angeles and rent a car or take the bus to Palm Springs (the bus station is just two blocks from the Palms). You can also take a commuter flight into the small but busy Palm Springs airport.

If you like driving, come east on Route 10 (the San Bernardino Freeway). Take 11 south into Palm Springs, then take a left at Alejo and left on Indian. The spa is on your right.

SUMMARY

The Palms is an attractive, well-run spa that caters to mildly affluent guests averaging between ages thirty and fifty. In the winter most guests are from out of state, especially New York and Canada, but in the warmer, off-season months, inexpensive specials are offered for teachers, mothers and daughters, fathers and sons, friends, and couples, and a slightly younger, less affluent crowd arrives.

The food and exercise program are first-rate, and the competent staff are all nice people who seem to like what they are doing.

Palm Springs itself will charm you. The best of everything is available there, including this well-priced and well-run resort.

FACT SUMMARY

NAME: The Palms

MAILING ADDRESS: 572 North Indian Avenue, Palm Springs, CA 92262

TELEPHONE: (619) 325-1111

ACCOMMODATIONS: Hotel rooms or private cottages

FEE: 3-day minimum—single, $145 per day; double, $69 per person, per day; deluxe double, $89 per person, per day; special rates in summer

MAXIMUM NUMBER OF GUESTS: 75-85

MAXIMUM NUMBER OF STAFF: 30

SEASON: Year-round

AMBIANCE: Casual; heart of posh Palm Springs; courtyard quarters

GENDER AND AGE RESTRICTIONS: Adults over 16; coed

DIET: Fresh, natural, American home style; 750 calories a day

FACILITIES: Pool, whirlpool, gym, saunas, massage and facial room, boutique, beauty salon, game room

PROGRAM: Permissive; aerobic based; body awareness, body dynamics, spot reducing, weight resistance, body contouring, yoga and pool exercise classes; lectures

SPECIAL FEATURES: Cellulite reduction program

LOCAL ATTRACTIONS: Shopping, Indian reservation museums

The Oaks at Ojai

A twenty-minute ride inland from Ventura, California, and close to the Los Padres National Forest, is the charming, small town of Ojai. The fertile valley surrounding the town is the home of several religious sects that settled there in the 1920s. They were drawn by the "spiritual vibrations" of the unique, east-west valley, which was thought to provide special receptivity to psychic and spiritual communications.

As if to belie these goings-on, a gracious and dignified wood-and-stone structure sits like a prim matron on the main street of town. This is the Oaks at Ojai. Built in 1920 as a lodge for vacationers from Santa Barbara, today, after a little sprucing up, it has a new life as one of the most popular spas in California.

The Oaks is owned by Sheila Cluff, once the spa's fitness director, and earlier a member of the Hollywood Ice Review. Ms. Cluff is one of the most active and visible national spokespersons for the importance of fitness in creating a quality lifestyle. As the Oaks began to prosper, she opened another spa, the Palms, in Palm Springs.

After checking in you'll be given a tour of the facilities. Almost everything is located in the spacious, well-appointed main lodge: dining room; exercise rooms; bar-recreation area; lobby with a pleasant, large fireplace and the inevitable, but in this case good, spa shop. Upstairs there are guest rooms. The tour guide explains the natural food plan and the general daily schedule. One learns there is a large staff, each with different abilities and duties. There are no amateurs here: most staff members have physical education or recreation degrees or both, and have taught extensively: a few are former professional dancers and all are warm and accessible.

Guests range in age from eighteen to seventy, with most people thirty to fifty. It's a lively, fairly fit group, who exude an air of success and far-ranging interests.

If you're looking for good talk and interesting company, you'll find it at the Oaks. As the spa is located near Los Angeles, there are almost always actors and actresses, producers, directors or writers visiting when you are. Lawyers, doctors, psychologists and successful business people also abound. About 80 percent of the guests are women, and 20 percent are men (who usually come as part of a couple).

ACCOMMODATIONS

You may stay in the main building, where the rooms are small but pleasant and inexpensive, or in the larger cottages, which are tucked among live oak trees and are connected by winding paths. Each cottage has a large bath with dressing area and two double beds. There are also telephones and color televisions in the rooms. If you came alone but would like a roommate to help cut the costs, just check with the front desk and suitable arrangements can usually be made.

FACILITIES

The main building is furnished in a contemporary manner that is indigenous to California: comfortable but attractively modern. The dining room is an open, airy room with comfortable seating at a variety of table sizes. Nearby is the large Winners' Circle with its handsome walnut bar (juice only) running the length of the room. This is where most of the guests congregate during free hours, and where the evening programs are held. In a wing off the lobby are the beauty salon, four massage rooms and two facial compartments. They are small but exquisitely furnished with antiques and muted fabrics.

There is a large, carpeted exercise room and behind it is an indoor whirlpool and sauna. Another whirlpool is located out by the swimming pool and is much more pleasant.

Outdoors, the large, graduated-depth swimming pool is set in the center of the complex of cottages and everything is surrounded by well-maintained flower gardens. The pool is the magnet for rest, sunning, casual conversation and blissful floating on high-quality rafts that feel as secure as your own waterbed.

PROGRAM

The Oaks staff is serious about fitness and the fourteen varied forty-five-minute class offerings a day reflect this attitude. Morning starts with a brisk morning walk or nature walk, followed by a body awareness class based on progressive stretches. If Sheila Cluff is there, don't miss her instruction in this class; you will learn a lot from her about your body and how it can function.

The body dynamics class is more challenging; it includes a real muscle workout with a sustained period of aerobics followed by a cooldown. You may notice some famous legs or torsos next to you as you work out. Frequent guests are Charlene Tilton of "Dallas," Gore Vidal and Jeanne Crain.

The pool classes at the Oaks are terrific. The ones we attended involved aerobic exercises and muscle toning. Large inflatable balls were used to help create resistance; moving them under water requires a lot of effort, and the exercises were strenuous but fun. One fanny and tightening exercise required balancing on top of a ball tucked under the buttocks. The pool looked like it was filled with bobbing human buoys.

In the afternoon, body contouring classes are offered. Here, guests have a chance to work on toning and tightening muscles using the ballet barre. In these as all other classes, both men and women are present, which always makes the time spent more fun.

The yoga class at the end of the day leads you through basic yoga postures, some good stretches, and a very complete relaxation sequence. We recommend it.

In addition to these classes, several times a week, you can participate in Sheila Can Show You How, which is a take-it-home exercise class tailored to your specific needs.

The quality of all exercise instruction at the Oaks is first-rate.

The teachers are thorough and energetic, encouraging guests to participate but warning them away from exercises that might be too strenuous. Classes are organized according to degree of difficulty, ranging from mild exercise (body awareness) to strenuous exercise (body dynamics), but even within these groups, a guest is encouraged to go at his or her own pace.

In the evening there are lectures or programs on a wide variety of topics including "The New Sexual Freedom: Now That We Have It, What Do We Do With It?" "Dance and Exercise to Music," "Learn to Batik" and "Holistic Health for Today." Other programs cover self-image, astrology, wills and trusts and designing your appearance. Following each program, there is usually a spirited discussion led by the lecturer.

A recent addition is the new yoga class offered at night, Bedtime Yoga, which teaches one how to gear down and relax for the night.

FOOD AND DIET

After you get settled you will have an appointment with the nurse, who will weigh you, take your blood pressure and a brief medical history and discuss your goals for your stay.

The food plan is based on 750 calories a day of natural foods. No chemical additives, salt, white flour or sugar are used. The menu features lots of fresh vegetables and fruit, with frequent seafood entrees, as well as chicken and veal. Occasionally, a special meal is planned such as "fried" chicken, corn on the cob (a very small ear) and trimmings. All still within the diet plan.

If you're a serious dieter, at least for the moment, you may want to consider the "calorie-cutter" entree: a large portion of chicken, fish or turkey on a bed of lettuce. Follow this choice and your calorie count for the day is a spartan, but pleasant, 525. Or, if you are able to eat more, ask for the "athletic portions," but note that they will add 200 to 400 calories per day to your diet. You may also order a "cleansing salad" (raw cabbage, oranges, sprouts and carrots), or a "living salad'" (raw vegetables with enzymes that aid digestion).

On the regular 750-calorie plan, breakfast is likely to be fresh fruit and a small bran muffin. Midmorning, a potassium broth is served. Lunch can be soup, a salad with tuna, boiled egg, mushrooms and mozzarella cheese accompanied by delicious diet dressings, or (another favorite) vegetable crepes, with fruit for dessert. "Cocktails" might consist of zucchini-pineapple juice. Dinner is soup, crackers, fish or veal, one or two vegetables, possibly a salad and fruit for dessert. The food is attractively presented and the service is pleasant and efficient.

Meals are usually eaten in the dining room, although you can arrange to have them brought to your room. If you wish, you may eat your lunch out by the pool. Sign up for this the day before, then pick it up at the kitchen at lunch time.

HEALTH AND BEAUTY SERVICES

At some spas the beauty treatments are an integral part of the program, but at the Oaks, they are strictly an option. The exercise staff doesn't refer to them much; they cost extra, and you have to make reservations to get them. However, they're worth seeking out.

The facials are some of the best that you will have experienced at any spa. Each takes an hour, and includes cleansing, one or more peels, toning, blackhead extractions, etcetera, depending upon whatever your skin type and condition needs. The treatment includes a hand-and-foot massage with heated lotion-filled booties tied on your hands and feet to soften the skin.

The beauty salon is modern and thoroughly complete: whether you bring your own or your acrylic nails, there is an expert to put them in the best of shape and color. A cellulite wrap is also offered. Massages are excellent and are available until 11:00 P.M. by appointment.

OTHER PLEASURES

The town of Ojai offers rewarding experiences for the adventurer. There is a surprising mix of shops: some offering elegant and costly European goods ($150 Italian shoes, for example), others selling herbs, used books, organic cosmetics and health foods. The morning nature walk winds through town while the more rigorous "brisk walk" takes you beyond the main village and along a glistening creek, via back roads where many of the people you see are riding horseback.

Ojai is also something of an art colony, and the front desk of the Oaks can make arrangements for you to go to artists' homes and studios, shop for antiques or see art shows in the many galleries.

It is also interesting to visit sites of some of the religious sects, such as the homes of members of the Theosophy movement, or the Krishnamurti Foundation. There are many psychics, astrologers, pyramid enthusiasts and other practitioners in Ojai, and many guests take advantage of their services during a stay at the Oaks.

The town has a marvelous bookstore, Bart's Corners, where used books, old magazines and sheet music are sold in an indoor-outdoor maze of bookshelves. There are even bookshelves built into the outer walls so that anyone who can't sleep can walk over to Bart's during the night, pick out something soothing to read and throw his coins (on the honor system) through the mesh fence. The fact that this works says a lot about the honesty and positive outlook that prevail in Ojai.

WHAT TO BRING

Bring shorts and T-shirts, a jogging suit and shoes, slacks or a skirt, leotards, bathing suit, swim coverup, sandals and a big beach towel. The evenings can get a little cool so pack a sweater or jacket.

For exercise classes, leotards are pro forma. For lunch and dinner as well as strolls around town, bring shorts and tops, or slacks, skirts and blouses. Dress is fairly casual but chic.

Men wear jogging outfits or sports shorts and casual sports shirts, and men and women alike can find a fine selection of clothes (even large sizes) at the spa shop. Prices there are spa prices: expensive, but no worse than most places.

The spa receptionist can make arrangements for golf, tennis or horseback riding, and if you plan these activities, bring the necessary equipment along.

HOW TO GET THERE

It is easiest to fly to Los Angeles or Santa Barbara and rent a car for the drive to Ojai. From Los Angeles, take Highway 101 northwest, to Highway 33 north, and 150 east to Ojai. From Santa Barbara, go south on 101 and then east on 150 to Ojai. The Oaks is located at 122 East Ojai Avenue, close to the center of town. You can also take the bus from Los Angeles or Santa Barbara.

SUMMARY

The Oaks at Ojai is a good, wholesome retreat for men, women and couples, just a short drive from Los Angeles. The exercise and diet program are sound and the small-town surroundings contribute to a feeling of relaxation and well-being.

This is not a fancy, high-powered resort, and many of its guests choose it for just that reason. It is like a coed summer camp for intelligent realists. Guests come away with renewed energy and (nearly always) a few new books from Bart's Corners bookstore.

FACT SUMMARY

NAME: The Oaks at Ojai

MAILING ADDRESS: 122 East Ojai Avenue, Ojai, CA 93023

TELEPHONE: (805) 646-5573

ACCOMMODATIONS: Cottages and rooms in the main lodge

FEE: $89–$94 per day, single; $64–$72 double plus tax and service charge, depending on accommodations. Two-night minimum stay; rates go down after 30 consecutive days

MAXIMUM NUMBER OF GUESTS: 80

MAXIMUM NUMBER OF STAFF: 20

SEASON: Year-round

AMBIANCE: Renovated country inn in picturesque California village; casual comfort

GENDER AND AGE RESTRICTIONS: Adults over 16; coed

DIET: Natural whole foods with no additives; fish, chicken, meat; low sodium; fresh vegetables and fruit; 750 calories a day

FACILITIES: Swimming pool, indoor gym, indoor and outdoor whirlpools, saunas, cosmetic center with facial and skin care department

PROGRAM: Superaerobics, body awareness, body dynamics, body contouring, pool exercise and yoga classes

SPECIAL FEATURES: Evening program includes nutrition lectures, behavior-modification talks, dance classes

LOCAL ATTRACTIONS: Local playhouse, art community

The Ashram

The Ashram, near Malibu, California, has the reputation for being "the toughest spa in the country." And in many ways, it is. Its director, Anne Marie Bengstrom, a former cross-country skiing champion in her native Sweden, knows about pushing personal limits. She once put herself to a test to discover those limits by spending five months in the Guatemalan jungle, an experience she says contributed to an almost mystical clarity about the essentials versus the nonessentials in life.

Most guests (male and female) who come to the Ashram are professional, fairly affluent, "with it" achievers who make their living with their minds, often at the expense of their bodies, and who deal with constant stressful influences in their work, social and personal lives. They come to the Ashram both to escape that stress and to learn how to deal with it.

Surprisingly, Anne Marie and her staff meet this need to escape stress by offering more stress. The secret is that it is a totally different kind of stress than that which the sedentary, sandwich-grabbing urbanite lives with daily. The philosophy here is similar to that of wilderness survival groups such as Outward Bound: by subjecting yourself to enormous physical demands that you have always thought were beyond your capabilities, and by meeting those challenges, you can undergo a transcendent, positive change in attitude toward yourself and life in general.

A week at the Ashram can function almost as a rite of passage to a new self-image, a time of ascetic purification and growth that tempts many guests to return once and sometimes twice a year.

Spa loungers and sybarites beware! The Ashram (a word that means "place of retreat") offers serious benefit, but it doesn't promise that it will come easily or without pain. But then, as one guest pointed out with a wry grin, real personal change seldom does.

ACCOMMODATIONS

The Ashram accommodates only eight guests, who room in four comfortable but unpretentious bedrooms of the main house. The overall atmosphere is not unlike a tiny dormitory. Because facilities are shared, and because of the group cohesiveness that builds as the program progresses, there is a very communal spirit to the place. There is also, however, a respect for the need to be alone; the other guests seem to pick up on that and you can retire to your room, sit out on the patio or retreat to the hillside solarium without comment.

The small group size, close living conditions and the intensity of the program contribute to the guests getting to know one another in an intimate way. A typical group is four men and four women, and although bathroom facilities are shared, there is never a problem since guests are usually aware, sophisticated people sensitive to one another's needs. Guests room with another person of the same sex, although couples who come together are welcome to share a room.

FACILITIES

The entrance to the Ashram is an unpaved road winding uphill to the two-story stucco house that is the heart of the Ashram. The surrounding terrain is rugged and rocky, with small gardens of bright wild flowers, cactus and herbs planted in open spaces.

The house itself is casual, comfortable and characterized by a truly ascetic simplicity. Downstairs is a comfortable living-room area with a fireplace. The earth-toned furniture is comfortable and attractive. One wall of this room houses an extensive library with samplings from literature, psychology, health, religion and metaphysics.

The dining area is just off the living room and looks out onto a covered, sun-dappled patio, where hummingbirds are frequently seen visiting the feeder. The patio is breezy and dotted with comfortable canvas furniture. Guests can choose to lounge in the sun or the shade.

The second floor of the house holds the weight room and gymnasium, hardly a typical workout room because it is actually a covered porch. One whole wall of the room is windows that look out on the hills and almost give you a feeling of being outdoors.

A small heated pool sits behind the house and is surrounded by towering sweet-smelling eucalyptus trees. There is a small winding path of stone steps leading up the hillside behind the house to a dome structure where early morning yoga and meditation takes place. The dome, like the house, provides a feeling of contact with the outdoors thanks to natural lighting. Next to the dome is the small solarium where guests may disrobe and relax in the sun during the short but very sweet rest period.

PROGRAM

The day begins at 6:30 A.M. with yoga, which is conducted in the dome. Stretching and breathing exercises help relieve some of the tightness that may have built up in the muscles from the previous day's exercises, and also reenergize the whole system in preparation for another active day. This is a quiet, contemplative time. It is just beginning to get light outside, the instructor speaks in a soft tone of voice, the room is amply carpeted and there is an attitude of peace and well-being.

A breakfast of fresh-squeezed orange juice follows yoga. Next, a two-hour hike. The leader keeps the pace relatively quick. Guests may choose to walk and talk at the same time, or hike silently and take this opportunity to think.

After the hike, there is a brief rest period that is followed by an hour of weight-lifting exercise with Maxie, a former sports trainer. This is followed by one hour of pool exercise. Though the exercises are strenuous and done at a quick clip, just being in the warm water in the sun feels magnificent after a hefty two-hour hike and a strenuous hour of lifting weights. Volleyball in the pool following the exercises is a great tension releaser—whether it be muscular or emotional/psychological or (as is usually the case) both.

Lunch is followed by an hour-and-a-half rest period. Many guests take this time to nap; some lie in the sun in the solarium and others rest in the warm pool water or take a book out onto the patio. Many of the guests started out using the rest period to do "work" they had brought along with them, but by the end of the week this "work" seemed less necessary than it had at the beginning of the week.

Every guest receives a one-hour massage at some time after the morning hike and before the evening hike.

After the rest period, heart and respiration rates are raised once again with calisthenics done to music. This goes on for an hour, at the end of which you put on your shoes and prepare for the evening walk, which is about an hour and a half. The strenuousness of the hikes varies from day to day.

The evening meal is served at about 7:00 P.M. and on certain evenings is followed by a lecture by Anne Marie and discussion. The focus of the discussion varies: from how to break unhealthy habits, to the energy centers of the body and what they mean, the importance and interpretation of dreams, and spirituality and sexuality.

All the guests participate in all the parts of the program. If someone is missing, it is noticed. Throughout the program, guests have a keen sense that the staff are not just there to whip them into physical shape in the same manner as a drill sergeant. Although each activity leader definitely works the group hard, she communicates in some way that the goal of pushing yourself so hard is not just to lose pounds or inches but to develop new sources of energy and strength that will make all aspects of your life more enjoyable. The staff exude a kind of joy, peace and love toward themselves and guests.

The Ashram is very well organized, but there is no feeling of rigidity in the course of the day's events. Strenuousness of activity varies from day to day, not at random but with purpose—the first two full days being tough, the second two a little less tough and the last two being very tough. The leader of the group for the evening hike stays overnight with the guests and leads the next day's activities. Every day and evening the staff leader is available for conversation and consultation; she is truly a part of the group and is not set off in any way as a guru.

Extreme attention is devoted at all times to the individual well-being of each guest: his or her nutrition, body condition and psychological well-being. At no time is anyone lost in the regimentation of activities, and although the time is heavily scheduled, there is no chance of feeling out of control, since guests have the assurance of support and of always knowing what comes next.

FOOD AND DIET

Though there is never any mention of numbers in relation to calories, calorie intake is low, probably hovering around the 600-calorie-per-day mark. Some adjustments are made according to individual weight, size and health needs.

Anne Marie espouses eating foods as close to their natural state as possible. Breakfast consists of freshly squeezed or

63

pureed fruit juice served in a large goblet. A typical lunch is a very small serving of a yogurt and cottage cheese blend, surrounded by a slice each of kiwi, papaya, apple, and orange. Dinner is the real meal of the day, and is actually the only time you really feel like eating a real meal because of the strenuousness of the activities. A salad of watercress with a sliced egg and tomato is set before you. In small crockery-type dishes set around the table guests can make their own salad combinations by choosing from a selection of onion, garlic, mung beans, lentil beans and alfalfa sprouts. A small serving of creamy Hidden Valley Ranch style dressing is served with each salad.

Snacks are available midmorning and midafternoon and consist of colorfully displayed choices of celery, zucchini and carrot sticks and other raw vegetables—as much as you care to eat. A special juice concoction of blended celery, parsley and zucchini is also available twice a day. Guests are encouraged to drink this green liquid because it helps to ward off symptoms that might result from the lowering of calorie intake and change of diet. A hydrochloric acid pill is offered each morning for the same reason.

The food tastes absolutely wonderful. The guest, having pushed his or her physical limits all day, seems satisfied on a small calorie intake. Some guests elect to fast one day out of seven.

The meals are set out on the table very attractively. The produce is fresh, and the colors of the food seem almost psychedelic. This visual sense is attributed not only to the bright natural colors of very fresh food but also, guests feel, to the perceptual effects of a slightly altered state of consciousness resulting from continual strenuous exercise. There is a great appreciation for the look, taste, texture and smell of every morsel.

All meals are served at a large rectangular table, and taken with the other guests. Mealtimes are a great opportunity to discuss and joke about the day's activities. There is a lot of tension released through interpersonal communication at this time—lots of laughing, lots of personal "in-house" jokes. The chief instructor of the day shares meals with the guests. This is important, since mealtimes tend to become important as strengtheners for the upcoming activities, and psychological encouragement becomes just as important as nutritional sustenance.

HEALTH AND BEAUTY SERVICES

Except for a competent daily massage given in your room, the Ashram offers no additional beauty or health treatments.

OTHER PLEASURES

The greatest pleasure of being at the Ashram is knowing that the experience will be one not only in which your fitness will improve but one in which you can stretch all your limits—physical, psychological and spiritual. The sense of anticipation is there the moment you meet the other guests. Layers of role playing, defensiveness and other stress-related inhibitors begin to fall away early, and the personal growth each person experiences is shared openly with members of the group. The Ashram experience is part religious retreat, part summer camp and part spring training, tempered with a holistic health approach.

WHAT TO BRING

Shorts, T-shirts and warm-up suits are provided. Bring sturdy hiking or running shoes. You'll need a bathing suit, slippers and coverup. It can get cool in the evenings so bring a jacket or heavy sweater.

HOW TO GET THERE

In keeping with the Ashram's slightly eccentric and reclusive style, guests planning to come are not actually told how to get there; the intent is to keep the location as private as possible.

When you make a reservation you can select one of three hotel locations for pick-up by the Ashram van. Most people fly into Los Angeles International airport, where the nearest pick-up point is the Marriott Inn at the airport. Other pick-up locations are the Holiday Inn on Sunset or the Valley Hilton.

The staff will cheerfully take you to the airport or other drop point after your visit.

SUMMARY

The Ashram is not a casual week in the country. It's a complete mind-body experience that will demand total commitment and a fairly fit body before you go. A week there is a totally absorbing experience, which will probably be radically different from any other week of your life. The Ashram is for people who believe in taking risks and who are willing to push themselves hard to stimulate new growth.

The sparse natural diet and punishing physical activity miraculously produce a euphoric energy and sense of well-being, but it's not easy.

FACT SUMMARY

NAME: The Ashram

MAILING ADDRESS: 2025 McKain Road, P.O. Box 8, Calabasas, CA 91302

TELEPHONE: (213) 888-0232

TRANSPORTATION: Spa van will pick up at 3 designated hotel points

ACCOMMODATIONS: No private rooms or private baths; dormitorylike

FEE: $1,200 per week

MAXIMUM NUMBER OF GUESTS: 6 to 8

MAXIMUM NUMBER OF STAFF: 4

SEASON: Year-round

AMBIANCE: No frills, spartan retreat; California stucco house in foothills; above Malibu Beach

GENDER AND AGE RESTRICTIONS: Adults over 16; coed

DIET: Vegetarian, primarily raw vegetables; limited fruit; spartan meals, approximately 600 calories per day; seeds, sprouts, nuts, herb teas

FACILITIES: 1 large building with gym and exercise areas; geodesic dome for yoga classes

PROGRAM: Very strenuous; rigorous schedule; maximum challenge, 7-day regime for people with a good degree of fitness: yoga, hiking, weight lifting, pool exercise, calisthenics

SPECIAL FEATURES: Cardiovascular training, fasting, meditation and yoga training; daily massage and facial

LOCAL ATTRACTIONS: None

Other Spas

Bermuda Inn

Bermuda Inn is a reducing resort located in the high Mohave Desert of California. Personal medical consultation is scheduled for all guests and a reducing program is then recommended. Exercise classes are scheduled throughout the day. Various social activities as well as points-of-interest trips are programmed, and transportation is provided. Participation in classes and activities is optional. Massages are available at a nominal fee, and a beauty salon and boutique are located on the premises.

FACT SUMMARY

MAILING ADDRESS: 43019 Sierra Highway, Lancaster, CA 93534

TELEPHONE: (213) 625-3115 (for reservations only); else (805) 942-1493

TRAVEL DIRECTIONS: San Diego Freeway north to Antelope Valley Freeway (Highway 14) to Palmdale/Lancaster to Antelope Valley exit; turn right onto Avenue L; turn left on Sierra Highway

TRANSPORTATION: Free pick-up service from Palmdale International airport and local bus terminal

ACCOMMODATIONS: Private, double and triple rooms, motel-like

FEE: Includes room, activities and medically supervised diets—single, $95 per day; double, $63 per person per day; triple, $48 per person per day

MAXIMUM NUMBER OF GUESTS: 85

MAXIMUM NUMBER OF STAFF: 45

SEASON: Year-round

AMBIANCE: Casual, relaxed

GENDER AND AGE RESTRICTIONS: None; however, facilities are not geared to children

DIET: 500-, 700-, 900-calorie balanced diets (recommended by doctor); can also work with vegetarians; low salt, low carbohydrates, low fat

FACILITIES: Indoor and outdoor pools, whirlpools, gym, outdoor lighted walking track, golfing, tennis and bowling facilities nearby; man-made lake, bicycles

PROGRAM: Diet and supervised exercise

SPECIAL FEATURES: Evening activities include lectures, fashion shows, movies, singalongs, bingo, disco dancing classes

LOCAL ATTRACTIONS: Edwards Air Force Base, Indian museums, Benedictine priory, shopping tours

The Grove

The Grove is a reducing and conditioning spa. Each guest is examined by a doctor prior to beginning the program. The doctor then prescribes the program best suited to the individual's needs. A full-time registered nurse records blood pressure and weight loss daily. Exercise and behavior modification sessions are part of the program and massages are available at a modest fee. Entertainment programs, as well as lectures and discussions, are held regularly.

FACT SUMMARY

MAILING ADDRESS: 32281 Riverside Drive, Lake Elsinore, CA 92330

TELEPHONE: (714) 674-1501; toll-free (800) 472-8583

TRAVEL DIRECTIONS: 75 miles southeast of Los Angeles and 75 miles northeast of San Diego on Interstate 15

TRANSPORTATION: Complimentary transportation to and from Ontario airport and from Riverside and Lake Elsinore Greyhound bus stations

ACCOMMODATIONS: 40 rooms consisting of 10 triples and 30 doubles

FEE: 1 day—single, $89; double, $65 per person; triple, $49 per person; 1 week—single, $623; double, $455 per person; triple, $343 per person

MAXIMUM NUMBER OF GUESTS: 80

MAXIMUM NUMBER OF STAFF: 45

SEASON: Year-round

AMBIANCE: A relaxed atmosphere that encourages one to participate in all of the activities; sunny and smog-free

GENDER AND AGE RESTRICTIONS: Adults over 17; coed; must have normal health except for being overweight

DIET: Standard diets of 500, 750, 900 calories per day; salads, fish, fowl, red meats, soups, fresh vegetables and dietetic desserts

FACILITIES: 40 rooms located on 5 acres with a gym, 2 pools (1 inside), a whirlpool, sauna, sun deck area, massage, body wrap, beauty salon, boutique, large-screen television plus Betamax for movies; golf, tennis and horseback riding nearby

PROGRAM: A controlled supervised diet, with 6 exercise classes each day; lectures in the evening on behavior modification plus entertainment and cooking demonstrations

SPECIAL FEATURES: On the 500-calorie program, a person can lose up to a pound a day

LOCAL ATTRACTIONS: Lake Elsinore, nearby historical town of Temecula, CA, and the Railroad Museum; for card players, a nearby casino offers pan, poker and lowball

Alive Polarity's Murrieta Hot Springs and Vegetarian Health Spa

Alive Polarity's Murrieta Hot Springs and Vegetarian Health Spa is located in the rolling hills of southern California. It lies on forty-five acres of lush, scenic grounds with fountains and gardens.

The hot springs were first used by the Temecula Indians, later by the padres and soldiers from the San Juan Capistrano Mission.

Alive Polarity is a blend of modern facilities and accommodations and holistic health programs. This is a seasoned, established spa program recently relocated to Murrieta Hot Springs.

FACT SUMMARY

MAILING ADDRESS: Alive Polarity, Murrieta Hot Springs, Murrieta, CA 92362

TELEPHONE: (714) 677-7451

TRAVEL DIRECTIONS: From Los Angeles take Pomona Freeway 60 to Riverside, then 15E south toward San Diego to Murrieta Hot Springs Road; turn left

TRANSPORTATION: Limo service for airport pick-up

ACCOMMODATIONS: Rooms and suites have total luxury and complete privacy with California decor; many have private patios overlooking a lake

FEE: Call for fee

MAXIMUM NUMBER OF GUESTS: 100

MAXIMUM NUMBER OF STAFF: 30

SEASON: Year-round

AMBIANCE: Quiet and casual with modern facilities

GENDER AND AGE RESTRICTIONS: None

DIET: Vegetarian and specially prepared diets

FACILITIES: Men's and women's spa, mineral pools, famous Tule mudbaths, saunas, 14 tennis courts, volleyball, badminton, shuffle board, Ping-Pong

PROGRAM: The spa is recently opened on this site; be sure to call in advance to see what accommodations and programs will be available by the time of your visit. They plan a full range of health programs from 2 day, 1 week, 6 weeks and some longer programs; programs for those who wish to make the health spa their home. (Inquire about Active Living Center.)

SPECIAL FEATURES: Smog-free air and hot springs, bubbling with mineral-charged 170° water

LOCAL ATTRACTIONS: Hot springs

Lakeshore Inn Golden Gate Spa

The Golden Gate Spa is a part of the Lakeshore Inn facility. The spa program is geared toward weight loss through diet and exercise. The inn accommodates those participating in the program as well as those who are not. (There are separate dining areas for dieters and nondieters.) The Lakeshore Inn is located in the Mohave Desert overlooking a large man-made lake and is directly adjacent to an eighteen-hole golf course. There is a bar with live music several evenings of the week and a spa lounge that is open twenty-four hours a day (serving soft drinks, coffee and tea).

FACT SUMMARY

MAILING ADDRESS: 21330 Lakeshore Drive, California City, CA 93505

TELEPHONE: (714) 373-4861

TRAVEL DIRECTIONS: 126 miles from Los Angeles, north on Route 5 from L.A., northeast on Route 14 to California City; or private planes can land at the California City airport

TRANSPORTATION: Pick-up service available from Bakersfield, Palmdale or Edwards Air Force Base; bus service to Lakeshore also available from Mohave

ACCOMMODATIONS: Standard hotel rooms and suites

FEE: Single, $60 per day; double, $40 per person per day

MAXIMUM NUMBER OF GUESTS: 80

MAXIMUM NUMBER OF STAFF: 50

SEASON: Year-round

AMBIANCE: Restful, pressure-free

GENDER AND AGE RESTRICTIONS: None

DIET: No additives, preservatives or anything artificial; fresh fruits and vegetables in season; two dining areas, one for dieters, another for nondieters

FACILITIES: Walking area, tennis courts, beauty salon, boutique, whirlpool, pool; horseback riding and golf facilities nearby; boating and hiking

PROGRAM: A nurse is on duty every morning for blood pressure and weight control checks. Orders for lunch and dinner are taken at this time. Weigh-in can also be done on a once-a-week basis. Various exercise classes are offered throughout the day, and behavior modification and group discussion round out the offerings

SPECIAL FEATURES: Overlooks a picturesque lake

LOCAL ATTRACTIONS: Edwards Air Force Base

Natural Environmental Health Center

The Natural Environmental Health Center is a holistic health community located in the Santa Cruz area in northern California. The diet, which consists only of organic foods, and the program are developed around individual needs. Other services offered by the center include iris diagnosis, bio-astro health analysis, herbal massage and vitaminology. The surrounding redwood forest provides a refreshing atmosphere.

FACT SUMMARY

MAILING ADDRESS: P.O. Box 11, Brookdale, CA 95007

TELEPHONE: (408) 338-2363 (accepts collect calls up to 6 minutes)

TRAVEL DIRECTIONS: Approximately 80 miles south of San Francisco in Brookdale, 40 miles from San Jose, 10 miles from Santa Cruz

TRANSPORTATION: Transportation can be provided from the San Jose air terminal or Greyhound terminal in Santa Cruz for small fee—50¢ a mile

ACCOMMODATIONS: Private room accommodations in lodge; shared or family-style rooms in an annex house are available at lower cost

FEE: Per person "plan" rates (see PROGRAM) range from $35 to $50 per day. Another alternative offered is to select from a schedule of $25 to $65 (in $5 increments) the amount one can afford to donate per day for a room; type of room is then worked around the amount donated

MAXIMUM NUMBER OF GUESTS: 75

MAXIMUM NUMBER OF STAFF: 8

SEASON: Year-round

AMBIANCE: Quiet, relaxed, very informal

GENDER AND AGE RESTRICTIONS: None

DIET: Diet is tailored to individual needs and consists of organic foods, herbs and natural waters

FACILITIES: Heated pool, exercise room, sauna and steam room, hydro-massage heated pool; tennis, volleyball on premises and other recreational facilities nearby

PROGRAM: Generally, programs are developed around a person's needs. Overall programs are offered at "plan" rates: *Plan A*—health vacation or weight reduction, no health problems; *Plan B*—health rejuvenation, disorders of less than two years; *Plan C*—health rejuvenation, disability of 2 to 5 years chronic durations; *Plan D*—health revitalization, disability more than 5 years, chronic duration

SPECIAL FEATURES: A special plan is available for those with limited income

LOCAL ATTRACTIONS: Redwood Forest State Park and Beach, Monterey Bay

Two Bunch Palms

A secluded desert hideaway with deep blue hot pools set among ferns and palms, Two Bunch Palms offers a wide variety of facials, massages and body treatments. There is no exercise or diet program; relaxation and retreat are the major specialties here.

FACT SUMMARY

MAILING ADDRESS: 67-425 Two Bunch Palms Trail, Desert Hot Springs, CA 92240

TELEPHONE: (619) 329-8791

TRAVEL DIRECTIONS: From Los Angeles take Interstate 10 to Palm Springs/Desert Hot Springs exit; follow signs to Two Bunch Palms

TRANSPORTATION: Car or bus to Palm Springs, taxi to Two Bunch Palms

ACCOMMODATIONS: Motel-like rooms (villas), 1- and 2-bedroom condos

FEE: Studios $45 to $60 per day; villas $45 to $125 per day; condos $95 to $135 per day

MAXIMUM NUMBER OF GUESTS: 120

MAXIMUM NUMBER OF STAFF: 30

SEASON: Year-round

AMBIANCE: Romantic hideaway

GENDER AND AGE RESTRICTIONS: Adults over 18; coed

DIET: None

FACILITIES: Double pools with grotto, sauna, steam room

PROGRAM: None

SPECIAL FEATURES: Secluded hot pools; shiatsu massage; salt rub treatment

LOCAL ATTRACTIONS: Rio Caliente Indian reservation, Palm Springs shopping

Monaco Villa Resort Hotel and Spa

Monaco Villa Resort Hotel and Spa is a small family-owned-and-run resort situated in the California desert community of Palm Springs. It features a weight reduction plan and a complete physical fitness program, including yoga and pool exercise classes.

FACT SUMMARY

MAILING ADDRESS: 371 Camino Monte Vista, Palm Springs, CA 92262

TELEPHONE: (619) 327-1261

TRAVEL DIRECTIONS: From Los Angeles go to Palm Springs; spa is 3 blocks south of Hilton Riviera, on Indian Avenue; turn left onto Camino Monte Vista

TRANSPORTATION: Spa offers transportation to various areas, to and from airport

ACCOMMODATIONS: Attractive, luxurious rooms

FEE: Single, $85.00 per day; double, $59.50 per person, per day (includes room, activity program and all meals)

MAXIMUM NUMBER OF GUESTS: 16 to 18

MAXIMUM NUMBER OF STAFF: 7

SEASON: September 20 to June 30; closed during summer

AMBIANCE: Charming, small and intimate

GENDER AND AGE RESTRICTIONS: No children; coed; must be mobile to participate

DIET: Nutritionally controlled diet geared for weight reduction; also plan for guests who do not wish to lose but are interested in healthful food

FACILITIES: Olympic-sized swimming pool; hot therapy pool, gym equipment

PROGRAM: Professionally conducted physical fitness program and diet supervision; massages available

SPECIAL FEATURES: Golf, tennis and horseback riding available by appointment

LOCAL ATTRACTIONS: Theaters, art museum, concerts, art galleries

Great Oaks School of Health

Great Oaks School of Health is located on an old estate, ten miles south of Eugene, Oregon. This holistic healing center, surrounded by organic gardens and orchards, emphasizes exercise, nutrition, fasting and meditation. Great Oaks is non-profit and nondenominational, offering guests a retreat for the restoration of health through simple natural living.

FACT SUMMARY

MAILING ADDRESS: 82644 North Howe Lane, Creswell, OR 97426

TELEPHONE: (503) 895-4967

TRAVEL DIRECTIONS: From Interstate 5 take Creswell exit; go west on Oregon Avenue (becomes Camas Swale Road) for 2 miles; left turn on Howe Lane; take Howe south 1 mile; right turn up driveway

TRANSPORTATION: Plane, bus or train to Eugene; 10 miles south of Eugene; pick-up available for $10

ACCOMMODATIONS: Private rooms, semiprivate baths; in summer there are three yurts—small rustic huts—in the forest above the main house

FEE: Room and board, $30 per person, per day

MAXIMUM NUMBER OF GUESTS: 10

MAXIMUM NUMBER OF STAFF: 6

SEASON: Year-round

AMBIANCE: Peace and quiet; forests

GENDER AND AGE RESTRICTIONS: None

DIET: Fresh fruits and vegetables, organic seeds, grains and nuts; no animal products; no caffeine, tobacco, alcohol or other drugs; no sugar

FACILITIES: Beautiful old estate of 85 acres with forest, swimming ponds, organic gardens and orchards, large weaving studio, woodshop, dance studio

PROGRAM: Full schedule from 6:00 A.M to 8:00 P.M. of exercise, meditation, singing and work; attempts to work on the physical (diet and exercise), the intellectual (extensive library, knowledgeable staff), the emotional (group living, counseling) and the spiritual (meditation, singing, tai chi)

SPECIAL FEATURES: Nutritional counseling, kinesiology, individual counseling, body work (massage), colonics

LOCAL ATTRACTIONS: Jogging and hiking trails, swimming ponds

THE WEST

Featured Spas

The Greenhouse

What looks architecturally like the New York Botanical Gardens greenhouse is hidden in a neighborhood of warehouses and comes with its own credit card?

The answer is the Greenhouse in Arlington, Texas, a spa that combines the marketing genius of Stanley Marcus of Neiman-Marcus and the sophistication and style of Charles of the Ritz. Everything you have ever admired about Texans and their way of life is epitomized by this consummate spa.

A circular drive delivers you to a discreetly columned entrance. A bell is rung. After careful scrutiny—security is tightly controlled here—the huge arched doors are opened by a gracious staff member and you are ushered into an elegant reception hall carpeted in ankle-deep seafoam-green carpet, filled with statuary, urns, plants and airy watercolors.

The enormous drawing room located just off the entrance hall is decorated in a tasteful eclectic style with Oriental touches such as rattan chairs and delicately figured porcelain jars and lamps and a great number of elegant chairs and loveseats. A huge black marble fireplace dominates the center of the room. Floor-to-ceiling breakfronts hold a collection of fine English, German, Austrian and American porcelain china dinner services. You might be reminded of the bridal registry department of your favorite department store.

The philosophy here is to create an environment exactly like the very fine home you've just left. But rich or just "comfortable" as you may be, everyone is made to feel at ease and at home. The spa's yellow terry-cloth robes and standard blue leotards are quite democratic, and an atmosphere of mutual encouragement and support is evident among the guests. It is this climate of support that draws a number of the guests to the Greenhouse in the first place, as they work out both stiff life problems and stiff muscles in carefully monitored exercise classes.

During a recent week, one guest had just ended a year's bout with cancer and was hoping to regain her lost sense of femininity after months of being treated as a body with a pathology. On the day she left she was glowing, her makeup carefully applied and her newly permanented hairdo bouncing jauntily as she strode out.

Another guest's husband had died suddenly six weeks earlier of a heart attack and she was dealing with the double problem of her personal loss and her desire to keep his business going. As she sat in his chair in his office, she felt depressed and small. "I realized I felt so small" she said, "because the *chair* was too low. So I raised it to a workable height. Suddenly I could see over the desk and into the future, so to speak. I figured the year ahead wasn't going to be easy, and that I was going to need stamina and a good feeling about myself to make it."

This take-charge positive approach is typical of the guests, who are mostly successful career women or busy, socially active women whose professions are their families or community.

ACCOMMODATIONS

When you are shown to your room you will discover a letter from the director, a complimentary sample of Charles of the Ritz perfume on your pillow, a Neiman-Marcus credit card with your name on it and (on a less frivolous note) a container for a first-day urine specimen, which will be discreetly fetched and analyzed by the nurse before you begin your program the next day.

The room itself is what you would expect in a very privileged private home, with some extra surprises tossed in. Soft peach damask hangs in heavy folds at the windows and in the partial canopy over the bed. Pastel green upholstery on Oriental-design chairs and benches complements the light ash tone of the wood, which is repeated in the ten-inch-deep moldings at the floor and ceiling. It all has the feeling of an enormous fancy jewelry box.

Several large mirrors promise ample chance to study your soon-to-be-diminished figure, especially in the large dressing area, which has wall-to-wall mirrors. The bathroom has a huge sunken tub and shower, and, of course, boasts that luxury staple for sophisticates, a bidet. The embroidered bed linens are changed every day by one of the ubiquitous maids.

Closets are roomy and contain a lot of sturdy hangers for evening clothes that you will need for dinner. Leotards and a big fluffy yellow robe are waiting for you; they will be exchanged each morning for fresh ones.

Just before you turn in, you may attempt to make the rounds to turn out the lights. Don't bother, since you won't be able to find the switches; virtually all lamps in the bedroom are controlled by a convenient master switch on the nightstand, near your pillow. At the Greenhouse, they think of everything.

FACILITIES

The Greenhouse is entirely self-contained; the wizard who designed it managed, through the skillful use of skylights and interior latticework, to give the impression of a snug sanctuary that is not confining.

The indoor pool with its three-story-high vaulted skylight and tropical setting is the heart of the spa. Here hundreds of potted flowering plants—bright yellow chrysanthemums in fall and poinsettias in winter—add clear washes of color to the dense background of palms, ferns and small flowering trees. The second-floor balcony is hung with more lush green plants suspended in Plexiglas hemispheres. Pots of tall hibiscus sway gently in the currents of the precisely monitored internal air control system.

This pool area is a perfect example of the careful thought that went into the structural design of the building. The pool itself is sixty feet long, four feet deep throughout and has an exercise bar built down the center of its length for support while one does underwater balletlike movements. No need to cling to the wet, slippery walls while one does frog kicks!

Another innovation is a wide ceramic-tile bench that runs the length of the pool and is used for exercises done in a seated position. At each rounded end of the pool is a small graceful fountain.

Because much of the nonpool exercise program takes place in the grotto surrounding the pool, and since the whole area around the pool is beautiful but slippery Italian marble, wide sections of bright green outdoor carpeting have been installed so that during stretch-and-flex class you won't run the risk of landing in the pool from an excess of enthusiasm.

Afternoon exercise classes are often held in the two smaller exercise rooms on the first floor, each of which is covered with thick gray carpet. There is also a carpeted platform for the instructor so that you can be flat on your stomach concentrating on an exercise to make your gluteus maximus more gluteus minimus and still have no trouble seeing the instructor as she demonstrates the proper movement. Double-level ballet barres line the walls for ease of use no matter how short or tall you are.

Just off the pool area in the west wing is the doctor's office and the whirlpool, sauna and steam area. Close by are several massage rooms, each equipped with a professional massage table. There is a small waiting area centrally located in case you arrive early for your massage.

Much of the second floor of the spa is devoted to beauty services. Here you'll find the facial department, equipped with eight private facial rooms; the beauty school classroom with its individual makeup stations, each with lighted mirror and an array of cosmetics and beauty tools; and a large hair salon with several stations, shampoo basins and nail-care tables.

PROGRAM

The typical Greenhouse day begins with breakfast in bed at about 7:00. A personal schedule for the day will be on your tray. At 7:40 A.M. everyone gathers near the front door to be taken on the morning walk on the one-sixth-mile track that threads through trees and shrubbery at the east end of the main building. More ambitious exercisers can strike off for a jog on the neighboring golf course.

After a stop in your room to change to the leotards provided, you are ready for morning wake-up exercises held around the perimeter of the pool. The instructors are excellently trained by the dynamic Toni Beck, who designed the exercise program and who (although reports are that she is in her sixties) has the trim body and clear energy of a teen-ager. She and her instructors consistently do everything right. For one thing, you can *hear* them, thanks to a microphone and their nearly perfect diction. For another, they give a demonstration of the exercise and a commentary on exactly how to do it and why it will benefit you. Exercise mats are placed so that you have a clear line of vision to the instructor. Two other instructors move among the guests, supporting, gently correcting and encouraging anyone who needs it. Another helper handles the music so that there is never an awkward break to adjust a record or turn up the volume.

The wake-up class, which lasts for thirty minutes, is basic easy stretches and limbering movements coordinated with proper breathing. It is followed by the stretch-and-flex class, which is forty minutes of more vigorous stretching and toning with a short period of mild aerobics. Some of the exercises incorporate the use of an exercise pole about three feet long, which helps you keep your balance.

At about 10:00 your schedule might take you to the whirlpool and steam room. The large bubbling whirlpool usually has only three or four guests in it at one time; this is so the facilities can be monitored under the careful eye of Mary Ann, the attendant, who simply will not allow you the dubious luxury of fainting or merely becoming prunelike. Five minutes is the limit, after which she will gently but firmly escort you to the shower, which she has already started and adjusted to a perfect temperature. You may then be scheduled for a massage or a beauty class, which will be your last activity before lunch.

After lunch around the pool you might have an appointment for a hair treatment. Then on to the toning class, which is about forty-five minutes of leg lifts, tummy tighteners and other repetitive (but not boring) exercises. Following this, an hour with the facialist will relax you. If you still want more exercise, the dance or aerobic class is the last class of the day. As alternative exercise choices there are two pool classes a day, one in the morning and another in the afternoon. These are a great favorite with guests; the pool temperature is kept very close to body temperature so it is similar to being in a big bathtub, complete with rubber toys—oversized inflated balls—to cling to while slowly circling the pool with various leg kicks. No one ever wants this class to end.

After a quiet rest in your room, "cocktails" (usually juices) are served at 6:30 with dinner at 7:00 P.M. After dinner, demitasse is served near the pool and then everyone gathers in the drawing room for the evening program. One night each week Neiman-Marcus presents a fashion show, after which guests can order their favorite items, which will be delivered before they depart. Other programs include a lecture demonstration on fine jewelry, a workshop on needlepoint, a talk on life and career planning or self-image and usually a live dramatic presentation.

Toward the end of the week, an afternoon is set aside for a

shopping trip to the Neiman-Marcus store in Dallas. Sleek limousines line up at the front door and well-dressed guests step in for the short ride downtown. At the store you are treated as visiting royalty. The store's public affairs director comes out to meet your limousine and asks with great concern what you might be interested in seeing. She will then arrange for you to have coffee while she contacts the buyer for that department, who will then be waiting for you when you arrive there.

FOOD AND DIET

About midweek in her stay one guest stormed into the kitchen office and challenged Bertha, the muse of the Greenhouse menu, to admit that the food served did not equal a mere 850 calories a day as claimed in the brochure.

Bertha confessed that the woman was right. "I *am*?" replied the guest.

"Oh, yes. It seldom gets that high except on the days we serve beef."

The interchange would have pleased the late Helen Corbitt, who originated the menus and recipes for the Greenhouse and trained the accommodating Bertha. The food is so fresh, the seasoning so delicate and the selection so varied, that the nemesis of spa food, boredom, is simply out of the question.

Breakfast in bed usually consists of a cleverly served piece of fruit, such as a zigzag-cut grapefruit with a sprig of mint; a coddled egg, presented in a porcelain egg coddler and a feathery-looking piece of toast sliced so thin that it is fragile to the touch.

This is all presented on exquisite china, with a linen napkin and silver utensils and teapot on a bed tray. A single rosebud in a tiny Lenox bud vase reminds you that the world is a nice place to be even if you *can* see through your toast (and you would have preferred Danish anyway).

At about 10:30 A.M. a potassium broth or vegetable juice is served to restore minerals lost during the morning's exercise.

For lunch a marvelous cheese soufflé with fruit or an over-sized lobster-and-crab salad with piquant dressing are examples of satisfying menus that provide plenty of energy to carry you through the afternoon.

Not everyone is on the 850-calorie diet. The lucky few who don't need to lose pounds are on a maintenance program and are served extras such as fruit and nut muffins or gooey-wonderful chocolate cake. If you think this might bother you, be sure to sit with others who are on the same diet plan. After the first meal you will know who they are.

At one meal several guests were discussing cooking diet-conscious meals at home when one woman remarked that she had lost thirty pounds in the previous year by using the Weight Watchers plan and recipes. Impressed, everyone asked her if that wasn't terribly time-consuming, what with attending the weekly meetings, then shopping and carefully following the recipes. "Not really," she replied offhandedly; she had just sent her cook.

The evening meals at the Greenhouse are the epitome of elegance and culinary perfection. Memorable roast game, lamb chops and fresh fish send many guests to the boutique the next day to buy one of Miss Corbitt's fine cookbooks. The salads and salad dressings are superb and don't taste at all low calorie. The mushroom-and-endive salad is a particular favorite. Each recipe has an interesting twist, such as the Cornish game hens, which have a mixture of shallots, parsley and Parmesan cheese stuffed between the skin and the breast meat. Delicious!

HEALTH AND BEAUTY SERVICES

Every day of your stay at the Greenhouse you will have a facial, a makeup lesson, a hair treatment and a massage. You will also get a complete manicure and pedicure throughout the week. Looking beautiful is considered serious business by the staff.

For each type of treatment you will have the same technician throughout the week, so that she can get well acquainted with your skin, hair or body and can try different products and conditioners to see what works best for you. For example, the facialist studies your skin type and condition before you go to your first makeup class and will give you a list of which products are best to use in skin cleansing or makeup.

Each day the facialist will do a mask or deep cleansing, or will remove excess facial hair by waxing, or will remove whiteheads or other matter clogging pores. It depends on what you and she agree that you need. This is always a relaxing session that includes a short nap while a machine sprays a light mist to replace moisture in the skin.

The makeup lessons are great fun and remind you of the first time you sat at your mother's dressing table, full of the wistful intent to make yourself gorgeous. Only here it actually happens. Makeup instructors show you a new technique every day: from cleansing rituals, to daytime makeup to fancy evening looks. All products are Charles of the Ritz, and everything you can imagine is provided to practice with, from eye colors to lip pencils.

Each person gets personal attention, including specific directions and sketches on what to use and how to apply it. The instructor will apply the eye makeup for one eye, then you practice by doing the other, and soon you are at ease with putting on your new look. You can purchase anything you like from the instructor, then practice in your room during the week and have her help you check your technique.

Massages are very thorough and take about forty-five minutes. The basic approach is a Swedish massage, with strokes especially designed to redistribute weight to more attractive locations. Nivea cream is used, and the finale includes a thorough going-over with a commercial vibrator. Guests speak very highly of the massages here, and it is considered to be the major reason no one ever feels sore or achy from the increased exercise.

The beauty salon staff's major concern is the condition of your hair. Each day they try a different conditioner, rinse or oil treatment. Although this means that you look less than elegant part of the time (you don't have a set and comb-out each time), it does give your hair a period of rest and recuperation that it seldom gets, and it will thank you by looking wonderfully shiny and healthy by the time you leave.

The only (tongue-in-cheek) complaint heard in this area is that the salon often smells too much like food and makes guests hungry! Apple, banana and rum hair rinses smell just like the real thing, and raisin toast and wheat toast nailpolish can give you ideas that the kitchen can't satisfy on the calories allowed.

OTHER PLEASURES

The biggest pleasure here is the highly personal service from every staff member. They all seem to have a talent for remembering your name and any special needs or preferences you might have. If you didn't have a compulsive mother or an English nanny, you probably have never experienced the kind of attention you will get here. When you approach the shower in the whirlpool area, you are helped out of your robe and your hair is tucked into a shower cap for you. When you step out, a big towel is wrapped around you by the assistant, who discreetly averts her eyes. Would you like a fresh leotard in the middle of the day? A glass of tea? Something you forgot ordered from the drugstore? You have only to whisper the word. In fact, if a staff person overhears you idly talking to another guest about how nice it would be to have such and such, it often miraculously appears.

While in the hot tub, one guest described a favorite exercise she does at home on a slanted exercise board. As she continued to speak, there was a sound of a heavy object being moved, and a slant board slowly moved into view from behind a wall. The guests watched, dumbstruck. "I overheard and thought you might like to have one here to show them," the attendant said apologetically.

This kind and concerned care from the staff has a healing quality. When one of the guests mentioned this to the likeable Charlayne, one of the hair dressers, she smiled and said, "Thanks, we do try. Of course there are some hurts so deep a massage can't reach them."

For those who want to take gifts home, there is a delightful boutique with good jewelry, clothes and objets d'art as well as practical items like slippers, hose and exercise tapes. These can be charged to your room.

The quality of the medical care here is excellent. Each guest has an appointment with the doctor soon after her arrival to discuss any health problems or medication that might conflict with the exercise program. A file is kept on each guest so that when she returns (about 75 percent of the guests any given week are repeaters), the staff knows already what care she might need. One guest has made sixty visits! Although most guests don't need to see the doctor after that initial visit, they like knowing that he or the nurse is available.

WHAT TO BRING

In some spas, even though regulation leotards are provided, it is considered more chic or "with it" to bring your own, more snazzy or colorful type. Not so here. Everyone wears the spa's simple blue short-sleeved Danskin leotards. You will need slippers but not a robe, since theirs does nicely and is likewise worn by everyone.

In fact, the only clothing items you must bring are jogging shoes, a warm-up suit or shorts for walking and tennis (depending on the weather), a bathing suit and the most elegant evening wear that you own.

Everyone dresses for dinner. The emphasis is on long silk dresses, evening skirts and elegant blouses or evening pants suits. Clothes by Chanel, Celine, Norell, Halston and other designers of that stratum are common, but any pretty evening suit is acceptable. Stop short of lamé, spangles or a low décolletage, for you won't be comfortable in them. Women who come here usually have fancy wardrobes, but if you don't, you can find what you need in the boutique.

HOW TO GET THERE

You may fly into the Dallas–Fort Worth airport and the Greenhouse limousine will pick you up by prior arrangement. It will also pick you up at any hotel or downtown location. You may also drive to the spa, which is in Arlington, a suburb west of Dallas. Request a map when you make your reservation.

SUMMARY

The Greenhouse is the place for you if you like being pampered, love beauty treatments and like being in a self-contained environment. You'll be absolutely carefree in this spa. You do not need to carry anything with you; all you need throughout the day is handed to you by a gracious staff member when you need it. Luxury is the norm and service is respectful and sincere. The group of guests is small, about thirty-five at most, and it is easy to meet people, develop a sense of camaraderie and feel at home. Although this is a sophisticated place, it is not a snobbish one. Everyone is here to relax and tone up, and the common goal makes for common acceptance.

The exercise and food plan produce good results. The average weight loss is four to six pounds a week, and inches go even faster. It is an easy program to take home, as the exercise tapes are the best around. The Greenhouse will undoubtedly remain one of the three or four most expensive spas in the country, but it is good value for your spa dollar.

FACT SUMMARY

NAME: The Greenhouse

MAILING ADDRESS: P.O. Box 1144, Arlington, TX 76010

TELEPHONE: (817) 640-4000

TRANSPORTATION: Spa limo pick-up at airport or hotel

ACCOMMODATIONS: Elaborate large rooms with bath and dressing room

FEE: $2,300 a week

MAXIMUM NUMBER OF GUESTS: 36

MAXIMUM NUMBER OF STAFF: 100

SEASON: Year-round except December

AMBIANCE: Lavish, sophisticated

GENDER AND AGE RESTRICTIONS: Women only; no age restrictions

DIET: 850 calories per day, gourmet meals

FACILITIES: Pool; exercise rooms; whirlpool; sauna, steam, massage and facial rooms; complete beauty salon; all under one roof in a semitropical setting

PROGRAM: Serious exercise program (6 classes daily), stretch-and-flex, dance, aerobics, pool exercise classes; complete beauty and health services

SPECIAL FEATURES: Total pampering, trip to Neiman-Marcus

LOCAL ATTRACTIONS: None

Canyon Ranch

The morning in Sabino Canyon is cool and fresh, and the air has the mildly medicinal tang of the creosote bush. The feathery branches of a mesquite tree rustle and from under it comes a family of Gambel's quail. Portly and dignified, they scoot across the path, head plumes bobbing, then disappear into a clump of ocotillo cactus. On the horizon are the rugged Santa Catalina Mountains, and to the east lies Tucson, the sunbelt city that has everything a metropolis needs while maintaining its small-town western flavor. It even has a few surprises, one of which is an $8 million, twenty-eight-acre coed vacation fitness resort called Canyon Ranch.

Bearing out the old saying that no one is more enthusiastic than a recent convert, Mel Zuckerman, the owner of Canyon Ranch, had a life-changing experience at a spa in California in 1978, where he lost thirty pounds and gained both a new perspective on life and a new career.

Full of this new energy, he returned to Tucson and bought the old "Double U" Dude Ranch. Eight million dollars later it has become one of the best coed spa choices in the country.

ACCOMMODATIONS

Part of the reason the Canyon Ranch has such a warm southwestern flavor is the scattering of stuccoed *casitas* ("little houses," in Spanish) that provide accommodations for guests. Many of them are original adobe structures from the dude ranch days, and these have open beamed ceilings. New structures are similar, without the beams, but all are good sized with adequate bathrooms, which have handheld showers, skylights and good counter space.

Rooms are decorated in desert tones of tan and rust with contemporary prints. Most have two beds (there are a few triples), a large bureau and a table and chair in natural wood. You can select a room with king-sized beds, regular or twins. Some quarters even have small sitting rooms.

Each air-conditioned room has a shaded porch.

FACILITIES

The centerpiece of the fitness resort is the 28,000-square-foot building, which houses a wide variety of spa, exercise, sports and service facilities. Here are three carpeted, mirrored gyms, four racquetball courts with viewing balconies and a fitness room filled with shiny chrome state-of-the-art weight-training equipment.

The lobby of the spa building, which is hung with colorful graphics, has a reception area, a juice break area and lots of comfortable chairs and couches for rest and conversation.

On opposite sides of the Mexican tiled lobby are double spa facilities, one for men and another for women. Each of these facilities has a whirlpool; sauna; steam room; inhalation room; a cold dip plunge; and rooms for massage, herbal wrap and skin care treatments. Each spa section has lockered changing rooms, fitted with floor-to-ceiling shelves stocked with immaculate towels, drapes for trips to the treatment areas and shower caps.

Deep into the building there is a coed spa equipped with a whirlpool, sauna and double shower that has blinds and an inside lock for privacy. Reostatic lighting and soft piped-in music complete the setting for a perfect sybaritic retreat for couples.

Also located in the spa building is a beauty salon offering a complete range of hair care and manicure services.

Near the spa building is the custom-designed outdoor aquatic exercise pool with retractable roof, which is necessary in the fierce heat of a Tucson summer. There is also a one-mile "exer-course" with twelve exercise stations at marked intervals.

The clubhouse at Canyon Ranch is the main nonspa facility. It includes a 150-seat dining room, a boutique, a library, lobby and reception areas and administrative offices. This is the basic entertainment facility with card and game rooms and movie and lounging rooms. It is furnished in upbeat contemporary style with lots of plants.

There are also tennis courts, volleyball and basketball courts and special areas for badminton and paddle tennis. For outdoor exercise classes there is a large covered outdoor gym.

PROGRAM

There is no vestige of a fat farm atmosphere at Canyon Ranch. It is definitely a fitness resort rather than a spa, and this approach is probably responsible for the high—up to 30 to 40 percent—percentage of men who go there.

There is an unstructured feeling: if you want to lie in the sun, that's fine. If you want to hike all day, that's fine too. But chances are you will be carried along by the energetic exercise staff, and by the end of the day will be able to reel off a long list of your physical accomplishments. There is a different set of classes for men and for women. An activity schedule is provided weekly so that you can plan your own daily schedule to include as many classes or sports as you like.

Each morning begins with a brisk walk. After breakfast you

can get in four forty-five-minute exercise classes during the morning. The first class of the day, Fitness First, is a good stretch-and-strengthen class. Several times a week you can take a Lower Back and Posture class. The toughest class offered is Positive Power, which leaves more than one guest huffing and puffing. After the juice break at 10:45 A.M., there is resistance weight training, or Aqua Trim, the popular pool class.

Afternoons are spent with slightly more unusual exercise programs, such as Energetics (a circuit weight program), creative movement and advanced Aqua Trim.

At least twice a day, after lunch and dinner, special programs are offered; examples are lectures on "self-control strategy," "herbs and your weight," "biofeedback" and a slide talk on "the changing Southwest desert." In addition, a series of different hikes is planned throughout the week and tennis and racquetball lessons and clinics are available. These are coordinated by the director of guest hospitality, who also plans trips and excursions off the ranch. Watch the bulletin board in the dining room for notices on what's coming up.

FOOD AND DIET

Any place that starts off your day with San Francisco sourdough French toast and strawberry jam can't be too difficult to endure. One of the menu secrets of Canyon Ranch is controlling portion size, so that guests wanting to lose, maintain or even gain weight can eat the same well-balanced and beautifully presented meals.

The ranch uses no artificial sweeteners, preferring small amounts of fructose instead. The diet is basically low in fats, high in fiber and devoid of refined sugars.

It includes about 42 percent complex carbohydrate foods, such as cereal, rice and vegetables. Guests who would like help with their diets when they go home can buy the book *Fitness First: A 14-Day Exercise Program for a New You*, written by Jeanne Jones, the food consultant, and the Canyon Ranch fitness director, Karma Kientzler.

Each of the weekly menus begins with a 520-calorie liquid diet the first day and continues with an 800-calorie weight-loss diet for each of the following days. For each meal a guest is offered several choices. Lunch might be a selection of artichoke bowls with shrimp salad and dill sauce, chicken enchiladas or a big vegetable salad. Dinners can be coq au vin, lamb or Chinese chicken with snow peas. Vitamins are offered at each meal, and decaffeinated coffee and herbal teas are available at all times in the lounge.

The dining room is airy and attractive, and a hostess will seat you and make an effort to introduce you to people.

HEALTH AND BEAUTY SERVICES

Canyon Ranch offers a complete range of beauty and body care treatments. Leah Kovitz, an Israeli woman trained in Europe, is the skin care director. Her staff will first give you a thorough skin analysis, and then prescribe one of a wide variety of facials with natural fruit and vegetable products.

One of their specialties is the Thermal Youth mask, a seven-step treatment of various creams that heat up when combined. The mask draws out skin soil and impurities, then hardens and lifts off in one whole piece—in a perfect hard pink sculpture of your face.

The treatment rooms are small, quiet and clean. Several of the treatments are unique. For example, Leah has a way of removing facial hair with special imported string that she twists deftly to painlessly remove the unwanted hairs—a Middle Eastern technique.

The newest beauty service is body peeling, and it's stiff competition for the standard loofah rubs. It is a French technique using European creams and crushed pearls (gasp). This is applied by hand to a small part of your body at a time and is then buffed off by hand. It's less harsh than a salt rub and certainly less messy. It is called the "Parisian Body Polish." Do this, or you'll never forgive yourself.

The massages offered are excellent; they are offered by both masseurs and masseuses. When making your appointment be sure to stipulate which you prefer. Herbal wraps are offered in a special herbal-wrap room with a fireplace. These treatments last fifteen to twenty minutes and are scheduled so tightly that it is a little hard to relax, as people are coming in and out all the time.

OTHER PLEASURES

Twice a week trail guide Phyllis Hockman leads small groups into the nearby mountains for hikes, like the one to the base of

Thimble Peak, an outcropping of rock 5,323 feet high in the Santa Catalina Mountains. It's a twelve-mile-round-trip climb, but the trail is clear and the vistas are stunning.

You can sign up in the dining room for side trips during your stay. Options are Nogales (a colorful Mexican border town), the Arizona-Sonora Desert Museum, a fascinating living museum with live desert animals and plants; a tour of Tucson; a tour of the Mission San Xavier del Bac, which is on a nearby Indian reservation; or Old Tucson, a western movie location.

WHAT TO BRING

Bring sports clothes for those activities you plan to take part in, such as tennis. Shorts and T-shirts or leotards are fine for exercise classes. A robe, slippers and a bathing suit are a must. Good hiking shoes, socks and moleskin will ensure that you won't miss any of the great scenery. Casual clothes are fine to wear to meals and after class programs.

HOW TO GET THERE

Guests can fly into Tucson International airport or take Amtrak into downtown Tucson. Greyhound and Continental Trailways bus lines also serve the Tucson area. Canyon Ranch provides complimentary transportation from the airport four times daily. Make arrangements when you make your reservation.

If you choose to drive, go east on Tanque Verde Road, then north on Sabino Canyon Road. When you come to Snyder Road, turn right, then right again onto Rockcliff Road.

SUMMARY

Canyon Ranch is one of the new breed of health and fitness resorts that appeal equally to men and women, making it an ideal spot for a couple to escape for a week. The desert air is clean and invigorating, and the Tucson sky offers some of the most spectacular sunsets you'll ever see.

The fitness program can be as challenging as you want to make it, and the food is varied and good. Unlike the situation at some isolated resorts, you won't go stir-crazy here; with miles of hiking and riding trails and easy access to the surrounding community, one could stay a month or more and not feel confined.

The staff is excellent, and the management is always trying new activities and services. The weather is beautiful until the summer months—June to September—when it can get quite hot. However, if you like dry heat, Canyon offers low rates during this period. If you are not a desert lover, you probably will be one after a stay in this beautiful canyon setting. The dignified saguaro cactus and the topaze-eyed coyote await you.

FACT SUMMARY

NAME: Canyon Ranch

MAILING ADDRESS: 8600 East Rockcliff Road, Tucson, AZ 85715

TELEPHONE: (602) 749-9000

TRANSPORTATION: Free pick-up at airport 4 times a day

ACCOMMODATIONS: 66 casitas clustered around landscaped areas—singles, doubles, triples

FEE: Single, $145 to $195 per day; double, $112 to $130 per person, per day; triple, $75 to $95 per person, per day

MAXIMUM NUMBER OF GUESTS: 100 to 125; 35 percent men

MAXIMUM NUMBER OF STAFF: 150

SEASON: Year-round

AMBIANCE: Luxurious vacation/fitness resort set in desert foothills, surrounded by mountains

GENDER AND AGE RESTRICTIONS: Adults over 14; coed

DIET: 800 to 2,000 calories per day, no salt, sugar; calorie control through portion size; vitamin supplements; juice breaks

FACILITIES: 3 exercise gyms, CAM II weight-resistance machines, tennis courts, racquetball courts, whirlpools, saunas, steam rooms, inhalation rooms, swimming pools, jogging track

PROGRAM: Unpressured program with choice of exercise classes and many sport facilities; mix vacation with fitness program

SPECIAL FEATURES: Lighted tennis courts, boutique; complimentary transportation to nearby golf courses and horseback riding

LOCAL ATTRACTIONS: Arizona-Sonora Desert Museum

The Phoenix

The Phoenix in Houston, Texas, one of the newest spas in the country, offers lush scenery (fifteen acres of woodsy charm), state-of-the-art fitness equipment (at the supermodern Houstonian Fitness Center) and as elegant an environment as you will find anywhere. But what makes this spa special (and it *is* special) is its intelligent and very warm staff members and their philosophy of "wellness."

"The Phoenix is not a spa per se but a progressive health retreat," says Director Chris Silkwood. "We want to help each guest become a vibrant, vital person, both physically and psychologically."

Although many of the staff, as well as the spa's owner, Judy Fatjo, are marathon runners, no one is pressed to overexert in any part of the Phoenix experience. "Ours is not a pie-in-the-face kind of drastic approach," notes Chris. "We simply try to give people pointers and suggestions on exercise, handling stress and eating healthy food."

Once during every week each guest is scheduled for an hour and a half to chat with the serene and caring Chris; what is discussed depends on what a person wants to talk about, but usually guests ask for help with how to handle the stress of both family and career, how to get a meat-eating husband to eat more healthfully or how to plan an exercise and diet program that a person can actually live with comfortably. She responds, reasons and suggests, but mostly she just listens, understanding the complicated process that lies between being what you are and becoming what you want to be. She's a good model, someone who seems to have life well figured out, and she is the primary reason for the young resort's rising fame in the spa market.

ACCOMMODATIONS

Guests stay in the sleek ultramodern Houstonian Hotel on the grounds of the security-gated Houstonian complex. Spa guests stay on a special wing on the fourth floor of the hotel, which is reached by following a path through the back yard of the mansion, crossing a wooden footbridge and then walking up four flights of stairs to their rooms. A sign at the top of the stairs reads "You have just consumed seven times more calories than you would had you taken the elevator." Firm discipline in a velvet glove, a hallmark of the Phoenix.

The rooms are expensively decorated in deep blues, tans and browns; and the heavy rattan furniture is better quality than most hotel furnishings.

Waiting in your room will be shorts, T-shirts, a warm-up suit and a black or light blue caftan for evening wear. Fresh clothing will be placed in your room throughout the week.

The bathrooms are generous, with a large dressing area that includes plenty of closet space. On the desk is a heavy red notebook with information on the week's activities, menus, facilities and the staff. At the end of the hall is an attractive lounge for spa guests, including a beverage bar, which makes decaffeinated coffee and tea available at any hour.

FACILITIES

It is hard to believe that in the midst of the bustling Houston area there could be an oasis of calm like the Houstonian complex. Located just off a main freeway on the west side of Houston, it is reached by a quiet dirt road that leads to a guard house, then winds through a beautiful woods past the hotel, newly built condominiums and the separate glass-and-brick Houstonian Fitness Center. In the virtual center of the complex is a lovely white Art Deco mansion that houses the Phoenix.

The mansion is beautifully decorated with contemporary glass, chrome and rattan furniture. The huge high-ceilinged living room, full of paintings, specimen shells and other objets d'art is a magnet for guests throughout their stay. Also on this level is a small carpeted exercise room. Down a few stairs is an enchanting formal dining room with a gleaming wood dining table and mirrors that reflect the dramatic floral wallpaper. Upstairs is the beauty salon and a classroom.

Although much of the program and activities take place in the main mansion, part of the program takes advantage of the Houstonian Fitness Center a few feet away across the drive. This is one of the most advanced fitness facilities in the country. It is basically for wealthy local businessmen who purchase memberships at a hefty $10,000.

The vast facility includes a gymnasium, a large pool, handball courts, men's and women's sauna, whirlpool and steam areas and a remarkable exercise equipment room circled on its outer edges by an indoor track. This is no ordinary track. It is treated with a special surface to cushion the feet, and it can be programmed via a computer so that lights in the track flash on to "pace" your progress.

Outdoors, there are several lighted tennis courts and another unusual track. This one is a rambling trail (almost a mile) that wanders through the woods up and down knolls, past streams and fields; it is a beautiful primeval setting and you can almost forget you're anywhere near a city, until you look down and find you are running on a strip of brilliant green Astroturf. This is Texas, all right.

PROGRAM

The program at the Phoenix is strenuous but oddly ladylike, probably due to the staff members who speak softly and move gracefully even while leading their charges in rigorous aerobic exercise.

The day starts with a 6:30 wake-up call and a brisk mile walk on the bright chartreuse trail through the woods. After breakfast the first exercise class of the day is held in the wine-carpeted exercise room. This half-hour class, called the Extender, is planned to stretch out your muscles for the day ahead. It is immediately followed by another class, the Toner, which shows you how to work on specific body parts for tone, strength and overall figure definition.

One of the nicest parts of exercise classes at the Phoenix is the running commentary that Chris and other staff members keep up as you go through your paces. You really learn useful information about your body. She has a no-nonsense approach to weight loss. "No one ever loses weight by doing toning exercises, such as hip rolls or leg lifts; fat is only burned up when you exercise the whole body enough to raise the heart rate, as you do while walking, jogging or jumping rope. This isn't to say toning exercises aren't useful, they are, but everyone needs both kinds of exercise to be truly fit."

She also points out that even thin people are often not fit. This becomes obvious when the calipers come out early in the week. This pincerlike device measures skin folds to determine body fat. Many guests blanche when they learn that 40 percent of their body weight is fat (25 percent is normal). Another interesting tidbit of advice that Chris offers those who can't seem to find the time to exercise regularly at home is to plan your exercise routine for the point in the day you feel most tired or *vulnerable*. For some women this is midafternoon; for others it is just after the workday ends at 6:00 P.M.

"Exercising at your most vulnerable time does several things," Chris says. "It raises your metabolism and produces a feeling of energy, it diminishes hunger and it contributes to a sense of well-being." Although many of the staff are long-distance runners, guests are advised that walking is the best all-around exercise, and they are asked to keep a log of how far they walk each day while at the Phoenix. A friendly rivalry springs up as guests compete with one another during the week. Toward the end of the week one guest who was lagging behind in miles walked tossed in a few extra miles in her total, claiming with an almost straight face that she walked in her sleep. The last regular class of the morning is the Toner, which is fairly vigorous and uses mason jars full of sand and lead shot as weights. Using these instead of fancy commercial weights is typical of strategies the Phoenix uses to show how easy it is to continue the program at home with very little expense.

Just before lunch everyone hops into the estate pool for the Revivor, a water exercise class.

The afternoon is the time for taking a dance or fitness class, working out on the space age exercise machines or indulging in the beauty treatments scheduled for you on your arrival. There is also time for tennis and racquetball for which instruction is available.

As the afternoon winds down it's time for a massage, then a final brisk walk through the grounds before retreating to your room to dress for dinner. Everyone gathers for low-calorie "mocktails" in the living room before dinner. This is a special hour at the Phoenix. The small size of the group and the warmth of the staff makes the conversation personal and animated.

After dinner a program is offered, such as a talk on low-calorie cooking, nutrition, wild flower arranging or the psychology of self-image. After the program many guests dash across the lawn to the Houstonian Fitness Center to get another mile or two of walking in on the indoor track before toddling across the footbridge and up those four long flights of stairs to their rooms.

FOOD AND DIET

The Phoenix diet is based on 850 calories of wholesome carbohydrates and protein foods. No added salt or artificial sweeteners are used. Everything served is absolutely fresh and the food is so beautifully presented that even foods guests ordinarily don't like look good enough to eat.

The food plan includes frequent small fruit and vegetable snacks throughout the day to maintain energy.

Chris Silkwood and nutritionist Nancy Fong give guests tips on eating well when they go home. "When shopping in the supermarket make only a U-shaped trip around the store," Chris advises. "This is because fresh vegetables, poultry, fish, and the dairy case are usually located on the perimeter of the store's floor plan. Avoid the inner aisles, where canned goods (high in salt) and sugary prepared foods are located. Make a healthy shopping list and stick to it."

It's certainly not hard to stick to healthy foods at the Phoenix.

Breakfast includes an egg or cottage cheese, fruit and whole-wheat toast or a muffin. Lunch is often a big salad of vegetables and tuna, ratatouille or (a favorite) low-calorie pizza and a salad.

Dinners usually include fish, veal or chicken with perfectly cooked vegetables, a salad and dessert such as carrot pudding or low-calorie cheesecake.

A cooking demonstration on how to prepare Oriental chicken in a wok is held once a week.

The staff plans carefully to include plenty of vitamin-C foods (citrus fruits, leafy green vegetables, potatoes) and B-complex vitamins (fish, grain and dairy products).

HEALTH AND BEAUTY SERVICES

Twice during the week each guest is given a makeup session with emphasis on the natural look and how to apply it. Facials are given twice a week, including a deep-cleansing, steam treatment and a skin mask using natural products.

On Tuesday a brisk scalp massage is followed by a conditioner that stays on until the next day, when it is washed off. Your hair will be styled simply so that it is easy to handle during the superactive spa days that follow. On Saturday just before leaving, each guest has her hair set and styled for a suitably glamorous reentry to real life.

A massage is offered every day in the women's locker room area in the Houstonian building, which for sumptuousness beats most luxury condominiums. There is a carpeted, cloth-walled waiting room hung with suede collages and furnished with beautiful birch-wood chairs. An attendant sits poised near a color-coordinated telephone waiting to be of service. The massage rooms themselves are ornate, with Byzantine wallpaper and red carpeting. You may take advantage of the sauna, steam room and elevated whirlpool. The staff is extremely careful about how long guests spend here, as it is Chris Silkwood's philosophy that more than a few minutes' exposure can be quite harmful after strenuous exercise.

OTHER PLEASURES

Since the Houstonian complex where the Phoenix is located is a self-contained world of its own, most guests do not go off the grounds during their stay. However, if a guest wants to go into Houston to shop, the staff will arrange transportation. Guests who want a complete physical examination and work-up can arrive a day early and take an extremely complete battery of tests at the Houstonian Fitness Center, which focuses on cardiac fitness and total body health. There is a hefty extra charge for this service.

WHAT TO BRING

You will need leotards, slippers and jogging shoes for the program, and resort wear for meals and forays into the public areas of the Houstonian Hotel. You might also prefer to bring your own warm-up suit. In the evening, you may wear the caftan the spa provides or you may want to bring your own hostess skirts or lounge wear for dinner. Most guests get tired of wearing the same simple but attractive house caftan every night, especially since dinner is such an elegantly served meal. It makes you want to dress up in your most festive outfits.

HOW TO GET THERE

Guests who fly into the Houston airport will be picked up by a member of the Phoenix staff and driven to the spa. There is no charge for this service; just let them know your flight number when you make spa reservations. For those who live in Houston or are visiting friends there, pick-up service is available at any home in Houston.

If you will be driving, take the 610 loop or "beltway" which bounds the city. Take the Woodway Memorial exit: if coming north, turn left on Woodway and right on North Post Oak Lane where you will see a discreet sign for the Houstonian complex. If traveling south on 610, take the Woodway Memorial exit, turning right, then right again on North Post Oak. The guard will stop you at the guard house and ask your name.

SUMMARY

The Phoenix is an isle of calm in the midst of one of the country's most aggressive and expanding cities.

The forestlike grounds and the spacious mansion combine to offer a perfect setting to rethink life priorities while learning new health habits. There are no gimmicks or quick weight-loss promises offered here. Instead, the tuned-up but toned-down staff members offer simple diet and exercise strategies to take home with you that actually can change the way you live.

The Phoenix has one of the best follow-up programs of any spa we visited. It is common for guests and staff to exchange phone calls, newsletters and correspondence after guests go back home. The Phoenix program is an interesting combination of no-nonsense and luxury; and for shy or private people, the small number of guests (thirteen) makes for an unusually warm and supportive atmosphere.

FACT SUMMARY

NAME: The Phoenix

MAILING ADDRESS: 111 North Post Oak Lane, Houston, TX 77024

TELEPHONE: (713) 680-1611

TRANSPORTATION: Free pick-up at airport or any home in Houston

ACCOMMODATIONS: Luxurious; located in Phoenix wing of Houstonian Hotel

FEE: $2,000 a week all inclusive

MAXIMUM NUMBER OF GUESTS: 13

MAXIMUM NUMBER OF STAFF: 6

SEASON: Year-round

AMBIANCE: Secluded, sensible program; gracious staff

GENDER AND AGE RESTRICTIONS: Women only, except for designated men's weeks

DIET: Low-calorie gourmet cuisine, elegantly served in dining room, by the pool or in your room

FACILITIES: Olympic-sized pool, handball, racquetball and tennis courts; padded jogging track; weight room; saunas, whirlpool

PROGRAM: Wide range of exercise classes, up-to-date equipment; walking emphasized

SPECIAL FEATURES: Private session with the spa director, very small group of guests, excellent follow-up, good sessions on handling stress

LOCAL ATTRACTIONS: Astrodome, shopping and museums in Houston

Other Spas

Maine Chance

Maine Chance is a luxury retreat located near Camelback Mountain in Phoenix, Arizona. This deluxe Elizabeth Arden spa emphasizes beauty with some exercise and healthful gourmet dining. Fine paintings, beautiful china and linen, antique furniture and marble floors create an ambiance of gracious living for the fifty female guests.

FACT SUMMARY

MAILING ADDRESS: 5830 East Jean Avenue, Phoenix, AZ 85018

TELEPHONE: (602) 947-6365

TRAVEL DIRECTIONS: Fly to Phoenix airport

TRANSPORTATION: Maine Chance limo from Phoenix airport

ACCOMMODATIONS: Distinctive feminine rooms, antiques, books, fresh flowers

FEE: $1,650 to $2,150 per week

MAXIMUM NUMBER OF GUESTS: 50

MAXIMUM NUMBER OF STAFF: 130

SEASON: Last week in September through end of May

AMBIANCE: Plush, old-line, aristocratic, 110 acres of tropical landscaping

GENDER AND AGE RESTRICTIONS: Women over 16

DIET: 950 calories per day, fresh fruits and vegetables with lean meat and fish; fresh fruit juices; outdoor luncheon and dinner, weather permitting

FACILITIES: Swimming pools, exercise area, sauna, extensive beauty areas for facials, massage, hair and nail care

PROGRAM: Primarily beauty with some emphasis on fitness and diet control; individually planned regimen

SPECIAL FEATURES: Excellent beauty and careful diet program; personal maid; Chagall and O'Keeffe works of art; French antiques; breakfast in bed

LOCAL ATTRACTIONS: Shopping and repertory theater; sightseeing of western art museums, Indian reservation

Aspen Health Center

The Aspen Health Center is part of the Aspen Institute for Humanistic Studies. The programs are geared to preventive medicine through the physical tuning of the body with exercise, massage therapy and beauty service. An additional program is the cardiopulmonary testing and conditioning lab. It is located in the majestic Colorado Rockies only thirty-five minutes by air from Denver.

FACT SUMMARY

MAILING ADDRESS: 25 Meadows Road, P.O. Box 1092, Aspen, CO 81611; reservations: Aspen Meadows Resort, P.O. Box 220, Aspen, CO 81611

TELEPHONE: (303) 925-3586 or 925-3426

TRAVEL DIRECTIONS: Stapleton airport in Denver, transfer to Rocky Mountain Airways or Aspen Airways to Aspen

TRANSPORTATION: Limo to and from Aspen airport

ACCOMMODATIONS: Chalets, 3-bedroom townhouses, studio apartments

FEE: Rooms range from $80 to $275 per person, per day; $80 per day single occupancy includes health center facilities and limousine service; beauty services extra

MAXIMUM NUMBER OF GUESTS: 25

MAXIMUM NUMBER OF STAFF: 8

SEASON: Year-round

AMBIANCE: Contemporary glass-and-wood chalets in the Rocky Mountains

GENDER AND AGE RESTRICTIONS: Coed; children under 14 must be accompanied by adult

DIET: Staff recommends individual diet plan from Aspen Meadow Resort restaurant

FACILITIES: Heated pool, 6 tennis courts, gym, sauna, cold plunge, steam, Olympic trampoline, weight machines

PROGRAM: Individual or group exercise and fitness programs

SPECIAL FEATURES: Miles of prime-quality fly fishing and hiking trails

LOCAL ATTRACTIONS: Sunlight ski area, Aspen music festival

Walley's Hot Springs

Located in the foothills of the Sierra Nevadas, overlooking the Carson Valley only twelve miles from Lake Tahoe's south shore, Walley's Hot Springs resort offers health club programs. Guests stay in charming turn-of-the-century cottages filled with antiques.

FACT SUMMARY

MAILING ADDRESS: P. O. Box 26, Genoa, NV 89411

TELEPHONE: (702) 782-7460, 782-4011, 782-5011

TRAVEL DIRECTIONS: Take Route 395, go 15 miles south of Carson City on Foothills Road to Genoa. The spa is 2½ miles south of Genoa on Foothills

TRANSPORTATION: Private auto or taxi to and from Tahoe-Douglas airport (4 miles) or Gardnerville Greyhound depot (6 miles)

ACCOMMODATIONS: Victorian cottages with hotel service; inn under construction (completion about mid-'83)

FEE: Cottages, 2 queen-size beds, $80 per day; 1 double-sized bed, $60 per day (both include breakfast and full use of spa facilities)

MAXIMUM NUMBER OF GUESTS: 12

MAXIMUM NUMBER OF STAFF: 20 per shift

SEASON: Year-round

AMBIANCE: Turn-of-the-century atmosphere overlooking the panorama of the magnificent Sierras and the Carson Valley

GENDER AND AGE RESTRICTIONS: None, except children under 12 are not allowed in spa area

DIET: No special diet; restaurant

FACILITIES: Crystal-clear hot mineral water in huge flow-through spas of variable temperatures; private lockers; saunas; steam rooms; complete physical fitness facility; restaurant, lounge; racquetball, tennis and handball courts under construction

PROGRAM: A general health club program with professional supervision; open to the general public with emphasis on tour groups

SPECIAL FEATURES: Historical heritage and superb mineral water in a breathtaking setting

LOCAL ATTRACTIONS: Tahoe casinos (20 minutes), Reno (45 minutes), skiing at Heavenly Valley (30 minutes) or Kirkwood (50 minutes)

Bermuda Inn at Lake Austin Resort

Located in the Texas hill country on the shores of Lake Austin, this reasonably priced spa provides as rigorous or easy a program as the guest chooses, with a calorie-controlled diet. A serene environment on the edge of a peaceful lake offers the guests an opportunity to participate in a wide range of outdoor activities.

FACT SUMMARY

MAILING ADDRESS: 1705 Quinlan Park Road, Austin, TX 78732

TELEPHONE: (512) 266-2444; toll-free, Texas (800) 252-9324

TRAVEL DIRECTIONS: From Austin take Ranch Road 2222 to Texas

620; turn west and go 2 miles to Quinlan Park Road, then left 6 miles. Or fly to Austin airport.

TRANSPORTATION: Free transportation to and from Austin airport, or any public terminal in Austin

ACCOMMODATIONS: Motel-style; all with view of lake and Texas hill country

FEE: Deluxe rooms (per day): single, $105; double, $75; triple, $55; regular rooms (per day): single, $93; double, $63; triple, $48 (beauty services extra; no minimum stay)

MAXIMUM NUMBER OF GUESTS: 90

MAXIMUM NUMBER OF STAFF: 38

SEASON: Year-round, closed December 23 to January 3

AMBIANCE: Informal

GENDER AND AGE RESTRICTIONS: Adults over 18; coed

DIET: 500, 650, 900 calories per day, low sodium and fats; primarily fish, seafood, chicken and turkey with some red meat entrees

FACILITIES: Gyms, indoor and outdoor pool, whirlpool, massage, facial and beauty departments, boutique

PROGRAM: Individually designed according to participant's own capacity, condition and desire, and includes a variety of exercise classes

SPECIAL FEATURES: Water sports, fishing, boating

LOCAL ATTRACTIONS: Theater at University of Texas, Lyndon Baines Johnson Library

The National Lifestyle Institute

The National Lifestyle Institute is a Utah mountain resort located in what is a ski area in the winter. The exercise program is vigorous and effective, and educational sessions on behavior modification are given. Sports enthusiasts will like the facilities, which include horseback riding, golf and sailing nearby. Open summer months only.

FACT SUMMARY

MAILING ADDRESS: P. O. Box 206, Bountiful, UT 84010

TELEPHONE: (801) 295-3819; toll-free: (800) 453-5757

TRAVEL DIRECTIONS: Fly into Salt Lake City airport and take Interstate 80 east, exit Park City turnoff, go 3 miles to Parkwest entrance and turn right at entrance; go to Red Pine condominium on left

ACCOMMODATIONS: Single or double rooms, or executive single—a 1-bedroom condominium

FEE: Single room, $450 per person, per week; executive suite, a 1-bedroom condominium, $570 per person (double occupancy), per week

MAXIMUM NUMBER OF GUESTS: 30

MAXIMUM NUMBER OF STAFF: 15

SEASON: June through September

AMBIANCE: Modern condominium resort complex

GENDER AND AGE RESTRICTIONS: None

DIET: Low-calorie balanced nutrition

FACILITIES: 4 swimming pools, tennis courts, exercise room, sauna, whirlpool

PROGRAM: Behavior modification, aerobics, dance, yoga, scenic hikes

SPECIAL FEATURES: Slim cooking classes, guest lecturers, personal evaluation

LOCAL ATTRACTIONS: Horseback riding, golf, sailing, rafting nearby

THE
MIDWEST

Featured Spas

The Kerr House

The musical tinkle of china cups and saucers sounds gently from the hall stairs. You awake in a perfect Victorian bedroom with delicate flowered wallpaper, an antique chest and lace-etched glass windows. Peeking out from under an authentic patchwork quilt you see graceful Brucilla in a long flowing robe bringing your breakfast on a woven basket tray.

This is not a revival of Louisa May Alcott's *Little Women*, but it's about as close as you can get in the twentieth century; it is the Kerr House near Toledo, Ohio, probably the most unusual private health retreat in North America.

On a cold winter day in 1977, Laurie Hostetler, an enthusiastic curly-haired former girl scout leader and yoga teacher, happened across a perfect Queen Anne Victorian mansion on the outskirts of the tiny but winning town of Grand Rapids, Ohio. It was suffering from extreme neglect, but with the foresight that she would later apply to her guests, she could see what a perfect specimen it would become with an ample application of loving care. The home was built in 1880 by the town's first and foremost merchant and owner of the general store, Mr. B. F. Kerr, whose benign and bearded presence beams down from the parlor wall, making you wonder what he would think if he could only see his very proper home host to changing groups of liberated ladies in various states of dress padding to the sauna or a sensuous massage.

ACCOMMODATIONS

Although the Kerr House is so large you can spend all week within its walls and not feel claustrophobic, unless you specifically ask for a single room (there is only one available, and at a considerable additional charge) or unless you bring a friend with you, you will find yourself sharing a room with another guest you have never met. Actually, Laurie is blessed with remarkable intuition and she carefully studies the guests' backgrounds in order to make the best pairing possible. Even if a crotchety guest actually appears at the door, there is something about the total loving and supportive attitude of the staff that makes it hard for a person to stay that way. The small number of guests (six to eight) guarantees that everyone, both guests and staff, knows your name and most of your idiosyncracies. If you want to lie in bed claiming the "vapors" (it seems an appropriate affliction in such a setting), you will be lavished with sympathy and gallons of the odd but satisfying house tea with lots of clucking and fluffing of pillows to go with it. We found that even for independent career types, a lot of coddling and sorority-house chatter in the crowded but cozy upstairs bath was more a delight than an annoyance.

The rooms, of course, are all different but exquisite, complete with antique bureaus, stained-glass windows, fireplaces, an occasional rocker and a profusion of well-placed antique objets d'art, silver dresser sets and period paintings.

The communal bath is complete with bidets, which the practical Laurie will cheerfully explain if you are unfamiliar with such an item.

FACILITIES

"I have abandoned my search for truth, and am now looking for a good fantasy" goes a popular quote by Ashleigh Brilliant. At the Kerr House you can stop looking. From the moment you step into the entry hall you are truly in another world.

The rose carpet and walls are a soft contrast to the handsome formal oak staircase, and the antique tile fireplace in the hall features at its center the image of the goddess Psyche. Everywhere you look there are stained-glass windows and antiques in perfect condition. Chairs and loveseats re-covered with authentic Victorian reproduction fabrics grace the rooms. The effect is of being in a new home in 1880, and the fantasy is supported by the serving of the special house tea (lemon, maple syrup and cayenne pepper) in the parlor on your arrival.

The formal parlor and equally elegant family sitting room are used for speakers and other group programs, or you can escape your schedule to sit here and read the 1887 issues of *Godey's Lady's Book* or just meditate in the fairy-tale surroundings. In the evening before dinner, a harpist appears and plays a lovely selection of melodies on a huge dignified harp.

The ten thousand square foot, thirty-five-room house offers many surprises. The cellar, for years host to glass jars of home canned fruits, barrels of pickles and galvanized tubs of sudsy Victorian laundry, now sports a sybaritic maze of mineral baths, a sauna, a ten-person whirlpool, showers and treatment rooms designed to soothe every part of the anatomy from your slightly oily forehead to the crusty soles of your feet. An area off the colorful beauty lounge provides space for additional facial treatments and tables for massages. Although these areas are separated only by curtains drawn around a frame, the feeling is private enough to allow for total relaxation and even a snooze as the kinks are worked out after a morning of exercise.

PROGRAM

"We work with the total person through exercise, nutrition, attitude, stress management and body treatment," says Laurie. "We don't much believe in spending time on makeup here, because we believe beauty starts on the inside. If a person wants to be useful to her family, work setting, group of friends or society as a whole she must start by maintaining a healthy mind and body."

The main program is planned around this holistic approach, whether a guest opts for the popular five-day Sunday to Friday program or only comes for the day. Often a group of friends will try the day program, then come back for a longer stay later.

The five-day program begins early. Studying the schedule at breakfast the first day one guest was aghast at the note "8:00 A.M. to 10:00 A.M. exercise." "What kind of exercise can go on for two hours?" asked the generously figured guest, commenting that too frequent trips to the hors d'oeuvres table had been her most demanding exercise lately.

There was no need to worry, since Laurie spends a lot of time at the beginning on basics such as proper breathing.

Breathing is big at the Kerr House. This is not surprising, since yogic movement is the core of the exercise program. "Proper deep breathing reaches down into your diaphragm and sends energy spinning into all parts of the body," says Laurie. "It can make everything you do easier from digestion to aerobic exercise, from thinking through a problem to dealing calmly with an angry boss.

"Good health is the natural state," Laurie says, beaming as she launches into the first exercise class of the week in the huge cloudlike former attic with its fascinating nooks and crannies slathered with deep soft baby-blue carpeting. The oddly shaped dormer windows and skylights make for interesting patterns of light, giving the room a cozy yet ethereal feeling.

In keeping with the spirit of the retreat—self-image and psyche are refreshed at the same time the body is energized by healthy food and exercises—Laurie helps get you started on relaxing and releasing the outside world by asking you to close your eyes and visualize a box. "Now you are going to take everything that is worrying you and place it in the box. Is a project at work bothering you? Put it in the box. Is there someone causing you concern or frustration? Put them in the box. Worried about money? Put that worry in the box, too. There is no past to regret, and no future to worry about, there is only you right now in this moment. Experience being here now."

Most guests are only too glad once they get the hang of it, as the "now" at the Kerr House is as close to nurturing perfection as most adults will ever get.

As the week progresses, exercises get more strenuous, almost imperceptibly, and the change is so gradual there is seldom any soreness or muscle strain. Complementing the yoga stretches and postures are aerobic exercises done on individual "rebounders." These are one-person-sized, low, mini-trampolines on which jumping, skipping and kicking take on a new dimension. It's hard not to grin with enthusiasm as you tramp through a routine feeling almost airborne. It is also supposed to gently massage internal organs, encouraging them to function well.

In the afternoon other activities include a second exercise session, or walking along the canal towpath or through the main street of Grand Rapids. Sometimes guests take a paddle-boat ride on the nearby Maumee River or just sit on the generous front porch, rocking or taking tea and chatting.

Throughout the day, usually in the morning, a guest appears to speak on a special topic like stress reduction or nutrition. A favorite is the graphologist who visits once a week and tells guests intimate secrets about themselves by studying handwriting samples.

Sometimes during these programs one is torn between feeling part of a classic English weekend house party or a Swiss clinic. The latter feeling is definitely stronger as the kinesiologist appears and demonstrates muscle weaknesses in everyone while pulling and stretching each guest into better body alignment. Scary at first but worth it.

Folk medicine and homeopathic treatments run throughout the programs. If you can't sleep, the staff offers calcium tablets. If you have trouble with digestion or bloating they offer hydrochloric acid tablets with meals. Herb laxatives are also offered. Even the cayenne pepper in the tea has a healthy purpose—it diminishes mucous in breathing passages. The whole approach here is holistic and gentle, from the programs to the exercise plan, and given this, most guests were amazed to learn how many pounds and inches they had lost in five days—from a low of four pounds to a high of nine and a half!

FOOD AND DIET

All those slightly smug Californians who can't believe fresh fruits and vegetables ever reach the midwestern provinces are in for a big surprise when they sit down to eat at the Kerr House.

The handsome and slightly shy Dean, who is in charge of the kitchen, has been known to drive like a person crazed (all the way to Cleveland!) to find just the perfect papaya, the freshest spinach or the best ginger root for his closely guarded (and delicious) recipes.

He does his magic without using salt, sugar or refined flour. He also juggles all fifty-two known essential nutrients (vitamins, minerals and amino acids) so that even on 750 to 1,000 calories a day guests don't have those ominous cravings that ordinary dieting sometimes produces.

Nearly everything is made fresh in the stone-walled kitchen in the basement of the mansion. For breakfast a rich, nutty homemade yogurt is served with a sprinkling of wheat germ, bran and granola. Because of its freshness it takes a minute to recognize what it is. A favorite lunch is garlic rouille, which consists of a piece of homemade seven-grain bread that has been toasted, then piled with fresh steamed vegetables blended into a garlic rouille sauce. Another is a salad that is similar to a Chinese chicken salad, piquant with lemon and a touch of honey, and served with zucchini bread.

Lunch is served in another cheerful stone-walled room next

to the kitchen, called the café, which is decorated in bright flower prints and hung with antiques. Small round tables encourage conversation, as does the fact that dress for lunch is simply the leotard or robe you happened to be wearing as you left your massage or herbal wrap. On the second day it is already hard to believe you haven't known these friends for years. After lunch Laurie sometimes leads singing around the player piano, which is stocked with more than a hundred schmaltzy, cheerful and romantic tunes.

Dinner in the formal Victorian dining room is as elegant as lunch is casual. Huge elaborate two-foot-high candelabra ceremoniously grace the table, which is set with exquisite antique china, and crystal that become prisms of light reflecting candlelight into rainbows on the linen tablecloth.

Before each meal Dean steps quietly into the room in his chef's coat and announces the menu. "This evening's dinner will be cold melon soup, spinach salad and eggplant Parmesan." His pronouncements are received in reverent silence. One of the guests joked that when she returned home, she would step up to the mirror at dinnertime and say solemnly, "This evening's dinner will be Velveeta cheese on saltines, with root beer." So much for the elegant life.

All the food is excellent, and there are some real surprises such as nutmeg in the chicken salad that make dishes quite special. The remarkable soups, however, run away with the highest honors. The cheddar cheese soup (made with yogurt), the fresh lettuce soup and the cantaloupe soup almost make the rest of the meal anticlimactic.

Laurie is always ready to alter the diet for a person with special needs. One guest with serious arthritis had special meals planned for her that avoided eggs, tomato, grapefruit and other foods known to aggravate the condition, and by the end of the week she was striding easily up and down the stairs, feeling terrific.

Meals at the beginning of the week are a little larger; they become more spartan as the week progresses, but you hardly notice as the body gets used to less food, served naturally without additives.

HEALTH AND BEAUTY SERVICES

The Kerr House offers a complete menu of body treatments. The five-day (Sunday to Friday) program includes two massages, an herbal wrap, a cellulite wrap, a "finger facial," a deep-cleansing facial and a foot reflexology treatment. There is, of course, a lot more—surprises are to be expected as normal here—but these are the basics.

If you choose a one-day program, you will experience a finger facial that is a thorough face and neck massage with a stimulating cleansing, an herbal wrap, a massage, an exercise class and a whirlpool or sauna, as you choose.

Massages are often given in your room—you will be told in advance if it is elsewhere. All of the masseuses are very well trained and give a massage tailored to individual needs, some of which you may not even have known that you had. The masseuse will notice if your body seems out of alignment or if a particular muscle is tight and will convey this to the other masseuses so that you get really personal care all week. Lying on the massage table in your bedroom surrounded by antiques and lace curtains, eye to eye with a low china cabinet so you can study each cup carefully as your knots are worked out is a unique experience.

This is the first place we experienced a massage that included having one's ears pulled, a practice that should be annoying but instead feels absolutely great, as if your whole cranium is getting a nice stretch.

The finger facial is a head-and-neck massage and cleansing usually accompanied by a peel. Heated mittens and booties soften the hands and feet as restful Indian string music plays softly in the background. A machine facial including steam treatment is offered for deep cleaning, using France Laure products. Shaklee products are also used throughout the spa.

An hour's foot reflexology treatment is offered for those who can stand it. The purpose is to stimulate the organs and work out calcium deposits from foot joints. Healthful but sometimes a little painful for the uninitiated.

Herbal wraps using herb-treated hot linens are soothing and administered lovingly, as are all the treatments.

Some guests tried the cellulite wrap, which is supposed to iron out some of those bumpy areas on legs and fanny. A lotion is applied, then you are wrapped in plastic wrap like a space age mummy. The treatment also helps you lose excess water.

The mineral baths, sauna and whirlpool are available to use at any time and usually are happily in use in the evenings, when guests are too tired to do anything else.

OTHER PLEASURES

The delightful town of Grand Rapids is located on the Maumee River and was a key station on the Ohio canal system, which carried everything from dry goods to livestock to rural areas in the 1880s.

Canal boats moved along the canals pulled by ropes attached to horses or mules, which trudged along towpaths on either side of the canal. Today you can walk or jog along these picturesque shady paths, with the river on one side and the peaceful old canal on the other. It's fun to poke around the old canal locks and the quiet round stone cove where boats came to drop goods before returning to the canal proper.

The town itself is in the enviable state of being charming but as yet undiscovered. Stores and businesses have been restored to their original appearance; and shop owners bustle around calling everyone by name. There is an herb store where soap making and other homely arts are taught, and a general store that sells calico, old-fashioned candies, gifts and antiques. A small cheerful restaurant boasts a little theater upstairs. In the fall the town holds an Apple Butter Fest, proceeds going to restore the old town hall.

Other interesting highlights of the area that guests may choose to visit include a fowl farm for endangered species, a glassblower's studio or Fort Meigs. Fort Meigs is the largest renovation of a fort in the country; it played a large part in the War of 1812. Lantern-light tours are offered there that feature living tableaus and incidents that might normally have taken place at the fort, such as a court-martial or a scene in a military tent. Costumed denizens of the night and the flickering lantern lights make one feel that the last hundred years never happened. Look closely at the characters—two of them are Laurie's husband and daughter.

WHAT TO BRING

Leotards, maillot swimsuits and fluffy white terry robes are provided. "Noppy" slippers are also offered, which make you feel as if you're walking on rows of rubber nails until you get used to them.

Although most of your day will be spent in leotards or robe, you will need jeans, shorts or slacks and shirts or T-shirts for the walks. It is the custom to dress for dinner; pretty caftans, long skirts or dresses, short dresses, or nice slacks are all appropriate.

Bring a jacket or sweater for cool evenings, and heavier gear if you'll be there during the winter, as Ohio can get Christmas-card cold and snow is common from December to February. Check the weather forecast.

Definitely bring a camera; the Kerr House and its proud town are full of great nostalgic images. In the summer when mosquitos can be thick along the canal, be sure to bring insect repellent.

HOW TO GET THERE

Most guests drive to Grand Rapids, which is twenty minutes from Toledo on Route 65, just fifteen minutes from the college town of Bowling Green. It is possible to fly to Detroit and rent a car; or take the jet port van to Toledo, the drive takes about two hours, or you can fly into Toledo and ask in advance to be picked up by a staff member. If you will be driving, when you make your reservation mention it, and Kerr House will send you directions and a clearly marked map.

SUMMARY

The Kerr House is for people who want to completely remove themselves to another world and time. It is a place of calm caring women; graceful, dignified surroundings; and homemade soup; where you inhabit a glorious Victorian house that is both stately and lively, located in an old-fashioned town small enough to walk to the post office. The food is superb, the yoga-based exercise program produces soaring energy and the staff will charm your socks off. This may not be heaven, but it's very close.

FACT SUMMARY

NAME: The Kerr House

MAILING ADDRESS: 17605 Beaver Street, Grand Rapids, OH 43522

TELEPHONE: (419) 832-1733 and 255-8364

TRANSPORTATION: Pick-up at airport by request

ACCOMMODATIONS: Shared rooms, filled with antiques, shared bath

FEE: 5 days, $1,500; 2-day weekend, $450

MAXIMUM NUMBER OF GUESTS: 8

MAXIMUM NUMBER OF STAFF: 20

SEASON: Year-round

AMBIANCE: Cozy, charming, Victorian

GENDER AND AGE RESTRICTIONS: Women only, but periodic couples' and men's weeks

DIET: Fresh fruit and vegetables; chicken, fish; low fat; no salt, sugar, white flour or additives; 750 to 1,000 calories

FACILITIES: Victorian mansion with hot tub, mineral baths, exercise rooms, rebounders, walking paths

PROGRAM: Goal is rejuvenation and behavior modification. Emphasis on relaxation techniques, yoga, walking, some aerobics, mini-trampolines

SPECIAL FEATURES: Wall-to-wall antiques, interesting lectures; serene, loving staff

LOCAL ATTRACTIONS: Paddle-boat rides, local parks, Fort Meigs, browsing in Grand Rapids

The Spa at Olympia Resort

The snow was falling quietly and a low wind blew the snow into sculptured drifts against trees and fences, giving form and definition to the usually flat Wisconsin landscape. Inside the Olympia Resort one guest broke the reverie of another who was staring out at the icy scene through a large picture window. "Feeling guilty?" she asked with a laugh, knowing her fellow spa-goer had a family at home coping with the elements. "No—just grateful!" her friend responded with enthusiasm.

This is the overriding feeling of women from the Midwest when they find the Spa at Olympia Resort. Many who don't want to spend either the time or the extra money for airfare to go to one of the more famous "glitter spas" in Florida or

California are delighted to find this excellent spa in their own back yard.

Since the Olympia Resort has a large convention business, many women are introduced to their first spa experience while their husbands attend convention sessions. Because there are so many first-timers, there is a feeling of personal amazement in guests. One grandmother was heard whispering, "I've never thought about this, felt like this, looked like this, ever thought I'd do this, in my whole life. I'm taking care of me!"

You'll find few jaded spa jet-setters here who complain about the temperature in the whirlpool being a few degrees off. Most of these women have never even seen a whirlpool before and they're hardly in the mood to be critical when they finally do.

ACCOMMODATIONS

Guest rooms or suites may be reserved in the main lodge, which provides easy access to the spa and dining area. In all rooms, sliding-glass doors give way to large balconies overlooking the golf course or quiet pond. Open fireplaces and bars accent the suites, which are equipped with sofa sleepers.

Though the complex is just seven years old, redecoration of living areas has been recently undertaken, and all rooms are tastefully furnished. Only fifty spa guests can be accommodated at any one time, and their rooms are generally located on a single floor so that camaraderie may develop more easily, and so that moral support in warding off caloric temptations is readily available.

If more space is desired, guests may opt for a villa on the Olympia grounds, a few hundred yards from the hotel. Originally designed for sale as condominiums, the villas are ideal for entertaining or to accommodate a family. They are available as an alternative to hotel accommodations on a nightly basis, or weeks may be purchased on a time-sharing plan.

FACILITIES

The Spa at Olympia Resort is a part of a richly varied resort complex, making it an ideal spot for a family vacation in that it not only offers "something for everyone"—it actually delivers.

Olympia Resort rambles over 400 acres in the lake country of southern Wisconsin. Oconomowoc, an Indian word for "where the water gathers," is the name of the nearby village. Not surprisingly, water sports are fully represented here: sailing, water-skiing and swimming (in Silver Lake or one of the heated pools) are all close at hand.

The first tee on an eighteen-hole golf course is within sight of the hotel. The course is 6,600 yards and is made treacherous by crisscrossing streams and other water hazards. Bag storage, lockers, carts and good advice are provided at the pro shop.

For the tennis player, the season is twelve months long at Olympia. When Midwest winters close down the outdoor courts, play continues at the Racquet Club, where handball and racquetball courts are also maintained. Private lessons can be arranged with Olympia's resident professional.

The resort is within a few miles of nationally famous recreational areas and the Kettle Moraine National Forest made distinctive by glacial action thousands of years ago. Hiking trails wend through the lake area, which can also be explored on bicycles rented from the resort. During most of the year, horses may be hired from stables within a half-mile of the resort, and hayrides can also be arranged.

When winter paralyzes the rest of the Midwest, a new world opens at Olympia. For downhill aficionados, a ski hill on the premises served by two double chairlifts and lighted for night skiing goes into operation. Ice skating and ice boating replace swimming and sailing, while the whoosh of cross-country skis is heard on the golf course and on jogging trails throughout the area.

For those who subscribe to the theory that a vacation is for loafing, and sport is work, Olympia Resort makes idleness easy. A huge beamed gathering room with a massive open fireplace and cozily arranged furniture does double duty as a lobby and center for socializing, and is only a few steps away from a quiet cocktail in the Polo Lounge. As the evening progresses, live entertainment is onstage in the Dram and Drum.

Spa guests may elect to dine in the Crown and Thistle (where the pastry cart will not be admitted), or may be seated in the main dining room, the Terrace, and served their selected spa entree while their companions order from the menu. A more cosmopolitan mood prevails in the Royal Cellar where many meals are prepared tableside with sauces to threaten the strongest of dieting willpower. Steaks and seafood are served nightly in a more casual atmosphere at the Beach House, which overlooks Silver Lake.

The spa is open daily from 9:00 A.M. to 6:00 P.M. The offices of the directress, nutritionist and physician are located just off the main reception area, adjacent to the ladies' gymnasium, which features exercise equipment to assist in toning and firming.

Down another hallway are the men's locker room, gymnasium with a Universal gym and running mill; sauna, eucalyptus and steam rooms and Grecian shower. Nearby are the treatment areas for men, where loofah rubs, massage and even facials can be administered in complete privacy.

The women's shower and treatment area was part of the original health club, and continues to be available to all hotel guests for a small fee. Here also are saunas, eucalyptus and steam rooms, and a Grecian shower. Also within the shower area is the loofah room, tiled from top to bottom in cheerful blue, and kept at a comfortable 85 degrees.

The newly opened area of the Spa at Olympia is dominated by the expansive Roman bath. Tiled in terra-cotta and accented in blue, the room is decorated with greenery and fresh floral arrangements. It features two large central pools, one maintained at 104 degrees, the other at 80 degrees. In both, continuous motion of the water soothes tired muscles and taut nerves.

At one end of the room are three individual whirlpool baths. Set on platforms somewhat above floor level and partially protected by redwood planters filled with trailing greenery, these pools are the ultimate in luxurious bathing privacy.

Nightly shows at the resort's twin cinema are first-run films, one of which is always suitable for children. In addition, during peak holiday periods, special programs are organized. Structured day care is available for little ones, and activities are arranged for teen-agers. There is even a busy electronic game room within the hotel.

Olympia is well known as a convention center and is equipped with meeting rooms and related facilities. Its Expo Center is reached from the hotel by an enclosed walk, along which a wide variety of shops and services are arrayed. An ice cream parlor, dress and gift shops and a cheese shop are open during regular business hours. Elsewhere in the hotel are a newsstand-smokeshop and shops where gifts and sportswear may be purchased.

PROGRAM

As originally constructed, the Olympia Resort hotel featured a lower level of indoor recreational facilities including a pool, sauna, eucalyptus rooms, whirlpool and exercise areas filled with the sort of equipment found in any suburban health club.

In 1981 plans to expand the health club were carried forward. Doris M. Hogue, formerly with La Costa and The Golden Door, was engaged to guide the expansion and serve as directress of the Spa at Olympia. With her came hundreds of thoughtful touches that make a visit to the Spa at Olympia a luxurious introduction to spa-going.

Although there are sauna and pool facilities for men and women, there is a formal program only for women. The staff at Olympia is dedicated to imparting to midwestern women what Californians have known all along—that spa life is not only for the fabulously wealthy; and that even a few days dedicated to restoration of body and spirit can work miracles.

One of the pleasures of the spa is its emphasis on individualized attention. Once settled in their rooms on arrival, guests are called and welcomed by Doris Hogue. A convenient time is then set for an introductory consultation, at which time the tape measure and scale make their awful statement, and (more happily) an individualized plan is developed to meet the goals for the week set by the guest. A medical history is taken, and where indicated, consultation with a physician is arranged before a fitness program is established.

Following this meeting, menus for the week are selected in consultation with the spa nutritionist.

While inch loss at Olympia is generally double the pound loss, Doris emphasizes that the spa's real goal is to make women guests feel "well and alive and a woman." The spa follows an active/passive program, which calls for alternating strenuous exercise with periods of quiet relaxation, such as a massage or herbal wrap. This helps ward off muscle strains associated with "too much, too soon" and assists in a gradual transition from a hectic life outside to the tranquil atmosphere of the spa.

"Women simply don't take the time they need for themselves in their normal routine. Our job is to give them a chance to relax," says Doris. It works. The most complex task to be addressed while at the spa is keeping an eye on strategically placed clocks to be sure the time set aside for exercise isn't snoozed away in the Roman bath. After the first consultation, there are simply no more decisions to be made, and most guests delight in padding about docilely or sitting quietly in the lounge sipping herb tea and waiting to be called for a facial.

A full range of dance and exercise classes are conducted at Olympia. Morning and afternoon classes of water exercises are conducted in the hotel's indoor pool, but exercise classes are held in the beautiful exercise room. Carpeted in mocha and peach, and equipped with ballet barres, the room has three mirrored walls, making it wonderfully easy to "get in step."

Instructors are experienced in yoga and dance, and they cheerfully lead their huffing and puffing charges through routines set to music. Although every class is a delight, when Rear Echelon is selected, no one can doubt that serious exercise is in progress. Rear Echelon is dedicated to those problem spots—hips, tummy and derriere—and gives evey guest a chance to realize fully just how much her thighs weigh.

However strenuous the exercise is, the emphasis remains on health. Heart rates are taken during aerobic class, and all classes incorporate a wonderfully relaxing cooldown phase. Special care is taken with exercises requiring use of the spine, and the stretching routines are peppered throughout by words of caution, "Gently, slowly, no bouncing—we don't want to pull or jar."

FOOD AND DIET

The routine diet for spa program guests of just 600 calories per day sounds like torture, but it is absolutely not. When a stay at Olympia concludes, honest guests will admit that it *is* possible to eat well when limiting caloric intake, and what's more, they will know how to do so at home.

Reeducation is the key. In her consultation with spa program guests, the nutritionist reviews existing eating habits and helps the guest identify areas needing more control. Together, they talk about how behavior can be modified and chart a realistic adjustment period.

Of course, several days in residence at Olympia make for a good head start. Guests attend classes in cooking taught by the spa chef to learn how to use arrowroot as a thickener in place of flour, and to substitute yogurt or cottage cheese for sour cream as a base for sauces. The spa menu makes heavy use of herbs and avoids salt and sugar entirely. Many spa recipes are already available to enthusiastic guests, and future plans call for a collection of recipes to be made into a book.

The menu from which the week's luncheon and dinner selections are made is incredibly varied. Each day, meat, poultry and fish entrees are offered for dinner, with salads or light meals available at lunch. And yet, appetizer, entree, vegetable and dessert never exceed 350 calories. Meats are served with sauces, desserts are luscious and the pounds still fade away.

Lunch might be melon balls with mint garni (20) and poached salmon (146) with a hot apricot compote (40) for dessert, while a routine dinner could include gazpacho (25), roast duck jardiniere (146), zucchini Provençal (16) and coconut custard (40).

For nondieting family members (and for spa-goers wishing to binge before their rehabilitation) the meal of the week at Olympia is Sunday brunch. Milwaukee residents make the trek weekly to feast on crepes, quiche, chicken, barbecued ribs, cold meats, smoked fish and fish spreads. Omelettes are made to order, incorporating any of a dozen ingredient options displayed on the table, including ham, tomatoes, green pepper and varied cheeses and vegetables.

One entire table is laden with fresh fruits, cheese and salads, while another offers breakfast sweets, other baked goods and desserts. If the end of a spa visit falls on a Sunday, do yourself a favor, leave early.

HEALTH AND BEAUTY SERVICES

To combat the soreness that is an essential by-product of Rear Echelon, sign up for a massage. The aches begin to fall away almost as soon as the massage room is entered.

An Olympia massage is challenged only by the spa's herbal wrap. The herbal wrap is a steam treatment that soaks toxins out of the body, conditions the skin and relaxes muscles after exercise.

In one of the most remote corners of the Spa at Olympia are a number of spacious bays where beauty treatments are administered. The emphasis is on skin care and makeup. Lancôme of Paris products are used because the emphasis the line places on individual care is a reflection of the Spa at Olympia's philosophy.

Unless French is a second language, spa guests may experience some difficulty remembering the product names. Somehow, no matter how many times an attendant patiently repeats "Douceur Demaquillante Nutrix," the fear remains that when the moment of truth comes at the cosmetic counter in Lord & Taylor, all will be blank. In anticipation of just this problem, at the close of the first facial session, each guest is presented with a VIP Beauty Chart on which skin analysis and products used are noted for future reference.

Facial treatments are adapted specifically to existing skin conditions, but all incorporate deep cleansing with a product in which fine clay particles are suspended, followed by applications of a bracing toner and a facial massage. Steam passed through ultraviolet rays en route to the face offers a germicidal effect, and pores are cleansed by means of a vacuum aspirator. The basal skin layer is reached and cleansed by ionization.

Masks of various kinds are available. A cooling seaweed mask is applied where hydration is in order, although for other skin conditions alternatives exist. But nothing can prepare the guest for the surprise received with a glimpse of her masked self in the mirror!

At least one facial during even a short stay at the Spa at Olympia will incorporate a complete head-and-neck massage. The full-length reclining chaise is tipped back, and a blissfully comforting rub ensues, reaching well down into the shoulders and upper back.

Unfortunately, a complete revamping is not possible, since hairstyling and cutting is not a spa service as yet. However, a hair-conditioning process using cholesterol is available, and the sheen and bounce it imparts is virtually guaranteed to make an exciting style look better.

Hands and feet do not go unattended. Manicure and pedicure can be arranged and will be solicitously attended to throughout the week. If a still-damp nail should accidentally be marred, chances are the beauty attendant will notice it the next day and insist on making an immediate repair.

A regular aspect of beauty treatment at the spa is conditioning of skin on the hands and feet. Rich cream is applied from fingertips to elbows, and toes to mid-calf, and then electric booties and mittens are worn to facilitate absorption by the skin. When the treatment is complete, calluses and rough spots have miraculously vanished and even the most ordinary of feet seem gorgeous.

OTHER PLEASURES

While extremely unlikely, the remote possibility exists that an Olympia guest would want to leave the complex in search of other diversions, and the Milwaukee area is glad to oblige. Tours of nearby cheese factories, wineries and breweries that close with free samples could easily form the basis of a day-long cocktail party, lest it be forgotten what made Milwaukee famous.

The area also boasts a fine zoological park and a number of historic and cultural attractions. Ethnic heritage is celebrated in annual folk and art festivals, and the city itself offers a broad range of shopping and dining options.

Closer to Olympia is the village of Oconomowoc (population 8,471). Just six blocks long, the main street reflects Oconomowoc's former life as a sleepy summer resort village. Frame cottages once closed up in September have now been winterized for occupancy year-round, and the old train station in the center of town has been transformed into a restaurant. The tastes of Olympia guests and those of other nearby resorts are reflected in distinguished clothing shops and excellent restaurants in and near Oconomowoc, making a trip "to town" a pleasant excursion.

WHAT TO BRING

If you are going to Olympia solely to enjoy the spa, nothing need be packed but a routine "weekend away" wardrobe. The atmosphere is informal, and in the wintertime dining attire can range from dresses and sports coats to ski wear still damp from the slopes. For the Royal Cellar, more elegant wear is in order, while the Beach House is decidedly casual.

On arrival, spa guests are issued a leotard, a warm-up suit, a luxurious terry robe and shower scuffs. These comfortable basics are absolutely all that is needed to get from one glorious treatment or class to the next. Freshly laundered articles are available daily or on request, and with luck, that fresh powder-blue wrap will be straight from the dryer and still warm as toast.

If organized sports are on your agenda, bring appropriate attire and equipment, although most articles needed to enjoy all the Olympia has to offer are available in the pro or gift shops on the grounds. While the necessary gear for water and snow skiing, golf and racquet sports are maintained for rental to guests, bellboys will cheerfully wrestle your own ski equipment and racquets to your room.

HOW TO GET THERE

The Olympia Resort is northwest of Milwaukee, a two-and-a-half-hour drive from Chicago. Situated just a few miles from Interstate 94, it is easily accessed by car.

Northbound travelers on Interstate 94 into Wisconsin bypass Milwaukee via Interstate 896, which rejoins 94 west of the city. Approximately twenty-five miles west of that junction, Exit 282 for Oconomowoc is reached. From the expressway ramp, follow signs for Oconomowoc, and travel one-and-a-half miles on Wisconsin Route 67 to the entrance of Olympia Resort, on the left.

Amtrak runs to Milwaukee, and air service is provided by several major airlines. From the airport, Olympia can be reached by rental car or limousine. Olympia and other motels in the western suburbs are served by reservation with the Oconomowoc Airport Limousine Service (414-367-4020). A call in advance of arrival is essential, because although a schedule exists, it is flexible and may not be followed to the minute. The service is operated by a lifelong Oconomowoc resident and former tavern owner who goes by the name "Torchy." He's a storehouse of knowledge about the area, and the asking of a well-timed question or two will ensure that a ride from the airport is accented by anecdote and trivia from Oconomowoc history and Torchy's life.

SUMMARY

The Spa at Olympia Resort is a large facility offering as full a range of services as many of the better known superspas. Women who live a good distance from either coast will be glad the spa movement has moved closer to home. But it's also a good choice for everyone in the summer, when the hot weather in the desert or Florida make the spas there less attractive.

Because of its location and the fact that it is fairly new on the spa scene, prices are low and classes are small. No crowding here. Doris Hogue and her cheerful staff make sure that the exercise programs are revised regularly so that boredom doesn't set in, and since most people who visit here have never been to a spa, morale is high as guests discover the joys of their first massage or delight in their first professional makeup jobs.

Husbands and children are welcome and will find plenty to occupy their time while Mom learns how to be a happy sybarite.

FACT SUMMARY

NAME: The Spa at Olympia Resort

MAILING ADDRESS: Oconomowoc, WI 53066

TELEPHONE: Toll-free (800) 558-9573

ACCOMMODATIONS: Hotel-like rooms and suites

FEE: 4-day plan—single, $463.00; double, $343.00 per person; 7-day plan—single, $788.00; double, $578.50 per person

MAXIMUM NUMBER OF GUESTS: 50

MAXIMUM NUMBER OF STAFF: 15

SEASON: Year-round

AMBIANCE: Slick, modern, full-service resort located in the lake country

GENDER AND AGE RESTRICTIONS: None

DIET: 600 to 1,000 calories; complex carbohydrates (fruits and vegetables), low fat; fish, chicken

FACILITIES: Separate spas for men and women, golf course, tennis courts, horseback riding, water and snow skiing, sailing, movie house, 5 dining rooms, indoor pool, Grecian showers, Roman bath, eucalyptus rooms, whirlpools, gift shops, game room

PROGRAM: Strong exercise program with sports options available, massage, pampering service; consultation with physician and nutritionist

SPECIAL FEATURES: Can begin program any day of the week; very personal service

LOCAL ATTRACTIONS: Village of Oconomowoc, tours of breweries and cheese factories

Other Spas

The Aurora House Spa

An eighteenth-century manor house completely renovated in Victorian style with beautiful antiques and the latest in spa equipment and facilities, the Aurora House Spa provides a comfortable country manor atmosphere with pampering and a balanced diet in a peaceful country setting. Aurora House offers year-round health, beauty and fitness programs for men and women.

FACT SUMMARY

MAILING ADDRESS: 35 East Garfield Road, Aurora, OH 44202

TELEPHONE: (216) 562-9171

TRAVEL DIRECTIONS: 20 miles southeast of Cleveland, Ohio, and 20 miles northeast of Akron. Accessible from Cleveland Hopkins airport. Located on State Route 82 east of Interstate 480; minutes from exit 13 of Ohio Turnpike

TRANSPORTATION: Chauffeured transportation by Aurora House from Cleveland airport

ACCOMMODATIONS: Small hotel located directly across from spa

FEE: 6-day, 6-night "spa retreat"—$1,495 per person; 3-day, 3-night resident—$700; 3-day nonresident (lunch only)—$450

MAXIMUM NUMBER OF GUESTS: 30

MAXIMUM NUMBER OF STAFF: 60

SEASON: Year-round

AMBIANCE: Victorian manor; Victorian charm with modern amenities

GENDER AND AGE RESTRICTIONS: Adults over 18; coed

DIET: 750 to 1,000 calories per day; high proportion of natural and organic food—high in fiber, low in sodium and fats

FACILITIES: Exercise studio, solarium, steam baths, saunas, environmental habitat, whirlpool, massage, full hair salon

PROGRAM: A pleasant balance of exercise classes, massage and beauty services

SPECIAL FEATURES: Victorian Tea Room, very extensive beauty services including paraffin wax skin treatment, seaweed skin treatments

LOCAL ATTRACTIONS: Shopping malls, Sea World, antique shopping, fishing, golf, horseback riding, skiing

Sans Souci

The resort of Sans Souci is located on a beautiful 80-acre tract of woods and meadows that adjoin a 600-acre park reserve, less than a half-hour from Dayton, Ohio. The focus of the activities is a colonial-type home that accommodates six guests at a time. The Sans Souci program combines fitness and reducing exercises and thorough nutritional education.

FACT SUMMARY

MAILING ADDRESS: 3745 West Franklin Road, Bellbrook, OH 45305

TELEPHONE: (513) 848-4851

TRAVEL DIRECTIONS: 14 miles south of Dayton; take Interstate 75 to Dayton, Ohio, or fly to Dayton airport

ACCOMMODATIONS: Single and double occupancy in luxurious rooms and surroundings

FEE: Private room, $842 per week; Semi-private room, $640 per week

MAXIMUM NUMBER OF GUESTS: 6

MAXIMUM NUMBER OF STAFF: 10

SEASON: May 1 through October 30

AMBIANCE: Luxurious and pleasant

GENDER AND AGE RESTRICTIONS: None

DIET: Balanced, low-calorie (700); low-salt, low-fat, low-cholesterol, high-fiber; natural diet

FACILITIES: Exercise room, heated swimming pool, parcourse with 18 exercise stations, 80 acres terrain and trails

PROGRAM: Diet, stretching, parcourse, swimnastics, aerobic dance, hikes, spot exercise, yoga, tai chi, lectures on behavior modification, nutrition

SPECIAL FEATURES: Individualized counseling on diet and exercise programs; beautiful 80-acre estate with lake

LOCAL ATTRACTIONS: Air Force Museum, art museum, King's Island Amusement Park

Oasis Spa

Oasis Spa is a fairly new spa at the French Lick Springs Golf and Tennis Resort. It's a good place to go as a couple; although men are not included in the spa program, they can enjoy golf, tennis and jogging on the resort grounds. The program includes low-calorie meals, mineral baths, an exercise program and a wide range of beauty treatments.

FACT SUMMARY

MAILING ADDRESS: Oasis Spa, French Lick Springs Golf and Tennis Resort, French Lick, IN 47432

TELEPHONE: (812) 935-9381; toll-free (800) 457-4042

TRAVEL DIRECTIONS: From Indianapolis on Highway 37, 100 miles south, then southeast on 56

ACCOMMODATIONS: Resort hotel rooms and suites

FEE: 5 days—single, $875; double, $763 per person

MAXIMUM NUMBER OF GUESTS: 12

MAXIMUM NUMBER OF STAFF: 14

SEASON: Year-round

AMBIANCE: Large resort in lush surroundings

GENDER AND AGE RESTRICTIONS: Women only

DIET: Low-calorie, high nutrition meals

FACILITIES: Mineral baths, pool, hiking trails, exercise rooms, golf, tennis courts

PROGRAM: Aerobics, dance, yoga and pool exercise; lectures on stress and wardrobe coordination

SPECIAL FEATURES: Cellulite treatment, aromatherapy (see Glossary), personalized makeup classes

LOCAL ATTRACTIONS: None

Solar Spring Health Retreat

Solar Spring Health Retreat focuses on weight control through diet and exercise. Techniques leading to permanent weight loss are also taught. It is located on seventeen acres of private woods and is for adults only. Smoking is not permitted.

FACT SUMMARY

MAILING ADDRESS: 58897 C. R. 115, Goshen, IN 46526

TELEPHONE: (219) 875-8151

TRAVEL DIRECTIONS: Approximately 6 miles southeast from Elkhart, Indiana; map available from spa

TRANSPORTATION: Bus and line service available from O'Hare International airport to Elkhart, with pick-up by resort in Elkhart

ACCOMMODATIONS: Single and double rooms or dormitory

FEE: Per person rates are approximately $15 to $40 per day depending upon occupancy; meals included

MAXIMUM NUMBER OF GUESTS: 11

MAXIMUM NUMBER OF STAFF: 6

SEASON: Open by reservation only—available year-round

AMBIANCE: Casual; rural wooded area

GENDER AND AGE RESTRICTIONS: Adults over 16; coed

DIET: Wholesome meals include fruits, vegetables, grains, legumes, seeds or nuts and dairy foods

FACILITIES: Library, indoor pool, jogging trail through woods, trampolines, sauna; golf facilities nearby

PROGRAM: Geared for weight control, consists of diet, learning habit control and individually planned exercise programs

SPECIAL FEATURES: Food preparation classes for fast, low-calorie gourmet meals

LOCAL ATTRACTIONS: Antiques auctions, theater

Wooden Door

The Wooden Door, with two locations—Lake Geneva, Wisconsin, and Woodstock, Illinois—offers women's fitness, beauty and diet programs that include exercise, yoga and dance. Classes on self-defense, self-awareness and beauty are also provided. A six-day weight-loss program is based on a 900-calorie low-salt diet.

FACT SUMMARY

MAILING ADDRESS: P.O. Box 830, Barrington, IL 60010

TELEPHONE: (312) 382-2888

TRAVEL DIRECTIONS: 2 locations: Lake Geneva, Wisconsin—90 miles north of Chicago; and Woodstock, Illinois—50 miles northwest of O'Hare airport; by car or bus from Chicago

ACCOMMODATIONS: Lake Geneva—fully modern cabins house 3 to 6 women comfortably (bring own linens); Woodstock—comfortable, air-conditioned, semi-private rooms with bath

FEE: Lake Geneva—1 week (Sunday to Saturday), $375 per person, does not include massages, facials, pedicures and manicures; Woodstock—1 week (Sunday to Friday), $560 per person

MAXIMUM NUMBER OF GUESTS: Lake Geneva—95; Woodstock—40

MAXIMUM NUMBER OF STAFF: 10 program staff people plus cooks, maids and waterfront staff; no maid service at Lake Geneva

SEASON: 14 weekends from March to October; write for specific dates

AMBIANCE: Woods and lakes; peace and quiet—a true getaway!

GENDER AND AGE RESTRICTIONS: Women only over 18

DIET: A daily diet of 800 to 900 low-salt, low-fat calories with well-balanced meals of fresh fruit and vegetables with chicken and fish often

FACILITIES: Lake Geneva—located on 54 acres of lakefront property, cabins, main lodge, gym, tennis courts, beach, sailing, water skiing; Woodstock—88 acres, pool, tennis courts, lodge, gym

PROGRAM: Hiking, yoga, running, slow-and-fast-paced exercise classes, beginning ballet, modern dance and beauty clinics; self-defense, self-awareness workshops offered each day; classes optional

SPECIAL FEATURES: Evening programs offer a variety of unique lectures for "women in today's society"

LOCAL ATTRACTIONS: 4-mile hike into city of Lake Geneva from Wooden Door, with shops for browsing, sailing, water skiing, fishing; Woodstock location is a short distance from a completely restored Victorian village with shops

THE
SOUTHEAST

Featured Spas

Turnberry Isle

If you are fluent in several languages, own a yacht large enough to park cars on and can step in and out of a helicopter with studied nonchalance, you probably already know about Turnberry Isle. If this description doesn't fit your lifestyle, think of the glittering excess of a James Bond movie and you'll get the picture.

Turnberry Isle is a resort for the very rich—a country club-yacht club-luxury condominium complex that also happens to have a completely equipped spa, just in case anyone got a trifle too enthusiastic over the fettuccine on the last trip to Rome.

The resort is located on an island in the Intercoastal Waterway opposite Miami. It is the pied-à-terre for the South American and European jet set and the wealthiest and best-known Americans in business, sports and entertainment. Princess Caroline of Monaco, Cheryl Tiegs, Lloyd Bridges, Vitas Gerulaitis and Oleg Cassini are all likely to turn up, looking tan and relaxed. One of the reasons they feel so relaxed is the remarkable security setup at Turnberry, which rivals that of the executive wing of the CIA. Everyone on the grounds must carry an identification card, and getting onto the grounds in the first place is not easy. The uniformed thirty-man security force is highly visible throughout all public areas. The very rich, for whom kidnapping and jewel thievery is a daily worry, don't have to worry while at Turnberry Isle.

ACCOMMODATIONS

Spa guests stay in the Marina Hotel, where rooms are mammoth (the smallest is 14,000 square feet) and beautifully decorated. Each room has a circular terrace that overlooks a marina packed with majestic yachts. There are two double beds and a sunken tub large enough for two in each bath. Some

141

rooms are complete with a full-sized dining table and bar. Furnishings are top quality and there is a slightly tropical feeling to the decor. Extra touches include a sophisticated stereo system, a whirlpool and a bidet; some rooms even have redwood hot tubs.

FACILITIES

The Turnberry complex includes a country club with its own hotel, a tennis club, a marina with adjacent hotel, two golf courses and the spa. The spa was built simply as another diversion for guests of the resort, but this does not mean that the management doesn't take the spa seriously.

Located in a separate building near the yacht club, it offers racquetball courts, indoor and outdoor pools, exercise rooms with Nautilus equipment and separate sauna and shower areas for men and women. There are indoor and outdoor massage areas, hot and cold plunges and locker rooms complete with shampoos, hair dryers and setters and every personal care convenience.

Winding through the complex is the Fit Trail (similar to a parcourse), which has exercise stations along its route.

PROGRAM

The Turnberry program begins with a visit to the spa doctor for a thorough physical. Complete blood and urine testing is done, and the results are very carefully analyzed as the basis for a guest's personal diet and exercise plan. Each guest also has a session with the spa director who asks about goals during your stay and then helps to plan your activities around them; a program for a person who simply wants to relax and de-stress will be quite different from one planned for a guest who wants serious body reshaping. However, general services offered to everyone in the four-day spa plan include two facials, two herbal wraps, four massages, a loofah bath and twelve group fitness lessons. It also includes three nights' hotel accommodations. Most people who turn up in the exercise classes are either hotel guests or residents who own one of the condominiums. Very few are at Turnberry strictly for the spa plan.

As most of the guests subscribe to la dolce vita, they seldom get up before noon, so the morning stretch and fitness classes are never crowded. The afternoon classes in fitness and yoga are more popular.

Each guest receives a personal schedule that may include private classes, if he or she chooses, at a substantial additional charge. There is also an extra charge for some of the group classes and all of the personal services such as massages, but this hardly fazes the typical Turnberry guest.

Racquetball instruction is available as well as instructor guidance on using the Fit Trail. This program is one of the most personalized available anywhere; an exercise instructor will even make a special exercise tape just for you to fit your particular needs. If you are shy (or just very rich) you can take every class as a private lesson and never see another spa-goer.

FOOD AND DIET

If Turnberry has a secret, it is Dr. Robert Haas, director of nutrition. Young and articulate, he has developed a very unusual diet plan for increased energy and weight loss based on grains, potatoes, pasta, vegetables, fish and chicken. The plan is low in fats and cholesterol, and no sugar, salt or additives are used. It was devised to prevent or alleviate circulatory and cardiovascular problems, high blood pressure, hypoglycemia, obesity and some forms of arthritis. The spa diet is based on 750 calories a day, and includes dishes you normally don't think of as diet fare. Breakfast is shredded wheat with bananas or buckwheat pancakes. Sample lunches are the Tuna Haas sandwich on pita bread or "eggless" egg salad. Another lunch option is a baked potato (big on the Haas plan) and a garden salad with diet dressing. Dinner might be barbecued chicken, corn on the cob, refried beans, a baked potato and fresh fruit.

Dr. Haas is available for consultation with each guest. His cuisine is so popular in Miami that several of the city's poshest restaurants offer Haas-designed dishes for their nutrition- and weight-conscious clientele.

HEALTH AND BEAUTY SERVICES

The most remarkable experience in beauty services at Turnberry is having a loofah salt rub treatment in the private third-level loofah room. One whole end of the room is glass, and lying on the table one can watch the clouds float by (or better yet, a storm gather) as your skin is gently massaged with avocado oil, salt and a loofah mitten. Cares seem to float away along with dry-skin cells.

Excellent facials, massages and herbal wraps are also available. The staff here is exceptionally well trained and can explain a treatment and its uses unusually well. This is the first place that we learned that an herbal wrap produces an artificial fever that raises the body temperature and metabolism rate, thereby cleansing the system.

The beauty shop is similar to many large metropolitan beauty salons, but with a more international touch. They understand the European styles requested by many of the customers, and technicians speak several languages.

OTHER PLEASURES

People who come to Turnberry know all about pleasure.

Enormous yachts glistening with brass and teakwood sit quietly at dock in the marina. If you have lent yours to a friend and are temporarily without, you can rent the Turnberry yacht, named *Monkey Business*, for the day or several weeks.

Since Miami is nearby, there is practically no activity a determined guest can't find. Theater, horse racing, dog racing, sport fishing, are all available and the concierge will be glad to help with arrangements and tickets.

The resort also offers sophisticated entertainment in its lounges.

WHAT TO BRING

A humble pair of tennis shoes is all guests need bring to take part in the Turnberry spa program; everything else is provided: robe, shorts, T-shirt, shower shoes and a white sweat top and pants are waiting when you arrive.

In the locker area, combs, brushes, soaps, shampoos, razors, hair dryers and curling irons are all provided; even suntan lotion is available.

Sophisticated sportswear is worn when guests are outside the spa itself, and dressy clothes are usual at dinner.

HOW TO GET THERE

Most guests fly into Miami and are picked up by a spa car. If you are driving, take Route 95 to 199th Street and follow the signs; you can also reach it by coming north on Route 1 or Route A1A.

If you do decide to drive, make sure the reservations staff know this so that they can arrange for your entrance at the guard gate. With their tight security system, no one "drops in" at Turnberry Isle.

Of course, you can always sail your boat to Turnberry; just make arrangements in advance with the dockmaster for a berth in the Turnberry marina.

SUMMARY

This is a resort for the person who has everything and wants to maintain it well. There is a ship store offering marine supplies needed for your yacht, a gift shop that stocks smoked oysters and caviar and a spa facility with the very latest equipment. The staff is superb and the Adonis-like spa director, Steve Martini, is on a first-name basis with all spa guests. This is no place for the unsophisticated small-town woman who wants to shed a few pounds, but it is a perfect place to retreat after finishing a multimillion dollar land deal or after completing your last film or blockbuster book. The golf, tennis and sailing are great. And you don't really have to get up until noon. Nobody else does!

FACT SUMMARY

NAME: Turnberry Isle

MAILING ADDRESS: P. O. Box 630578, Miami, FL 33163

TELEPHONE: (305) 932-6200; toll-free (800) 327-7028

TRANSPORTATION: Spa car from Miami Airport

ACCOMMODATIONS: Yacht & Racquet Club Hotel; Marina Hotel; Country Club Hotel—118 total deluxe accommodations

FEE: Spa plan holiday (7 days, 6 nights)—single, $1,162 to $1,500, depending on season; double, $833 to $1,000 per person, depending on season

MAXIMUM NUMBER OF GUESTS: 200

MAXIMUM NUMBER OF STAFF: 45

SEASON: Year-round

AMBIANCE: Exclusive international and residential setting

GENDER AND AGE RESTRICTIONS: Adults over 16

DIET: The Haas Diet is a scientifically proven lifetime nutrition program with a well-documented record of success. Unlike other low-fat, low-cholesterol diets, the Haas Diet does not punish a dieter's taste buds.

FACILITIES: Turnberry Health Spa, 24 tennis courts, 4 racquetball courts, 2 18-hole Robert Trent Jones golf courses, marina, jogging fitness trail, shops

PROGRAM: Varies according to a person's physical wants, needs and restrictions

SPECIAL FEATURES: Disco, nightly entertainment in lounge, dining room—gourmet food, charter boats, tournaments held here: PGA International Gold Cup (Great Britain vs. U.S.); Elizabeth Arden LPGA; International Backgammon Tournament; Bacardi Trophy Race

LOCAL ATTRACTIONS: Gulfstream Racetrack, Hollywood Dog Track; Dania Jai-alai, Bal Harbour Shops, Neiman-Marcus, Saks Fifth Avenue, Bonwit Teller, five minutes to the beaches

The Saga Club

Pass in, pass in
The angels say
Into the upper doors
Nor count compartments
 of the floors
But mount to paradise
By the stairway of surprise
　　　　—*Ralph Waldo Emerson, "Merlin II"*

Chances are that Emerson did not have a spa in mind when he wrote these lines, but they fit the Saga Club well enough to make one wonder. In the middle of historic Georgetown, surrounded by dignified red brick Federal residences, cobblestone streets and restored buildings housing chic shops, you come across a door so unassuming you might miss it. A small plain sign, SAGA CLUB, gives no clue as to what surprise lies behind it.

Open the door and you will find yourself in another world. The Saga Club was created on two levels of a renovated flour mill, and while the red brick outer walls have been retained, the angular interior spaces have been opened up to light with skylights, giving the place a clean contemporary feeling. The effect is a blending of the brick-and-wood building materials of the original structure with a dash of urban savvy. This is the spa of the future.

Located in the busy heart of a sophisticated city, the Saga Club was created to serve busy people who likely wouldn't be able to take a full week or more to visit a more isolated spa. The major part of the Saga Club's business is in annual memberships of men and women who live in the area and use the facilities several times a week. However, by arrangement with the posh Four Seasons Hotel nearby, it also offers one- or two-week residential programs.

The Saga name comes from the word *Sagateller*. In the days of the Vikings, the sagateller was the person in the village who entertained young and old with his epic tales of the adventures and accomplishments of important Norse families. The staff here believe that we can all create our own fitness sagas—that we each have the potential to shape our own health history. The name reflects the Scandinavian feel of the place, which is evident in the interior design, and which is epitomized by the spa's attractive Norwegian founder and director, Lisa Dobloug.

Miss Dobloug, who has spent sixteen years as a director at such spas as the Golden Door, Palm-Aire, the Greenhouse and Bonaventure Inter-Continental Hotel and Spa, is certainly one of the foremost spa professionals in the country. Her concept in starting the Saga Club was to provide a total health and fitness facility with a very personalized program that would help each member and guest realize his or her fitness potential through conditioning and strengthening exercises, diet programs and treatments devoted to reducing daily tensions.

ACCOMMODATIONS

Accommodations for the Saga Club participants from out of town are available at the Four Seasons Hotel just a few blocks from the club on M Street. It is a grand and elegant hotel in the European tradition, complete with Oriental rugs, antiques and a French concierge.

Rooms range from moderate to deluxe to presidential suites

and are all beautifully decorated in understated colors and fine furniture.

The location is great, not far from the Kennedy Center, and close to the shops of Georgetown.

The service is superb; the staff is multilingual; there is twenty-four hour room service, and they even accommodate pets. As you might imagine, this hotel is a busy place, especially during fall and winter when the political and social life of Washington goes into high gear, so a two- or three-week advance reservation for spa guests is a must.

FACILITIES

Although the Saga Club has only 9,000 square feet, the space has been designed to make good use of every foot, and full spa services are available.

On the first floor, alongside the lobby is an airy glass-walled women's exercise room, the floor of which is covered with a specially woven carpet that makes exercise mats unnecessary. Women's lockers and treatment rooms for facials and massages are also on this floor, as well as a well-equipped Universal weight room, which is open to both men and women.

A beautifully furnished guest lounge overlooks the pool—and what a pool it is! Long and deep, it is a jeweled centerpiece in an enormous vaulted room with a high-arched glass skylight. Potted palms and hanging plants in straw baskets complete the scene. Comfortable cushioned chairs are placed around the pool, making it a good place to relax after pool class. You can sit (or float on your back in the pool for that matter) and watch the changing weather over the city's famous skyline. Imagine the view when it snows!

Near the pool are steps leading to the brick patio and sun deck overlooking the Potomac, with the Washington Memorial and the Kennedy Center in the background.

A refreshment bar is located to one side of the guest lounge. There is a spacious dressing room complete with Lancôme cosmetics and an attendant who will provide towels, exercise togs and anything else you may have forgotten.

PROGRAM

Your Saga day begins after breakfast in the Four Seasons dining room and a cab ride to the club. There you will have an interview with a staff member and take a fitness test so that they can design the right program for you.

A sample program begins with a fifty-five-minute exercise class. Class offerings are divided into A classes (beginners), B (for regular exercisers) and C (the very fit). Most guests start at level A and progress to B after several days. The selection ranges from water fitness to body awareness to aerobics to fencing. For men there is more emphasis on the use of the Universal machines and on cardiovascular workouts.

Lisa Dobloug teaches several classes a day and they are superb. She doesn't like the word "exercise" to describe what she does; she prefers "movement," as it connotes more enjoyment. Lisa is able to teach an exercise class and evaluate how your body functions, then make suggestions on exercise to improve your weak areas and contribute to total body strength.

A facial might follow, then on to another exercise class. Lunch is served around the pool or at the hotel.

After lunch, you choose among exercise classes, such as yoga or aerobic dance, body conditioning or perhaps a repeat of the water fitness class, a real favorite. A pleasant way to wind up a day is with a makeup application class or a special body treatment.

Guests are impressed with the dedication of the staff. Most of the fitness staff have master's degrees in physical education or physical therapy and many have extensive dance backgrounds. The tone is set by Lisa, who is calm, soft-spoken, organized and warm. Everyone seems especially pleased with the individualization of the program and the personal interest shown by every staff member.

FOOD AND DIET

There is not really a diet program available to guests who go through the Saga program, and you will have to discipline yourself. Most of the meals will be served at the Four Seasons Hotel, which serves breakfast, lunch and dinner in its classy Beaux Champs restaurant. In the future, it is expected that a special spa menu will be available. Meals are not included in the spa fee.

The breakfast menu offers a wide selection of eggs, fruit and teas. The health club breakfast on the menu lists grapefruit or yogurt, two eggs (hard-boiled or poached), whole-wheat bread or rye crackers and coffee, tea or milk. Possible lunch choices are salads, omelettes, broiled rockfish, or fillet of chicken in champagne-vinegar sauce. Dinner is dangerous for the calorie counter, but breast of chicken in pink grapefruit and lime sauce, or fillet of red snapper with chive sauce are both possible selections.

Throughout the day at the spa itself, fruit and vegetable juices are available at the refreshment bar.

HEALTH AND BEAUTY SERVICES

The body massage here is very professional—the fifty-minute deep-muscle massage is available from male and female technicians.

Facials are given with Lancôme cosmetics by European-trained aestheticians and are available for men and women, although there are three skin care treatments for women only. The Saga Glow is a treatment in which a special cream is applied to your entire body, then rubbed off, taking with it excess body hair and smoothing the skin in the process. The Saga Contour is aimed at stimulating circulation and smoothing bumpy cellulite areas from thighs, hips and buttocks. The Saga Loofah Scrub is a brush rub with a natural sponge and creamy soap. It is designed to remove dead skin cells and soften the skin.

OTHER PLEASURES

Because it is so close, don't miss the Kennedy Center for the Performing Arts. Depending on your taste in art and artifacts you could spend months wandering through the Smithsonian, the National Gallery or the Hirshhorn Museum. Of course, another more simple pleasure is walking the quiet tree-lined streets of Georgetown, or following the Potomac canal as it winds through the residential area.

Georgetown is crowded with shops that sell clothing, jewelry, antiques, ice cream and plants. There are even food markets, but hardly of the type you know back home. One such market is staffed only by young good-looking Frenchmen who have a nicely flirtatious approach and insist on calling you "madam."

Thirty minutes out of town is the Wolf Trap Farm Park for the Performing Arts. This open-air concert facility presents summer concerts from jazz to symphonic music.

WHAT TO BRING

Since the Saga Club is in the center of a sophisticated city, you will want to bring clothes appropriate to the urban environment. Suits for sight-seeing and dresses for dinner at the hotel will be useful. Sports jackets or suits are good for men.

As for the spa itself, towels, shorts, T-shirts, bathing suits, slippers and robes are provided. You might want to bring leotards and your own sandals; you might also prefer your own bathing suit.

HOW TO GET THERE

Most guests will probably arrive at National airport and take a cab from there. If you want to avoid traffic, not always an easy task in Washington, stay on the south side of the Potomac and cross the Francis Key bridge. Then, turn right on M, right again on 33rd Street/Duck Lane, crossing over the old Chesapeake and Ohio Canal, then left on Water Street, left again on Potomac, and the Saga will be on your left.

If you wish to sight-see a bit, take the 14th Street Bridge and then turn left on Pennsylvania Avenue (the White House will appear on your left), go left when you reach M Street and follow it to 33rd Street/Duck Lane where you again turn left.

From Bethesda and the north, come down Wisconsin and then turn right on M and follow the route described above.

SUMMARY

The Saga Club is a sophisticated spa in an urban setting that caters to both residents and visitors. It is a great resource if you will be in Washington on business and need a place to work out or simply to rest and recharge, whether for one day or several days.

The staff is top-notch, and the guiding presence of Lisa Dobloug ensures that each guest gets personal attention.

It's likely that more of these plush urban spas will be opening in the future. Meanwhile Saga is definitely first with its total care approach to the busy city-dweller.

FACT SUMMARY

NAME: The Saga Club

MAILING ADDRESS: 1000 Potomac Street N.W., Washington, D.C. 20007

TELEPHONE: (202) 298-8455

ACCOMMODATIONS: At the Four Seasons Hotel

FEE: $95 per day (includes lunch). Hotel additional; from $150–$180 per day including breakfast and dinner

MAXIMUM NUMBER OF GUESTS: 35

MAXIMUM NUMBER OF STAFF: 16

SEASON: Year-round

AMBIANCE: Spare, bright, modern interior

GENDER AND AGE RESTRICTIONS: Children permitted with adult

DIET: No special diet; director recommends items from the menu at Four Seasons

FACILITIES: Pool, exercise rooms, sauna, steam, massage rooms, lounges, snack bar

PROGRAM: Rigorous exercise; dance, yoga, weight training, pool exercise

SPECIAL FEATURES: Fencing

LOCAL ATTRACTIONS: Museums, Georgetown streets and shops, historic monuments, Kennedy Center for Performing Arts, Wolf Trap Park

The Greenbrier

Who among us has not, once in her life, yearned to stay somewhere with an imposing white façade, stately pillars and a "North Portico." If it can't be the White House, the Greenbrier will do nicely. This Georgian-style hotel, tucked into the middle of hilly West Virginia, is a national historic landmark. A winding lane from the main gate to the north entrance is shaded by 350-year-old oaks that grace an endless expanse of velvet lawn.

The Greenbrier has the quiet elegance, luxury and mannerly service of bygone eras. Good manners are a way of life here: required from the staff and generally extracted from the guests who come here to play golf, relax and enjoy these 6,500 acres of West Virginia.

This is a family resort and there is something, indeed a lot of everything, for everyone to enjoy at the "Old White," which can easily accommodate the golf-playing husband, the wife who needs quiet pampering and the teen-age tennis addict.

ACCOMMODATIONS

Guest quarters at the Greenbrier vary widely in size, ambiance and cost. The rooms and suites in the hotel are individually decorated in the bold red, blues, greens and yellows of the lobbies and public rooms. Each room has a personality of its own; for a genuine down-South experience, ask for a room with a canopied bed. You'll find spacious bathrooms with ample lighting, ceramic tiles and mirrors, and marvelous walk-in closets are equipped with shelving and shoe racks. Guest houses are located within a short walk of the main hotel; they provide large families and small groups with the privacy of a homelike atmosphere. Most have wicker-filled porches and parlors, and some boast fireplaces and secluded patios. Some of the large cottages include a small dining room and adjoining kitchen.

Paradise Row is the most recent renovation project at Greenbrier. Each of the white wood guest houses in Paradise Row features a spacious bedroom with a king-sized bed, a tiny parlor with brick fireplace and an adjoining wet bar and an expansive porch that affords a view of the vast Greenbrier estate.

Color television with a music channel, fresh linen twice daily and evening turndown are provided whether you're staying in the hotel or in one of the guest houses.

FACILITIES

At a luxury resort you expect perfection, and at the Greenbrier you get it. The public rooms, elegantly decorated in the Dorothy Draper style, are replete with genuine antiques and nineteenth-century paintings, elaborate chandeliers and the famed rhododendron wallpaper.

Indoor sports and fitness facilities include billiard and pool tables, indoor tennis courts, table tennis, an exercise room and a game room.

Also on this level is the spa. The mammoth Roman mosaic-tile indoor pool is surrounded by a fantasy of green and white wicker; beautiful, decorative tile; green plants and giant arched windows. The spa features the famous White Sulphur Springs baths, pools, bathhouses, hydro-tubs, massage and resting rooms. Here one "takes the waters."

On the lower level a shopping arcade is filled with a terrific collection of shops selling books, flowers, jewelry, shoes, newspapers and magazines, gifts, toys and games and clothing: just about anything the acquisitive traveler might want. Authentic Appalachian crafts—attractive quilts, children's clothing, toys, Christmas decorations and other inventions of the mountain people—are sold at a small nearby cottage. Other cottages house a variety of contemporary artisans displaying and creating pottery, metalwork, weaving and paintings.

The grounds are meticulously maintained and there are many breathtaking gardens, flower beds and special plantings. In spring the rhododendron are in bloom everywhere, and throughout the year, except for winter, there is always something in flower at the Greenbrier.

The Greenbrier Clinic located in the spa area can provide a three-day medical evaluation including complete health analysis and consultation with an expert medical staff. Guests can combine a golfing vacation with a thorough physical, an option which many business executives prefer.

Outdoor sports and exercise facilities include: three championship golf courses (one designed by Jack Nicklaus), 200 miles of riding trails, a sea of tennis courts, platform tennis courts, measured (1- to 5-mile) jogging or walking trails, trap and skeet fields, croquet, cross-country skiing and ice skating (in season). If you just want to watch others exercise, take a ride around the grounds in an old-fashioned carriage.

The golf courses are so beautiful that some guests walk them just to enjoy the mountain scenery. The golf club, open from early spring to late fall, has a lively relaxation area where one can enjoy drinks before an informal dinner at the club. The pro shop is excellent.

At the tennis courts there is videotape replay equipment to help you see your faults and expert coaches to help you improve your game. Ball machines are available for individual practice, but one can usually find a game with a comparably skilled player.

If fishing is your sport, good rental equipment is available and the creek is stocked with rainbow trout and large-mouth bass. A chef will prepare your catch, if you wish.

The large outdoor swimming pool is surrounded by an attractive brick terrace and a stand of pine trees. A maze of seasonal flowers provides the color accents that are so popular throughout the Greenbrier. Here, as at other sports facilities, snacks are available.

PROGRAM

The Greenbrier does not have a formal physical fitness program, but any guest with self-discipline and the inclination can devise one of the most complete schedules of athletic and fitness activities imaginable.

This is a distinctive resort that treats its guests as adults and expects them to decide what activities will please them most. Then the ever-attentive and polite staff will heed your whim and make it easy to indulge.

FOOD AND DIET

The Greenbrier is not without hazards, for it is patterned after the European concept of "taking the waters" while enjoying sumptuous meals and first-rate service. So, pack your strong moral fiber and good intentions if you plan to lose weight on this trip.

The breakfast menu offers sixty choices, the dinners have six courses and the staff of thirty-five chefs has won many national and international awards for its cuisine. If you look carefully, the menus offer some fine choices for the calorie-conscious. Although there is no one to watch over you, you may choose the Health Living Breakfast, which offers fresh fruit, plain yogurt and tasty pumpkin muffins; or if you want to be even more serious, try a single poached egg and dry wheat toast and a glass of skim milk.

One need not go to the dining room for delicious food, for the golf club luncheon buffet offers more than ninety items to choose from, including attractively arranged fruit and vegetable salads, thinly sliced meats and fresh seafood. If you want to indulge yourself, and that's a popular pastime at the Greenbrier, then remember to leave room for the delights of the incredible dessert table.

Happy hour cocktails and complimentary hors d'oeuvres are available in the Old White Club in the Virginia wing of the hotel, or you may have cocktails on the golf club's glassed-in porches, or on the open-air deck overlooking the tennis courts.

Dinner in the dazzling crystal-chandeliered dining room, with a string ensemble playing background music, is an elegant experience. The menu changes daily and dieters will never be bored. Dinner is also served in the Tavern Room, which features a fine continental menu.

Alternate food service is available at the coffee shop (10:00 A.M. to 6:00 P.M.) and from room service (7:00 A.M. to midnight).

HEALTH AND BEAUTY SERVICES

The healing properties of the mineral springs have been heralded since 1778, when White Sulphur Springs attracted its first visitors, and the resort makes good use of the slightly odorous waters in a variety of baths. The spa area offers cleanliness and private treatment rooms.

Giant porcelain tubs are used for the mineral water soak. Your head is cradled on a cushioned support and you lie submerged to the neck and covered with a giant towel to retard the heat loss. After ten to fifteen minutes, an attendant helps you extract your limp self from the bath. After the bath you are wrapped in a large white sheet and can choose to spend time in the sauna or steam room for cleansing and relaxing, followed by a Scotch spray. The spray directs fine jets of water over your entire body while the attendant applies higher pressure jets on specific muscle areas. A short stop in the mineral water whirlpool and you are again wrapped in a sheet and guided to your own private massage room. The Swedish massage is expertly administered by one of the twenty-five masseuses. After the massage you return to your own dressing room, which is equipped with a day bed for the nap that by now seems mandatory. It also has a table of toiletries so that you can prepare yourself for the return to the hotel.

All spa services are à la carte, and if you prefer one masseuse over another, it's best to book your favorite twenty-four hours in advance. If you prefer a heavy or deep massage, tell the booking receptionist and she will select the correct technician.

The beauty department of the Greenbrier is surprisingly out of date. The drab fixtures and outdated equipment remind one of the small-town beauty salon of the 1950s.

Full hair services, manicures and pedicures are available. A facial using mineral oil–based cosmetics is neither a surprise nor a highlight. It's odd that a resort with otherwise impeccable accommodations and services should neglect the beauty services area.

OTHER PLEASURES

The Greenbrier packs scrumptious box lunches that will brighten your trip home. The deluxe box has three sandwiches, fried chicken, a fresh fruit salad, German potato salad, relishes, hard-boiled egg and pastry *and* cheese and crackers. Other take-home treats are homemade candies and baked goods, including petit fours, tarts, brownies and a wide variety of breads and sweet rolls. They won't help your diet, but they're great for rabid self-indulgence.

The Greenbrier *is* a family place and a children's activities program is conducted June through Labor Day by college-trained counselors. Arts, crafts, supervised swimming, class instruction in various sports and movies are available.

Thanksgiving, Christmas and Easter are celebrated with decorations, special programs and menus.

During the winter there are periodic five-day gourmet cooking classes offered at an extra charge.

A resident historian conducts humorous tours weekly to acquaint guests with the heritage and history of the resort and the surrounding countryside.

WHAT TO BRING

At the Greenbrier one dresses "properly" or feels out of place. You can hardly plead ignorance of the dress code because a guide to apparel is sent when you make reservations or request information. For dinner at the tavern or the dining room, men must wear coats and ties and women dressy dresses.

The Brooks Brothers look is "in," and one sees lots of wrapped cotton shirts with little frogs or strawberries, cotton polo shirts, and cotton/canvas espadrilles. Preppie green and pink combinations are in, and Lilly Pulitzer dresses are very popular. Crisp khaki or cord slacks and madras or alligator sports shirts with pastel crew-neck sweaters complete the "proper" look for men. Shorts and tennis dresses are acceptable only in the golf and tennis areas, and, of course, bathing suits are worn only at poolside.

Remember, you're in the mountains, so pack a sweater as the early mornings and evenings are cool, even in the summer months. Layered clothing is recommended for warmth and flexibility. At the coffee shop or the dining room of the golf clubhouse, open-necked shirts are allowed. Decide in advance what activities you'll pursue and bring the appropriate footwear.

HOW TO GET THERE

The Greenbrier is located in White Sulphur Springs near Interstate 64; exit at the White Sulphur Springs exit, then take U.S. 80 one-half mile west to the Greenbrier entrance. The Greenbrier provides a handy map showing how to approach the resort from eighteen major cities.

Greenbrier has its own airport. Daily scheduled flights are available on Piedmont from LaGuardia airport in New York, and from Atlanta. Connecting flights are also available from other major cities, and the airport is just a fifteen-minute ride in the hotel limousine. Private and charter aircraft also use the airport.

Once, the best way to get to the Greenbrier was the Chesapeake and Ohio Railroad, on luxurious sleeper cars. Now there are two trains a day (one east, one west) from Chicago, via Cincinnati in the West, and from Washington, D.C., in the East.

SUMMARY

You have to be able to slow down and relax in order to enjoy the Greenbrier. It is an absolutely first-rate resort, staffed by 1,400 attentive, capable and ultimately polite people; rushing around and doing things for yourself is seen as unnecessary and even slightly rude.

The food is superb, the scenery breathtaking and the variety of activities and sports offered is staggering. It will take several stays to see and do everything the Greenbrier provides—from taking formal tea in the afternoon to a leisurely horseback ride through the piney mountain woods. Scarlett O'Hara would have loved it. So will you.

FACT SUMMARY

NAME: The Greenbrier

MAILING ADDRESS: White Sulphur Springs, WV, 24986

TELEPHONE: (304) 536-1110; toll-free (800) 624-6070

TRANSPORTATION: Hotel limo to and from airports

ACCOMMODATIONS: 700 rooms and suites; individual guest houses

FEE: Depending on accommodations, $80 to $300 per person, per day

MAXIMUM NUMBER OF GUESTS: 1,200

MAXIMUM NUMBER OF STAFF: 1,400

SEASON: Year-round

AMBIANCE: Antebellum South; elegant five-star resort in Allegheny Mountains

GENDER AND AGE RESTRICTIONS: None

DIET: Award-winning restaurants; no spa dining room

FACILITIES: 3 golf courses; indoor and outdoor swimming pool and tennis courts; spa treatments: mineral baths, sauna, whirlpool, Scotch hose, massage; skeet and trap shooting; fishing; cross-country skiing; ice skating; shopping arcade; game room; beauty salon

PROGRAM: No structured exercise program

SPECIAL FEATURES: Diagnostic medical clinic, arts and crafts colony, horse-drawn carriage rides, historic tours of resort, take-home box lunches, programs for children

LOCAL ATTRACTIONS: Mountain scenery

Bonaventure
Inter-Continental
Hotel and Spa

The newest spa in the country, the Bonaventure Inter-Continental Hotel and Spa, looks more like a page from *Interiors* magazine than a spa. Immaculate, uniformed staff move with single-minded efficiency about the sleek glass, tile and chrome rooms of the separate men's and women's spas. There are few plants and art pieces to disturb the clean sparse lines. There is no smoking, no idle chatter, no tipping and no nonsense.

This is serious business, from the twenty-page health questionnaire each guest is expected to complete before coming, to the rigorous individual exercise program planned by a computer based on each guest's needs.

Cozy it isn't. But it isn't cold either, thanks to Lisa Dobloug, the director, who with her warmth and energy makes the place hum with efficient and purposeful activity. "The spa will be the vacation for the eighties, and not just for women," says Lisa. Urban male executives are turning up at the Bonaventure in increasing numbers to trim down and de-stress, and for most it is a new experience. The biggest crisis most men encounter at Bonaventure is whether to go along with the regularly scheduled pedicure (if real men don't eat quiche, do they dare get their toenails done?). Evidently the answer is yes, since those who do gruffly admit it feels great.

ACCOMMODATIONS

This is a resort hotel and a spa, and the rooms are what you might expect of an Inter-Continental hotel, commercial but very pleasant.

The rooms are located in nine four-story guest buildings clustered about the main building. About half of them look out over the golf course and lake.

The doubles with queen-sized beds are the smallest of the spa rooms, but they have large baths and dressing rooms, a roomy shower, twin sinks, a bidet, lots of light and strategically placed mirrors. The color scheme is tan and cream, pleasant enough, and to compensate for the small casement windows they give you a giant TV with twenty-five cable channels.

The king-sized rooms feature an overstuffed couch, twin chairs, a glass-topped coffee table and a king-sized bed. Some of these rooms also have a wet bar and all have a terrace where you can take in the view. The best strategy is to ask for a king-sized room on arrival. They're priced the same as the others, but they're a much better accommodation.

The two-bedroom suites have a parlor, a bedroom with a king-sized bed and another bedroom with twin accommodations, two baths, a wet bar and a terrace.

FACILITIES

The facilities are decorated in a spare but elegant style. The main lobby of the spa building has a gleaming black marble floor, walls covered in gray quilted velour and overstuffed velour couches in a 1940s style. The lobby is one of the few areas of the spa that has plants and paintings, which soften the effect of the chrome-and-glass tables and chairs.

There are entrances to both the men's and women's spas off the lobby. Here also is a boutique that stocks expensive resort and casual wear, including the gray velour warm-ups that are used by the spa guests. The men's and women's spas have the same layout—only the color scheme is different: cranberry for the men and gray and cranberry for the women. The men's section has a barbershop and facial section.

Within the spa proper you receive your personal daily program. An attendant provides you with spa gear (velour warm-ups, cranberry leotards, T-shirts, shorts, tank suit, bath shoes and mauve terry robe and towels), and assigns you a locker. You don't have to carry anything with you, since hair dryers, brushes, creams and so on are provided, and a copy of your schedule is posted on your locker so that you don't need to search aimlessly to find out where you are to go next.

The large guest lounge in each spa has one wall entirely of glass, which overlooks the pool. Just outside is a 105-to-110-degree whirlpool under an ornate gazebo. Nearby is the outdoor four-foot-deep exercise pool in a walled, landscaped setting. Around the pool are comfortable lounges for sunbathing and a special secluded spot behind some discreet plantings for nude sunbathing.

The sunny wet area is really the heart of the Bonaventure spa. In the center, under a huge skylight, are the cold and hot plunge pools. Surrounding this area are eight elevated balcony whirlpools, which guests must step up to enter so that they can sit or recline in a whirlpool and have privacy but still hear and see what is going on in the central area. Also in the wet area are a sauna and steam rooms, and a four-table herbal wrap area.

Down the hall are two large skylighted exercise rooms, each fully carpeted. The one nearest the men's spa has Paramount weight equipment and a computerized rowing machine.

Separate massage and facial areas are located in the quiet parts of the spas. The tile in this area was selected from hundreds of samples—for its perfect ability to ensure quiet. No clanking carts or noisy footsteps will spoil your post-massage snooze at the Bonaventure.

PROGRAM

There are three plans to choose from at the Bonaventure. There is a four-day and a seven-day spa plan, which include all meals; a fitness and nutrition program; Swiss showers; massage; body and skin care treatments; manicure, makeup and hair set for women; blow dry and comb for men; plus use of the sauna, pools and exercise rooms.

The seven-day deluxe fitness plan is for the serious spa-goer who aims for maximum results in the time allowed. It runs from Sunday to Sunday and includes a medical screening complete with lab work, a hair analysis and treatment, and for women, depilatory services. After test results are in, a computerized personalized schedule is devised for each guest, based on his or her strengths and needs.

There are three class levels. The first is a light stretch or yoga workout class or a vigorous walk, which is recommended for most guests on either plan during the first few days and is mixed with other classes as endurance increases. Intermediate level classes focus on body awareness with a heavy emphasis on abdominal work, aerobics and water classes. The highest level class is a high-intensity program, and guests are required to be on the intermediate level for several days before they advance to it.

The staff members here go to great lengths to accommodate guests' needs, which is particularly evident in their flexibility in scheduling. This is one of the few spas that will actually change your schedule if you request it. No questions asked.

A typical day might start with a walk-jog along the golf course, followed by breakfast. At midmorning, an hour-long exercise class is held. Then guests pad off to the whirlpool followed by a sauna, a Swiss shower and a massage or an herbal wrap.

After lunch, an aerobic activity or water class might be planned for you, followed by yoga or a late afternoon walk. If full days are too much for you, you can arrange for a half-day program, and spend the rest of your time golfing or lying in the sun.

In the evening, programs are given on nutrition and lifestyle, or you can take advantage of the hotel transportation into Miami for plays and concerts. There is also evening tennis, and the hotel lounge offers live music.

FOOD AND DIET

The dietary program at Bonaventure is based on an analysis of your current dietary habits and condition. The famous Dr. Gayelord Hauser's receipes are incorporated into the spa diet. Everything is fresh: no canned, frozen or preprepared foods are allowed.

The complete nutrition program provides a 900-calorie diet each day with an emphasis on variety. Breakfast could be a grapefruit half, a hot bran muffin with corn oil margarine, and acidophilus milk. Lunch might be vegetable broth and a fresh gulf shrimp salad plate; and dinner could be a bibb lettuce salad with lemon mustard dressing, breast of chicken with raspberry-vinegar sauce, sesame broccoli spears and apricot cream with whipped yogurt. You don't pile on calories at Bonaventure, but the food is very tasty.

Meals are taken in a separate spa dining room a few steps down from the main hotel dining area, or they can also be taken in your room if you're too tired to make yourself presentable.

HEALTH AND BEAUTY SERVICES

At Bonaventure the world is divided into two parts: the spa plan and the deluxe plan. The difference between the two is akin to the difference between tourist and first class. If you're on the Spa Plan you get a half-hour daily body massage, while the deluxe fitness plan guests get a one-hour massage. Shiatsu is offered on both plans at extra cost and lasts an hour and a half. Reflexology is also offered in both plans at special request and extra cost.

The skin care program uses German Numectron machines, but the beauty products are all French. This is a serious, comprehensive skin care program, and guests are given a recommendation regarding specific products and procedures most effective for their skin.

Several types of facials are available including the one-and-a-half-hour deep-cleansing facial and a massage of the face, neck, shoulders and upper chest. Every full-service beauty option imaginable is available, including waxing, permanents and makeup consultation. Herbal wraps are available daily, and you can choose from mint, hibiscus, eucalyptus, spearmint and camomile.

Men's manicures and pedicures, hair analysis and treatment are available. Hair analysis, coloring, permanents and conditioning care programs are thorough, professional and fastidious.

OTHER PLEASURES

There is excellent shopping at the Broward and Galleria malls and a wide selection of shows and museums nearby. Miami Beach is alive with nightlife, and on almost any evening you can find several of your favorite stars performing there.

The marine pleasures are really boundless. You can take an air boat through the Everglades, or you can go deep-sea fishing. College students discovered these magnificent beaches long ago. Scuba diving and snorkeling are popular as are riverboat tours and cruises along Millionaires' Row and Biscayne Bay, and visits to the Miami Seaquarium. Don't miss the Fairchild Tropical Gardens in Coral Gables.

Sports fans will find everything from winter season major league baseball, horse racing, harness racing, jai alai, football, or even polo at Boca Raton.

WHAT TO BRING

You don't need to bring many things to the Bonaventure, since the spa provides velour warm-ups, leotards, T-shirts, shorts, a tank suit, bath shoes and a terry robe. Add jogging or walking shoes, and shoes for racquetball or tennis. If you wish to ride horseback you should bring your riding clothes with you. For dinner wear, informal clothes will do: sports jackets and slacks for men and nice evening sportswear for women.

HOW TO GET THERE

You can fly into either the Miami or Fort Lauderdale airports and take the spa limousine from there. If you select the Deluxe Fitness Plan the limousine service is one of the many extras that are included.

If you are on the Spa Plan, the mini-bus shuttle will transport you.

If you drive, take Interstate 95 to State Highway 84 and head west, following the sign to the Bonaventure.

SUMMARY

The Bonaventure is a first-class place, catering to both men and women. Most guests are successful-looking people in their forties and fifties in fairly good physical shape. Busy men seem to like this spa; many come alone first, then return with their wives for a longer stay.

The staff is exceptionally well trained and meticulously groomed. Anyone determined to make a real change will be guided and encouraged here. The spa is delighted to have guests who are serious about fitness.

FACT SUMMARY

NAME: Bonaventure Inter-Continental Hotel and Spa

MAILING ADDRESS: 250 Racquet Club Road, Fort Lauderdale, FL 33326

TELEPHONE: (305) 474-3300; toll-free, Florida (800) 432-2673; out of state (800) 327-0200

TRANSPORTATION: Limo or shuttle bus from airport to spa

ACCOMMODATIONS: Rooms and suites

FEE: 4-day spa plan—single, $640; double, $520 per person;

7-day spa plan—single, $1,120; double, $910 per person; deluxe fitness plan—single, $2,188; double, $1,889 per person

MAXIMUM NUMBER OF GUESTS: Men's spa, 100; women's spa, 125

MAXIMUM NUMBER OF STAFF: 125

SEASON: Year-round

AMBIANCE: First class; uncluttered and elegant

GENDER AND AGE RESTRICTIONS: Adults over 16; coed

DIET: 900 calories, low fat, no red meat, fruits and vegetables, whole grains

FACILITIES: 3 pools, wet area, exercise rooms, Swiss showers, massage, sauna, beauty salon, Paramount weight equipment, spacious grounds

PROGRAM: Varied fitness classes including stretch, yoga, pool class, fencing, aerobics

SPECIAL FEATURES: Individualized fitness program emphasizing correct body movement

LOCAL ATTRACTIONS: Horse racing, the Everglades, the beach, jai alai, Millionaires' Row, Seaquarium

The Spa at Palm-Aire

This coed Valhalla for the sun-loving elite is a 1,500-acre combination country club, resort and spa in Pompano Beach, Florida. Three hotels provide visitors with the ultimate in creature comforts, and the spa offers an excellent diet and exercise program that will help you get back into shape without losing your sense of humor.

They know what they're doing here, they do it well and expect guests to faithfully embrace a 600-to-1,000-calorie diet and an exercise program based on an "exercise prescription" determined by a medical examination given shortly after you arrive.

It's all very grand. The pools are Olympic in dimension; there are five golf courses, endless rows of tennis courts and top-quality facilities for every sport and exercise endeavor.

The buildings are "resort-y" in design, but each is in a superbly landscaped setting that makes you forget the sheer size of the hotel, resort condominium and spa complex.

This is an ideal place for couples because of the variety of activities and programs. There is an executive health spa program for men, and a total spa program for women: the twin spa pavilions are adjacent but separate. If one partner is into golf, not conditioning, he or she can play one of the Palm-Aire courses or select from a host of others nearby. Or one can follow the fitness program at the spa while the other plays tennis, shops, goes sight-seeing or just lounges by the pool or ocean.

ACCOMMODATIONS

The rooms are large, bright and well appointed. There are a good variety of rooms, suites and master suites to choose from. Walls and modular furniture are white, and the Parsons table also houses the color TV on which a feature film is shown four times a day on a special channel. There are small terraces overlooking the golf courses, separate dressing rooms with spacious closet and makeup counters with well-lighted mirrors. The bathrooms are large and so are the counter spaces. Some accommodations feature two baths and two private dressing rooms.

FACILITIES

Palm-Aire is an inland resort with a beachfront facility nearby, five golf courses (four championship and one executive par 60), thirty-seven tennis courts, five racquetball courts, a parcourse, twin spa pavilions for men and women, Roman baths, exercise pools, an Olympic pool, two pro shops, and 425 golf carts. Add three hotels, four major dining rooms, full and expert personal services for men and women and you begin to understand the magnitude of Palm-Aire.

The men's pavilion features a solarium garden; a secluded solarium for nude sunbathing; a facial room; a Nautilus equipment room; an enclosure for outdoor massage; Roman baths; a stress-testing room; a barber shop; an exercise pool; whirlpool baths; warm and cool contrast pools; locations for sauna, herbal wraps, Turkish bath, Swiss showers and siesta/napping rooms and a gymnasium. It's all there, convenient and close.

The women's pavilion has similar facilities as well as two

areas for facial treatments and a pair of massage rooms, an outdoor massage area, a beauty salon, a well-stocked boutique, loofah scrub and salt glow areas and two gymnasiums.

In both pavilions there are excellent locker facilities with convenient showers, and safe deposit boxes for valuables.

Coed facilities include an adjacent Olympic-sized swimming pool, the half-mile parcourse–jogging facility, indoor racquetball courts and the nearby golf courses and tennis courts.

PROGRAM

The Palm-Aire exercise program starts long before you even pack for Florida. As soon as you register, the spa requests a medical history and suggests a prearrival exercise routine. On arrival a variety of tests are made to determine your current condition and this provides a basis for your personal exercise program. The spa physical examination includes a stress test, a urinalysis, strength and flexibility tests, a body fat percentage measurement, a risk factor profile and a physical fitness profile. This information is fed into a computer, which uses it to determine your program. They are very careful at Palm-Aire and you grow to appreciate that, a lot.

The goal is to teach the guests to appreciate their own bodies, to realize how exercise can improve their health and sense of well-being and to develop their own at-home fitness program.

The day starts at 8:30 with about ten minutes of stretch exercises followed by a one-and-a-half-to-two-mile walk. Your computer printout schedule for the morning will look something like this:

    9:20 Whirlpool
    9:40 Spa Special, level II
  10:00 Spa Special, level I
  11:00 Advance toning
  11:40 Aerobics, level I
  12:20 Yoga
  1:00 lunch

Spa Special, level I, for the novice exerciser is an excellent, mildly paced all-around workout that includes aerobic exercises for arms, shoulders, chest, back, waist, midriff, abdominals and hips. The benefits are toning, firming, endurance and strength. The techniques range from fencing to floor work. Spa

Special, level II, is for those who exercise regularly and is similar except that it has a faster pace and is more strenuous.

Afternoons involve more exercise classes, a massage, facial, relaxation, meditation and the salt glow beauty treatment.

At Palm-Aire you don't just exercise, you learn the philosophy of exercise, the necessity and wisdom of the warm-up, exercise, cooldown cycle. By the second day it's an ingrained habit, a habit that will serve you well when you exercise at home.

The programs are complemented by a series of luncheon and evening lecture-discussion-demonstration programs to provide the latest information on every phase of health and beauty care. Typical daily lectures include: toning and flexing, lifestyle, nutrition, the stock market (mental condition), spa life and diet, skin care, exercise and weight control, and back care. The special programs for a sample week also cover stress management seminars, fashion shows, habit control seminars, lectures on China bronzes and plastic surgery techniques and benefits, lessons on backgammon and bridge, a seminar on goal setting and motivation and a night at the Pompano harness track.

FOOD AND DIET

Andrew Adriance, the dietician and director of food service, insists that foods can be attractive, tasty and still low in calories. He proves his point, starting with an orientation lecture on the correct attitudes toward food and eating, moving from concepts to specifics. The goal is to teach guests how to balance their diet, eat well and lose weight both at the spa and after they return home.

The diet, just like the exercise program, is programmed only after the staff has the results of your entrance physical. Be it the basic 600-calorie or a weight-gaining 2,200-calorie choice, it's planned just for you. Those who doubt the success of this program need only listen to the tales of how Elizabeth Taylor pared 20 pounds in three weeks and 8 pounds in one!

Here is a sample menu of "first week" meals for serious dieters. Because many guests stay more than a week, menus are rotated to provide variety and interest for the longer-term guest.

Breakfast: one serving of fruit, such as melon wedges, or

juice, such as orange or grapefruit; one protein item, such as an egg or a serving of cottage cheese.

Lunch: an appetizer, such as chicken consommé or romaine salad; an entree, such as a cottage cheese fruit plate with cinnamon yogurt dip or a Spanish omelette with green beans. Dessert can be fruit torte or fresh fruit.

Dinner includes an appetizer, such as spinach soup or tossed salad; an entree, such as flounder marinara or broiled lamb chops; a vegetable such as steamed artichoke and a dessert of vanilla tart with blackberry sauce or fresh fruit. Both lunch and dinner total only 230 calories each!

The summary of rules is: no snacking between meals, omit added fats and oils (butter, mayonnaise, oils, etc.), limit simple sugars (white sugar, honey, syrup), increase intake of crude fibers (fresh vegetables and fruit), drink five to eight cups of water, preferably between meals, avoid caffeine (coffee, soft drinks, tea), limit beef to three portions weekly, omit high-fat meats (luncheon meats), control portion sizes and don't eat salt.

HEALTH AND BEAUTY SERVICES

Beauty services here are no exception to the overall excellence of the spa. A woman will be scheduled for six massages, six herbal wraps, six whirlpool baths and six facials in her first week and the same operator will be with her throughout her stay. On the days that your masseuse is off, you will be given a salt glow.

Other beauty services include a makeup consultation; manicure; pedicure; a lip, body and bikini wax; a shampoo and set. These services are provided once for each guest during a week's stay. The full line of Lancaster products is used and you will be an exception if you don't go home with a collection of them.

Massages are given indoors or in a delightfully landscaped and very private outdoor area. They're head-to-toe bliss, but as with all beauty treatments, you must be on time. You can't take the 2:00 P.M. massage at 3:00 P.M., and if you miss an appointment you don't get a makeup. As one staffer said, "It's an adult spa, and we expect the guests to follow the schedule." Most do, and rather religiously.

The whirlpool baths are kept relatively cool and the force of the jets is really quite strong. It's great while you're in the bath, but don't be surprised if you're pleasantly tired afterward.

It's a good idea to book the beauty services shortly after you check in and as soon as you have time to assess the variety that is offered.

OTHER PLEASURES

For shoppers, the choice ranges from nearby Loehmann's Plaza to the fancy boutiques and shopping areas of Miami, Deerfield, Fort Lauderdale and Palm Beach.

If you like racing, you may choose among thoroughbred racing (at Gulfstream, Hialeah and Calder), greyhound racing, harness racing (November to April) and quarter-horse racing (May to August).

If boating is your sport, you may rent a boat or yacht and cruise the intercoastal waterway, the ocean or nearby lakes. Fishermen and women will find charter, drift or party boats available at Hillsboro Inlet and at every other inlet on the coast. There is also superb bass fishing at Loxahatchee.

You might enjoy a sail on the *Paddlewheel Queen,* which docks in Fort Lauderdale, or a cruise down the New River on the *Jungle Queen.*

Anyone interested in "the world's fastest sport" will want to catch jai alai at either the Dania or Palm Beach frontons.

Between December and April some of the finest polo in the world is played at the Royal Park Polo Club near Boca Raton. Those who wish to move from the sublime to the ridiculous may watch alligator wrestling at the Seminole Indian Reservation.

WHAT TO BRING

Palm-Aire provides green leotards for exercise classes, swimsuits and togas. To fill out the wardrobe, pack flat-heeled sandals, a coverup or warm-up to wear to the spa from the hotel, dressy sportswear or city clothes for evening. (Jackets are required for men's evening wear.) A visor for pool class and your own bathing suit for your trip to the private ocean beach club will be useful. Gym clothes may be worn at breakfast and lunch. Tennis shoes and a coverup for your hair, sun block (the Florida sun is fierce) and a straw hat will all come in handy.

Men bring normal resort wear, slacks, sport shirts, tennis/ jogging shoes, sport shorts and bathing trunks.

A well-stocked boutique at the hotel can fill in for anything you might forget to pack.

HOW TO GET THERE

Palm-Aire is located on South Pompano Parkway, just south of Atlantic Boulevard, opposite Pompano Park Harness Racing track. Take the Florida Turnpike to Exit 24, follow Atlantic as it goes south and east, then turn right on South Pompano Parkway. If you're traveling on I-95, exit at Atlantic Boulevard, go west on Atlantic and then South on South Pompano Parkway.

If you fly into Miami International or West Palm Beach airports you are about forty-five minutes away. Fly to Fort Lauderdale and you're less than thirty minutes away. If you have your own plane, the Pompano Beach Airpark can accommodate DC-3s and is just ten minutes from the spa.

There are a host of commercial ground transportation services between the spa and the airports. The Grayline van will take you from the Fort Lauderdale airport for $7.50 and *to* Miami International for $15.00. The Red and Top Coach (van) goes to and from Miami for $11.00 each way; Yellow Cab is $45.00; and Sherman Limousine Service is $85.00.

If you come by train aboard the Seaboard Coast Line, disembark at the nearby Deerfield Beach station, and take a cab to the spa.

SUMMARY

Palm-Aire is a top-drawer spa that gives real fitness results. Its reputation is for luxury accommodations, very extensive facilities, excellent dietary offerings and superb physical conditioning programs.

FACT SUMMARY

NAME: The Spa at Palm-Aire

MAILING ADDRESS: 2601 Palm-Aire Drive North, Pompano Beach, FL 33060

TELEPHONE: (305) 971-6000; toll-free (800) 327-4960

ACCOMMODATIONS: Attractive hotel-like rooms

FEE: Single, $242.50 per day; double, $190.50 per person, per day

MAXIMUM NUMBER OF GUESTS: 100 men, 100 women

MAXIMUM NUMBER OF STAFF: 150

SEASON: Year-round

AMBIANCE: Luxurious, resort-y atmosphere

GENDER AND AGE RESTRICTIONS: None

DIET: Low-calorie, complex carbohydrates, emphasis on fresh food

FACILITIES: Pools, sauna, Turkish and Roman baths, Swiss showers, solariums, gymnasiums, beauty salon, barber shop, boutique, 5 golf courses, 37 tennis courts, 5 racquetball courts, dining room

PROGRAM: Strong exercise program with wide variety of health and beauty services; lectures

SPECIAL FEATURES: Medical examination on arrival, seminars, fashion shows

LOCAL ATTRACTIONS: Nearby beach, jai alai, horse racing, polo

Safety Harbor Spa

On a bright Sunday in May 1539 an armada led by Hernando de Soto sailed into a spacious spring-fed bay on the southern tip of a recently discovered continent. Because it was the day of the Feast of the Holy Spirit, de Soto named the bay and springs Espiritu Santo. De Soto proclaimed that in Espiritu Santo Springs he had found the original fountain of youth, and ever since people have flocked to the springs in what is now Tampa Bay.

A booklet describing the springs in 1902 provided evidence about their curative powers in the case of Mr. Henry B. King:

> This gentleman came to the Springs in a most deplorable and desperate condition: age 55; sick some time; so swollen that his pants, drawers, socks, and shoes had to be slit

up with scizzors; so weak that he could hardly walk. . . .
He began to improve soon after his arrival at the Springs,
and, after spending 30 days returned home free from all
symptoms; . . . was strong, active and hopeful, and was
happy and rejoicing over his restoration to a normal state
of health.

Others claimed to be cured of dropsy, catarrh of the stomach
and torpid liver. In 1946 a naturopath, Dr. Salem Baranoff,
started the Safety Harbor Spa. Today, the Safety Harbor Spa
focuses on exercise, diet and relaxation, although the mineral
waters are still available for spa-goers to soak in or drink. Most
guests are fairly fit men and women in their fifties and sixties,
who come for several weeks. About 75 percent are repeaters, so
the atmosphere is very friendly.

ACCOMMODATIONS

Rooms range from simple singles to deluxe suites, depending
on how much you are willing to spend and how long you have
been a patron of the spa.

Rooms in the original main building are large and comfortable, newly decorated with two double beds and two easy chairs
and ottomans. There is a dressing table and mirror and a table
and two chairs for cards, plus a color TV with remote control. A
small dressing room and a small bath with lots of counter space
complete the scene. Some of the rooms even have a telephone
in the bathroom. Suites in the main building are just slightly
larger than the regular rooms but are divided to accommodate
a small sitting area, and there is a small balcony overlooking
the swimming pool or the bay, depending on location. In the
newest and most expensive accommodations, the Tower
Suites, there are two double beds and a couch that makes up
into a bed for one. These rooms also have terraces that look
onto the bay. There are *two* televisions (one in color in the main
room, one black and white in the bathroom) and two telephones (one in the bathroom), lots of mirrored closet space and
two separate vanities. These suites are exquisitely furnished.

FACILITIES

The spa is housed in a sprawling group of slick modern buildings on an expanse of flat green lawn. The first floor contains a

reception area filled with plush, overstuffed furniture, a dining room, a movie theater, card rooms and a gift shop.

Downstairs are separate men's and women's bath and so- larium areas, a beauty shop, a gymnasium with exercise equipment, exercise and yoga room and studios for art and ceramics. A coed indoor therapy pool is also on this level.

Just outside is a four-hole golf course, which is situated on a bluff looking onto Tampa Bay. On the eastern edge of the prop- erty there are eleven tennis courts and a golf driving range.

PROGRAM

The general activity plan at Safety Harbor allows for vigor- ous activity in the morning, then more relaxed activities—a trip to the mineral pools or a massage—in the afternoon.

Breakfast is offered from 8:00 A.M. to 10:00 in the dining room. At 9:45 there is scheduled the most unusual "yoga" class we've seen anywhere. The instructor, a rather solidly built woman in her fifties, barks out commands and directions in a rapid-fire auctioneer's monologue that is difficult to follow. There are few classic yoga postures performed; instead this appears to be more of a stretch class taught by a drill sergeant in leotards. The room is usually crowded with sixty or so people all straining to hear and understand the leader's no-nonsense instructions. The spa management has plans to expand the exercise/yoga room in the near future.

The next class of the morning is called "stick conditioning," which is basically a stretch class in which everyone moves a three-foot stick into various positions, as directed by the in- structor. There is no music, and again, the instructor speaks in a fast, clipped monotone, as if she has memorized the routines and is bored with them. There's very little personality or en- couragement in her delivery.

Since both of these classes are quite crowded, most people slip in before class and "save" a place to exercise by placing their tennis shoes on one of the exercise mats.

At 11:00 A.M. there is a body workshop in the gym, where an instructor demonstrates how to use equipment such as exer- cise cycles. This is popular with the men, but women are also welcome.

Lunch is served from 12:30 to 1:30 in the main dining room. A host seats guests, first asking if they want to sit alone or with a group. After lunch every day there is a tour of the facilities for

175

newcomers. This is when you meet one of the social directors, who also handles such niceties as arranging a fourth for bridge or organizing a trip to a local shopping center.

For the rest of the afternoon guests can choose from another stick conditioning class, a free golf clinic, another yoga class or a water exercise class called "Aquajetics" in the indoor or (weather permitting) outdoor pools. The latter offers the best workout of any of the classes and is well attended by both men and women.

In the evening, guests play cards, work in the art or ceramics studios, which are staffed by helpful instructors, attend a live instrumental concert in the theater or catch a fairly recent film shown by the spa staff.

On Mondays free dance lessons are given. At other times guests can sign up for private or group lessons on a fee basis. There is dancing nightly to live music and many guests are real whizzes on the dance floor. Twice a week a house bus takes guests to nearby shopping malls and every night transportation is available to local movie theaters and the nearby dog track.

Every guest is given a brief physical exam on arrival before he or she begins the program; and guests with a serious weight problem are also asked to see the doctor twice a week during their stay.

FOOD AND DIET

All meals at Safety Harbor Spa are taken in the main dining room where most guests tend to sit at the same tables at each meal.

There is no breakfast menu, since the choice is always the same: an egg white omelette with a small amount of low-fat cheese, a bran muffin with a small bowl of cottage cheese, or cold cereal. The dietician thinks that because of its high sugar content fruit should be limited to one serving a day, so you may have it at breakfast if you choose.

The lunch and dinner menus change daily; at breakfast, guests order their lunch and at lunch they give their dinner choices. Salt and sugar substitutes are used. The food always looks appetizing, but it is not gourmet—it's more home-style, with the calories taken out.

The waiters and waitresses are all well versed on the calorie content of each dish and know by the color of the card next to your plate whether you are on a plan that allows for 600 calories, 700, 800, 1000, 1200 or unlimited. A dietician is on duty in the dining room at all meals to answer questions, and she is very strict about allowing substitutions or additions. There is no butter or margarine on the table, and no liquids are served until the meal is over.

Lunch and dinner usually offer a small portion of fish or chicken (spiced with lemon and garlic or baked with Dijon mustard, for example), a salad, and one or more vegetables, depending on your dietary allowance. Desserts consist of fruit or diet gelatin.

There are two breaks—one at 3:00 P.M. and one at 9:30 P.M., when diet gelatin, grapefruit, juices, coffee and tea are offered.

HEALTH AND BEAUTY SERVICES

There are separate men's and women's bathhouse areas in the main building, where saunas, showers, whirlpools and massages are available. The physical facilities are not particularly fancy, but the service is solicitous and pampering. One can hardly towel off an appendage by oneself without an attendant rushing over to do it for you, and it is not possible to get into a tub or out of a shower without a hovering attendant assisting your every move.

In the steam room there are plastic buckets of salt so that guests can rub salt on themselves (the only thing the attendants allow you to do for yourself!) to slough off dry skin.

Massages are given in a large room filled with massage tables separated by partitions. Massages last a half hour— longer ones are not available—and are primarily based on Swedish massage techniques. A hot pack treatment is available for those with sore joints or injuries. Hot, wet towels are placed on the affected area by technicians and one is left to rest. A large mineral water whirlpool surrounded by small private tubs for individual soaks is set in the center of the bathhouse area.

OTHER PLEASURES

There are many sight-seeing attractions close to the spa. Disney World, Cypress Gardens, Busch Gardens and Tarpon Springs are nearby and transportation can be arranged easily. Check with the bell captain. He can also arrange deep-sea fishing and boat trips around the bay. Horse and dog racing are nearby, and for those looking for something a little esoteric, there is the underwater ballet extravaganza at Weeki Wachee.

WHAT TO BRING

This spa does not provide any clothing articles, so bring a robe or coverup, slippers, a bathing suit, leotard, T-shirt and shorts for men, a jogging suit and running shoes. Dress on spa grounds is informal during the day; exercise clothes or shorts are fine for lunch in the dining room. Bring tennis or golf clothes if you want to play and your own equipment if you prefer your own clubs and so on. The evenings at Safety Harbor are very social—everyone dresses for dinner; men wear coats and ties. Bring your prettiest dressy sportswear or dresses to wear to dinner and for the concerts or the ballroom dancing in the dance studio after dinner.

HOW TO GET THERE

Guests fly into Tampa International airport, and although airport regulations there prohibit resorts from offering transportation from airport to resort, it is easy to take a taxi or limo to the spa. The usual fee is approximately $8.

SUMMARY

Safety Harbor is a health-oriented spa and resort for guests in their middle years. The management is trying to lure younger people, but at times the average age is about fifty. This by no means implies that the place is stodgy or dull; it's actually quite lively and has a healthy, jovial social atmosphere. Many couples come here, and families are common too, but single guests will not feel out of place. Many guests have been coming here for years and know one another and the staff well. It's encouraging to see people over fifty looking so fit and vital, enjoying life to the hilt. There is a genuine friendliness here and you can't be a stranger for long.

FACT SUMMARY

NAME: Safety Harbor Spa

MAILING ADDRESS: Safety Harbor, FL 33572

TELEPHONE: (813) 726-1161; toll-free (800) 237-0155

TRANSPORTATION: Free bus to Tampa International airport when departing

ACCOMMODATIONS: Spa Building: standard; Bay and Spring Pavilions: superior; Terrace, Palm and Tower suites: deluxe

FEE: Single, $130 to $195 per day; double, $90 to $125 per person, per day

MAXIMUM NUMBER OF GUESTS: 400

MAXIMUM NUMBER OF STAFF: 300

SEASON: Year-round

AMBIANCE: Friendly, social; health-oriented

GENDER AND AGE RESTRICTIONS: None

DIET: Individual diets for effective weight control ranging from 600 calories per day to unlimited

FACILITIES: Medical examination on arrival, daily massage and mineral baths (except Sundays), tennis, golf, gymnasium, indoor and outdoor swimming pools, solariums, entertainment, full American plan and spa plan

PROGRAM: Monitored and organized on a daily basis: yoga, stretch, water exercise classes

SPECIAL FEATURES: Golf clinics, dance lessons, ceramic studio, house bus to shopping malls, movies and city of Clearwater

LOCAL ATTRACTIONS: Disney World, Busch Gardens, dog racing, jai alai, thoroughbred horse racing, Weeki Wachee, Tarpon Springs

Other Spas

Harbor Island Spa

Harbor Island Spa is a spa that caters to middle-aged urban guests from the Northeast. The exercise program is geared to special physical needs and the diet is modified Pritikin. Couples are welcome.

FACT SUMMARY

MAILING ADDRESS: 7900 Harbor Island, North Bay Village, FL 33141

TELEPHONE: (305) 751-7561; toll-free (800) 327-7510

TRAVEL DIRECTIONS: Fly into Miami airport, 15 minutes from airport by taxi or limo; located on Biscayne Bay between Miami and Miami Beach

ACCOMMODATIONS: Hotel rooms and suites

FEE: 7 days—single, $95 to $140 per day; double, $65 to $98 per person, per day; 11 days—single, $60 to $85 per day; double, $41 to $62 per person per day

MAXIMUM NUMBER OF GUESTS: 300

MAXIMUM NUMBER OF STAFF: 200

SEASON: Year-round, closed Labor Day to October 10

AMBIANCE: Florida resort-type

GENDER AND AGE RESTRICTIONS: None

DIET: Modified Pritikin

FACILITIES: Pool, exercise room with equipment, golf course, tennis, nightclub

PROGRAM: Slimnastics, yoga and posture classes

SPECIAL FEATURES: Free massage daily

LOCAL ATTRACTIONS: Horse racing and dog racing

Lido Spa

The Lido Spa is a medically oriented spa situated on Biscayne Bay at Belle Island, Florida. A free physical examination and consultation are offered to those staying at the spa. The examination and a brief medical history are used as a basis for the diet and physical therapy routine followed while staying at the Lido Spa. A staff dietician checks with those guests on special diets on a daily basis. Various social activities are scheduled during the day, and there is entertainment nightly in the Lido Spa Theater. Guests are usually mature, but there are no restrictions.

FACT SUMMARY

MAILING ADDRESS: 40 Island Avenue, Miami Beach, FL 33139

TRAVEL DIRECTIONS: 15 minutes by taxi or limo from Miami International airport

TRANSPORTATION: A house car will transport you back to the airport, or anywhere within a 50-block radius of the hotel; buses run outside the door; taxi from Miami International airport

TELEPHONE: (305) 538-4621; toll-free (800) 327-8363

ACCOMMODATIONS: 122 guest rooms, includes 4 suites

FEE: Single, $45 to $85 per day

MAXIMUM NUMBER OF GUESTS: 180

MAXIMUM NUMBER OF STAFF: 90

SEASON: October 29 to May 5

AMBIANCE: Friendly and casual; homey atmosphere

GENDER AND AGE RESTRICTIONS: None

DIET: Dietician provides any of many low-calorie diets (salt free, sugar free also available), tailored to the individual

FACILITIES: Complete spa including fully equipped gymnasium, steam rooms and cabinets, Swiss showers; 3 pools, putting green, boating and fishing docks

PROGRAM: Includes daily massage and exercise classes, use of spa facilities

SPECIAL FEATURES: New guests are usually seated with other people of similar age and within 2 days know most of the other guests; strong entertainment program

LOCAL ATTRACTIONS: Ballet, concerts in Miami, movies, Parrot Jungle, Seaquarium, the Everglades

Palm Beach Spa

The weight control and conditioning program at Palm Beach Spa begins with a physical examination. Based on this, an individualized exercise routine is developed by the spa director and a diet is planned by the dietician. Various social activities are offered by the spa daily; there is also nightly entertainment in the spa's nightclub. Although there are no age restrictions, this spa tends to cater to mature adults.

FACT SUMMARY

MAILING ADDRESS: Everglades Avenue, Palm Beach, FL 33480

TRAVEL DIRECTIONS: Along Intracoastal Waterway in Palm Beach; or taxi from Palm Beach International airport

TELEPHONE: (305) 833-8411; New York booking office (212) 746-8755

ACCOMMODATIONS: Hotel rooms and suites, deluxe villa (1 room and terrace), and deluxe lanai (2 room suites)

FEE: Double, $42 to $84 per person, per day

MAXIMUM NUMBER OF GUESTS: 375

MAXIMUM NUMBER OF STAFF: 204

SEASON: November to mid-March

AMBIANCE: Resort atmosphere

GENDER AND AGE RESTRICTIONS: None

DIET: Individually tailored after consultation with a physician and dietician

FACILITIES: Boulder steam room, sauna, mineral whirlpool baths, lakeside pool, heated pool, lake trail, separate gymnasiums for men and women, beauty and barber shop, dance studio, putting green, solarium; golf and fishing facilities nearby

PROGRAM: Program is individually prescribed after consultation with a physician

SPECIAL FEATURES: Overlooks Lake Worth

LOCAL ATTRACTIONS: Royal Poinciana Playhouse, Four Arts Galleries and Library, Norton Gallery, Flagler Museum, jai alai, greyhound races

Shangri-La Natural Health Spa

The main emphasis of this coed spa, which caters to mature guests, is getting back to a natural way of living. This is reflected in the diet, lectures and classes offered by the spa. Lectures and classes promote a learn-by-doing attitude, with topics such as mental and emotional poise, meditation, movement, rhythmics, yoga, organic gardening and permanent weight loss. Shangri-La Natural Health Spa is on ten acres in the village of Bonita Springs, Florida.

FACT SUMMARY

MAILING ADDRESS: Route #3, P.O. Box 1, Bonita Springs, FL 33923

TRAVEL DIRECTIONS: 25 miles south of Fort Myers on old U.S. Highway 41

TRANSPORTATION: Call spa for taxi pick-up service

TELEPHONE: (813) 992-3811

ACCOMMODATIONS: Dormitory-style, double and single occupancy

FEE: Dormitory, $29 per person (not air-conditioned) to $52 per person, per day; 10 percent rise in winter season; single, from $45 to $52 (air-conditioned); double, from $32 to $42 per person (air-conditioned)

MAXIMUM NUMBER OF GUESTS: 90 (class size, 15)

MAXIMUM NUMBER OF STAFF: 50

SEASON: Year-round

AMBIANCE: Quiet, restful

GENDER AND AGE RESTRICTIONS: None

DIET: Natural vegetarian health foods, supervised water fasts, no dairy products, no caffeine

FACILITIES: Tennis courts, heated outdoor pool, paddle boats, white sand beach nearby, badminton, shuffle board, nude sunbathing solarium

PROGRAM: Unstructured; dancing, classic in yoga, rhythmics, meditation

SPECIAL FEATURES: Lush gardens and citrus groves, nude sunbathing facilities, shopping trips

LOCAL ATTRACTIONS: Everglade/Wonder Gardens, Kennel Club, Corkscrew Swamp

Sea Pines Behavioral Institute

This is a serious weight control and fitness program located on Hilton Head Island off the coast of South Carolina. The four-week program features behavior modification and an educational approach to nutrition. The spa is medically supervised and has an excellent reputation for permanent weight loss. The island setting is breathtaking.

FACT SUMMARY

MAILING ADDRESS: Sea Pines Resort, Hilton Head Island, SC 29928

TRAVEL DIRECTIONS: Fly into Savannah, Georgia, airport, take limo service to Hilton Head, Sea Pines Visitor Center of Sea Pines Plantation; limo will take guest directly to villa on request

TELEPHONE: (803) 671-6181

ACCOMMODATIONS: Villas near the institute

FEE: 26-day program, $3,500

MAXIMUM NUMBER OF GUESTS: 25

MAXIMUM NUMBER OF STAFF: 5

SEASON: Year-round, except mid-December to mid-January

AMBIANCE: Casual atmosphere but serious program in beautiful setting

GENDER AND AGE RESTRICTIONS: None

DIET: 700-calorie low-cholesterol, low-sodium diet

FACILITIES: Beach, tennis courts, swimming pools, bicycle paths, golf courses, gymnasium

PROGRAM: Specializes in permanent weight control through behavior modification, classes and demonstration on nutritional dieting

SPECIAL FEATURES: Good spa for the very overweight person; warm supportive staff help with lifestyle change

LOCAL ATTRACTIONS: Sailing, boating, fishing, horseback riding, beach, sight-seeing in Savannah and Charleston

The Homestead

The Homestead is located on 16,000 acres of forest, stream and meadow in the Virginia Alleghenies in Hot Springs, Virginia. It has a history that dates back to before the Civil War. During World War II Japanese diplomats were interned there, and it has served several presidents and other well-known politicians. It originally became known for the medicinal value of the mineral waters. Today the spa facility at Homestead provides a medically supervised hydrotherapy program using the same mineral waters. Homestead is a full-service year-round resort with luxury rooms, gourmet meals and many sports and activities.

FACT SUMMARY

MAILING ADDRESS: Hot Springs, VA 24445

TELEPHONE: (703) 839-5500; toll-free Virginia (800) 542-5734; out of state (800) 536-5771

TRAVEL DIRECTIONS: 80 miles north of Roanoke in the Virginia Alleghenies

TRANSPORTATION: Limo service from Ingalls Field, Roanoke and Greenbrier Valley airports; charter flights directly into Ingalls Field at nearby Warm Springs also available

ACCOMMODATIONS: Rooms with or without balcony, duplex suites, cottages, rooms with or without parlor and fireplace

FEE: Per person rates range from $83 to $102 per day, depending upon type of room accommodation. Cottages for 4 persons are $340 to $392 per day. Room rates do not include such charges as green fees for golf, use of tennis courts, daily service charges, etc. Several special package rates are available. Full American plan.

MAXIMUM NUMBER OF GUESTS: 1,100

MAXIMUM NUMBER OF STAFF: 1,200

SEASON: Year-round

AMBIANCE: Peaceful; formal; grand resort

GENDER AND AGE RESTRICTIONS: None

DIET: None; international cuisine; medical director will advise

FACILITIES: Medical clinic, exercise rooms, mineral sauna, ultrasonic and hot-pack baths and massage facilities, whirlpool, indoor swimming pool, bowling lanes, 2 outdoor pools, sunning terrace, sand beach, children play area, casino, 3 golf courses, 19 tennis courts, 2 lawn bowling greens, skeet and trap-shooting fields, badminton, Ping-Pong, billiards, bridle trails, trout fishing, winter skiing and ice skating

PROGRAM: Medically supervised hydrotherapy program at spa facility

SPECIAL FEATURES: Hot mineral springs, also used in indoor swimming pool

LOCAL ATTRACTIONS: None

Coolfont ReCreation Spa Retreat

Coolfont ReCreation offers several types of programs through-out the year. A Health Happening is five days of exercise, diet-ing and health counseling; a fitness weekend offers a combina-tion of body-conditioning activities; and a massage weekend teaches its participants body stress points and the release of fatigue through proper massage. Coolfont ReCreation is lo-cated on 1,200 acres of mountain forest in West Virginia and offers a variety of recreational activities, including water sports on the two nearby lakes.

FACT SUMMARY

MAILING ADDRESS: Coolfont ReCreation, Berkeley Springs, WV 25411

TRAVEL DIRECTIONS: Two hours from Washington, D.C., or Baltimore—from Washington, Beltway (495) to 270 to 70, south on 522, to Berkeley Springs: from Baltimore, 70, south on 522, to Berkeley Springs; can use BWI, National, Dulles or Hagerstown airports

TELEPHONE: (304) 258-4500; toll-free from D.C. (800) 424-1232

ACCOMMODATIONS: Participants housed in 24-room lodge or A-frame chalets

FEE: 5-day program—single, $395; double, $325 per person (in-cludes everything except massage, which is $15; enrollment guests receive 15 percent reduced price on beauty services)

MAXIMUM NUMBER OF GUESTS: 25 to 30

MAXIMUM NUMBER OF STAFF: 6

SEASON: At present, first and last week of every month except December

AMBIANCE: Quiet, mountain lake resort

GENDER AND AGE RESTRICTIONS: Women over 17 on 5-day program; coed on fitness weekends

DIET: 750 to 1,200 calories per day basic balanced diet—fish and chicken, turkey

FACILITIES: Tennis courts, hiking trails, horseback riding, lake swimming, paddle boats and canoes, volleyball, ice skating, cross-country skiing, roller skating in the barn, nature walks

PROGRAM: 5-day Health Happenings begin on first and last Sundays of each month; consists of exercise, dieting and health counseling

SPECIAL FEATURES: Coolfont is a haven—only televisions or phones are in lodge; cabins hidden in woods

LOCAL ATTRACTIONS: Berkeley Springs is the oldest spa in the U.S.; near famous Civil War battlefields, historic castle, London Fog outlet, chamber music concerts, Coolfont Foundation for the Arts

THE
NORTHEAST

Featured Spas

International Health and Beauty Spa at Gurney's Inn

Nestled against a bluff overlooking one of Montauk, Long Island's finest white sand beaches is Gurney's Inn and its International Health and Beauty Spa. The inn is a large and very private retreat that has provided relaxing vacations for generations of Easterners. Now, at the spa, it also provides some of the best physical conditioning and psyche-pampering treatments available anywhere.

There are really two spas, one pavilion for men and one for women, and both are available for full-schedule spa visits, or for single-day treatments. Gurney's is a favorite spot for the busy executive of either sex, to relax and get the body back in shape: the ultimate repair shop for stress and overindulgence.

The spa is a labor of love for its owner, Nick Monte, who firmly believes that if everyone would live close enough to the ocean there would be no need for psychiatrists. His philosophy is personified by the sculpture based on Botticelli's *Birth of Venus* that greets spa guests. The sculpture symbolizes the sea giving birth to life, to beauty, to health and to love.

ACCOMMODATIONS

Gurney's Inn, now grown to 215 rooms, has long been *the* seaside choice of elegant Easterners, some of whom have been coming to this hideaway on Long Island's south shore for fifty years. Guests choose from rooms, cottages or suites and all come with a great view of the white sand beach and the ocean.

Cottages accommodate from two to six people; each has a living room with a fireplace, kitchen pantry with refrigerator, sun porch with a private lawn facing the ocean and from one to three bedrooms. Rooms and suites are large, wood-paneled and simply furnished; most have double beds.

FACILITIES

Near the inn are twin spa pavilions, one for men and one for women, and they are open from 8:00 A.M. until midnight. Each pavilion contains a small mirrored and carpeted exercise room for the fitness classes of twenty people. Close by are the sauna, steam room and whirlpool baths, which are immaculate, quiet and softly lit. The settings are luxurious throughout; a marble, mirrored area surrounds the whirlpool, which is filled with ocean water heated to 105 degrees. In the dim light, twenty-six Jacuzzi pumps circulate the salt water to relieve aches, pains and tensions. In the same area is a Finnish rock sauna with birch reclining shelves, and a Russian steam room with a peaked ceiling that prevents the annoying drip of steamy water on the bare skin. A siesta room, equipped with a full assort-ment of relaxation tapes and variable-level lighting, provides comfortable cots and fluffy white blankets.

On the minus side, the locker room is small and tends to be overcrowded as guests stand up to struggle in and out of their leotards or shorts because seating is so limited. The massage rooms, separated only by curtains, afford full access to conver-sation from the next cubicle—not the best arrangement if you're a private person who wants total silence and relaxation. To get around this, request an outdoor massage on the deck. Dick Cavett, a frequent visitor to Gurney's, requests that his massages be outdoors at night, under the stars. So can you if you put in your order twenty-four hours in advance.

A parcourse winds its way through the resort, along the bluffs and the beach. Ask the staff for assistance in locating and then following the route. They will also guide you in the use of the weight-training and exercise room equipment.

Use the beach as part of the spa facilities. Fly a kite, jog or speed walk and breathe in the crystal clear air. Organize a sandy volleyball game; swim in the surf in view of the expert, licensed ocean lifeguards or flop down on one of the big cushioned wooden lounges.

If you're a winter guest, you're in luck: the lunch area over-looking the sea becomes an ice-skating rink from Thanksgiving to Easter.

PROGRAM

Gurney's program combines three approaches; the major focus is European-style hydrotherapy using the sea waters of the Atlantic for water treatments. The second focus of the spa is a holistic approach to disease prevention and wellness, incorporating lectures on stress management, private and group biofeedback sessions and holistic therapies including shiatsu, reflexology and polarity therapy. The third part of the program features aerobic and cardiovascular fitness with a selection of fitness classes. The combination of these approaches makes up a complete program that includes health and beauty services, stress reduction, a credible fitness program and a low-calorie diet.

When you arrive at Gurney's you are asked to complete a two-page health questionnaire (to screen guests for coronary problems, hypertension, allergies, etcetera) and are then given a blood pressure check, after which measurements are taken. Then the staff works with you to create a personalized program that combines and spaces exercise classes, beauty treatments and therapies, and offers such options as weight lifting, pool exercise, stretch-and-strengthen exercises, disco aerobics, calisthenics, yoga and swimming (ocean, pool or both).

A private exercise class tailored specifically for you is available with Nesha, a superb instructor and a wonderful role model for physical fitness. A cassette tape from this session for home use is available at $15, an excellent value.

The weakest link in the fitness program seems to be the irregular length of the exercise classes, which makes adhering to your regular daily schedule (posted on your locker) difficult. If you like structure, you'll resent the fact that although each class is supposed to last thirty minutes, you may find that some are only fifteen minutes long, others go on for fifty minutes and no one seems to know in advance what to expect. Classes are, however, widely available, both morning and evening; also in the evenings you can choose from lectures on stress management, nutrition and biofeedback, or you can have one of the available beauty treatments. The spa is open to guests in the evening after the dinner hour. This may be the perfect time to enjoy the sauna, steam and pool facilities; it is certainly the time when they are the least crowded.

Massages and exercise classes that are held outdoors on the seaside deck in the summer are held indoors during the blustery winter months. There is something wonderful about swimming in the buoyant 80-degree seawater pool while a January storm is brewing outside, as you view it all through the mammoth windows surrounding the pool. The program offers a good balance of therapy and exercise, and with careful planning you can make it as rigorous or relaxing as you wish. A typical day might include three exercise sessions and a massage before lunch, and an aerobic dance class followed by yoga in the afternoon.

Later in the afternoon or evening you could have thalassotherapy or a fango (mudpack) treatment. After the evening lecture and discussion, most guests are ready for early turn-in.

FOOD AND DIET

Gurney's is the place to have seafood. Take advantage of this spa that stretches out into the Atlantic and eat your fill of the fruits of the sea, fresh daily, still staying within the recommended 1,000 calories per day.

You'll enjoy fresh littleneck clams with lemon slices and horseradish sauce or fresh oysters (in season); melons, tiny asparagus and giant beefsteak tomatoes (used to make the most wonderful gazpacho) are also a part of the daily diet. The chef tends to overbroil or poach the tiny local scallops and fresh local fish, so request undercooking if seafood is your choice. Your entree will be more moist and flavorful.

For nonseafood fans, there's a wide range of choices including chicken, veal and vegetable main dishes, nicely prepared with continental flair.

Lest you think meals at Gurney's are a free-for-all, diet *is* emphasized, with the accent on a modified Pritikin diet. There is little oil used and lots of fruit and vegetables.

A description of Gurney's kitchen would not be complete without mention of the bakery, where homemade Italian whole-wheat hard rolls are baked daily. Eaten with a poached egg and a slice of golden melon, these can make for a terrific breakfast.

The Gurney's spa dining room is small but airy, with large windows overlooking the beach. Service is not up to par with the food, perhaps because the spa dining room is located so far from the main kitchen. All spa meals can also be enjoyed in the main resort dining room, a more spacious room that has a menu to challenge any dieter. The seemingly endless breakfast buffet features mounds of scrambled eggs, giant platters of sausage and bacon and mountains of starchy homemade sweet rolls.

Eating a diet dinner is easier, but we were very tempted by a neighboring table where a few couples were attacking a monstrous chocolate-cherry anniversary cake covered with globs of real whipped cream.

The spa menu, changed daily, offers five or six appetizers, a choice of three salads, a minimum of five entrees and three desserts. The calorie count is listed beside each item for your review in the morning; select your choices carefully so that you can enjoy each meal but not exceed your calorie limit for the day.

If your goal is serious weight loss, and 800 calories per day meets your requirements, drop the appetizer and dessert at lunch and dinner. This deprivation is barely noticeable.

If you must have between-meal snacks, the spa refrigerator offers juices and a platter of crudités with a low-fat cottage cheese or yogurt dip.

HEALTH AND BEAUTY SERVICES

Institut de Beauté, the full-service salon located within the spa building, is designed to accommodate both men and women and offers privacy for most of its services. There were several male guests when we were there, including an ex–New York Knicks basketball player and a conservative, fortyish Xerox salesman.

Where else can you get the combination of superb view of the Atlantic Ocean and really professional beauty services? If you have a manicure or pedicure, be sure to ask for the heated mittens and booties, which really soften the skin. The natural and biogenic facials are great favorites among the guests who seem to enjoy the Christine Valmy and Georgette Klinger products.

A special facial, offered irregularly but worth asking about, is the Loving Hands, an East Indian technique that combines gentle skin manipulation with a mask of yogurt, fresh fruit and vegetables. The materials are prepared and the treatment given by Nagis, a woman from Bombay.

Skin and hair analysis and treatments are available and include a warm oil hair conditioning and scalp massage. Body waxing, makeup application and brow shaping are standard at many spas, but here coloring and permanenting are also available.

The beauty services are available at any time from 8:00 A.M. until 6:00 P.M., with a few services available until midnight.

The list of offerings is endless, but the specialties of the house are the European-style treatments that use seawater. The German thalassotherapy is an invigorating, twenty-minute session in a tub where underwater jets circulate 125 gallons of warm sea and fresh water to ease your tensions. At the same time, the spa technician treats special areas with a high-velocity hose. It's a must!

The Scotch hose treatment at Gurney's uses a unique combination of hot and cold, fresh and salt waters. The Swiss shower contains rows of jets, where fresh water is directed at the body following the saltwater treatment. French Vichy showers use an overhead needle spray using hot and cold, fresh and salt water. In conjunction with this hydrotherapy they offer salt glows (rubs), using salt taken from the Dead Sea.

Herbal wraps at Gurney's use kelp leaves (full of aloe, potassium, magnesium and vitamins), which are harvested daily. Kelp is draped over the body and then you are wrapped like a mummy in giant steaming terry towels with an outer layer of plastic sheeting, and covered with a warm blanket. Cool, herb-scented towels are available to wipe a perspiring brow as you rest supine and listen to classical music. If the kelp treatment is too rich for your blood, standard herbal wraps using sheets dipped in camomile, eucalyptus and lavender are available.

Even experienced spa-goers will be amazed by the special fango therapy. A mixture of Italian volcanic mud rich in minerals and warm soft paraffin is applied and molded in heavy sheets to the specific ache or pain. The heat and weight of the mudpack are contained by wrapping the body in a large, soft blanket. You awake relaxed and refreshed.

The range and quality of massage and therapy is impressive. In addition to treatments already mentioned, the adventurous guest may participate in several kinds of therapeutic massage: Swedish massage (gentle kneading and stroking), shiatsu (the 3,000-year-old Japanese pressure-point massage), polarity therapy (very light pressure at various points to release energy), deep fascia manipulation (deep massage of muscle tissue) and reflexology (pressure-point massage of the feet), all by-products of the wellness or holistic movement concept.

The loofah scrub uses an invigorating natural vegetable sponge to apply organic soap to the entire body, leaving skin smooth and soft. The Norwegian sponge rub features giant soft sponges and warm, foamy water for a mild, soothing cleansing.

In the field of beauty services, Gurney's is exceptional, certainly one of the choice elite. Very few commercially oriented spas offer this range of services. If you're slightly overwhelmed by this array of body work or preventive therapies, ask the helpful staff for guidance.

OTHER PLEASURES

Montauk is perhaps the most attractive coastal area on Long Island, a photographer's paradise. There are activities to please every whim and interest.

Deep-sea fishing is superb off Montauk where a riptide literally churns up the fish, and the question is not whether you'll catch any fish but rather how many. Wind surfing is another popular sport here and sight-seeing cruises are available. If you can afford it, the New England Airlines' charter flight to Block Island is a real delight.

The village has a good collection of arts and crafts shops. It will amaze some to learn that the oldest cattle ranch in the United States is located in Montauk where cattle grazed as early as 1660. This is also the location where Teddy Roosevelt and his Roughriders trained. The Second House Museum, constructed in 1746 as a shelter for cattle herders, is the oldest house in Montauk.

If you like to meander, the Walking Dunes, so named because of their shifting contours, provide a great spot for hiking. It's the scene of many of the 1920s movies, including *Beau Geste* and *The Sheik*.

Kite flying, an increasingly popular sport, is big at Montauk, where there is almost always a pleasant breeze. Bicycle riding and horseback riding (with either English or Western saddles) are big.

Montauk is located at the crossroads of major migratory bird patterns and is a superb place for birdwatching.

Naturally, all the aquatic sports thrive here: swimming, surfing, sunning, sailing or water skiing, and these may be supplemented by trips to freshwater ponds, a balloon ride, golf, clamming, tennis or beach walking. If the latter seems a little tame, remember brisk walking in soft sand can be a real calorie burner.

HOW TO GET THERE

If you have a small private plane you can drop in to the short (3,500-foot runway) Montauk airport, or if you have your own boat it is possible to step ashore at the Montauk harbor, but most people will come by car from New York City or from La Guardia or Kennedy airports.

Drive east on the Long Island Expressway to Exit 70 and then go south to Route 27, the Old Sunrise Highway, and proceed east to Montauk. As you leave Amagansett you will enter the Napeague Highway. This is a straight stretch of highway and about six miles past Amagansett you will observe twin radio towers on your left, clearly visible as towers by day and identifiable by their flashing red lights at night. Proceed two miles and take the right fork on the Old Montauk Highway. Gurney's Inn is about two miles past the fork on the right. Be careful to observe speed limits as enforcement is strict.

You can go from New York City to Montauk by train via the Long Island Railroad, a trip of about three and a half hours. For information on train schedules call (212) 739-4200.

Gurney's provides complimentary transportation to local airports and railroad stations.

WHAT TO BRING

Towels, spa shoes and heavy terry robes are provided by the spa. The list of personal gear to bring depends on which sports or activities you want to take part in. Leotards are good for the exercise classes; and elastic waist shorts and T-shirts are acceptable for men and women. Since you will be in the water much of the time, bring several bathing suits, and if your hair is long, a bathing cap. Take along slip-on shoes or sandals for walking to and from the spa and your room; and don't forget jogging shoes for running the parcourse or jogging on the beach. As Montauk temperatures can drop in the early morning and evening, a warm-up suit will come in handy for protection from cool ocean breezes; you can also use it as a coverup around the resort over your leotards or shorts. For the evenings, women will want to bring dresses, skirts or dressy pants outfits. Men are expected to wear a jacket and tie.

SUMMARY

Gurney's Inn is a gracious old seaside resort with a snappy new spa addition. It is a great place to come as a couple, but it's also a comfortable place to come alone, since it is easy to meet people here. The food is excellent and the health and beauty treatments available are the most extensive offered at any spa. The usual guest is a dynamic urban professional person in fairly good physical condition.

Every activity at Gurney's is made more enjoyable by the breathtaking view of the ocean from nearly every part of the facility.

FACT SUMMARY

NAME: International Health and Beauty Spa at Gurney's Inn

MAILING ADDRESS: Old Montauk Highway, Montauk, Long Island, NY 11954

TELEPHONE: (516) 668-2345 or 668-3203

ACCOMMODATIONS: Wide variety of rooms, cottages and suites

FEE: Day of Beauty for $100, 7-day Rejuvenation Plan for $400; rooms $90 to $130 per person, per day double occupancy

MAXIMUM NUMBER OF GUESTS: 215

MAXIMUM NUMBER OF STAFF: 280

SEASON: Year-round

AMBIANCE: Gracious, comfortable with breathtaking views

GENDER AND AGE RESTRICTIONS: None in resort; adults over 18 in spa

DIET: Low-calorie continental cuisine; emphasis on fresh seafood; modified Pritikin; 800 to 1,000 calories per day

FACILITIES: Indoor saltwater pool; beach; separate spa facilities for men and women; beauty salon, gym, Roman baths, steam rooms, saunas, Scotch hose, many hydrotherapy choices; parcourse; 2 dining rooms

PROGRAM: Permissive, moderate exercise program; emphasis

on hydrotherapy, stress reduction and diet; classes in yoga, aerobics, cardiovascular fitness; lectures; jogging

SPECIAL FEATURES: Scenic Atlantic Coast setting; use of seawater in many spa hydrotherapy services; 1,000 feet of private beach on Long Island; extensive beauty and body treatments

LOCAL ATTRACTIONS: Montauk harbor for deep-sea fishing and cruises, clamming, balloon riding, wind surfing, arts and crafts shops

New Age Health Farm

If a friend invited you to go along to a resort where no coffee drinking or smoking was allowed, where most guests were denied solid food, no radios or televisions were permitted and where anyone who had a headache was not allowed to take aspirin, chances are you would politely decline the invitation. However, every week men and women flock to the New Age Health Farm in order to be denied these very things, and many swear that it has led them to a healthier, happier life.

The owners, Elza and Graeme Graydon, certainly look healthy enough. Lovely blond Elza, who often dresses in authentic Austrian costume (she is a former Miss Austria), has impressive energy and a lively no-nonsense manner; her husband, Graeme, is a ruggedly handsome Heathcliff type (without the stormy temperament), and a former New Zealand farmer and ethnic museum director.

Guests are invited to share the Graydons' healthy lifestyle in a carefully developed program of fasting, exercise, meditation and whole body detoxification (which is a health farm euphemism for enemas). They have one simple policy: you must follow their rules; no exceptions.

ACCOMMODATIONS

Guests stay in two-story buildings just a few feet from the main house. Rooms are simple and clean, and usually have two single beds and a roomy chest of drawers. Bathrooms are small but certainly adequate. You will notice that there are towels but no washcloths. You will also notice an odd coat hanger device hanging on the towel bar; its use will be revealed when you attend Elza's orientation session, the day after your arrival.

FACILITIES

The New Age Health Farm sits at the base of the blue-green Catskill Mountains in upstate New York. The cluster of buildings, including a rambling white wooden farmhouse, are located on a rise from which grassy pastures extend in every direction. The farmhouse, the heart of New Age, has a cozy living room dominated by a stone fireplace and a large airy dining room that fills with light from walls of panel windows. Elza and Graeme have offices in the house and there is a check-in desk where you can schedule beauty treatments and buy health-related books.

The renovated barn has a carpeted exercise room, sauna and whirlpool, plus massage and facial rooms. Outside, where the meadow dips into a natural bowl, a swimming pool is nestled in a copse of trees. The property slopes upward about one hundred yards from the buildings to the edge of a forest; no ordinary stand of trees, but the deep, dark, awe-inspiring forest of Grimm's fairy tales. The virgin growth of trees is 200 feet tall and the floor of the forest is covered with a knee-deep sea of waving ferns. Miles of trails wind through this wood where guests come to meditate, walk off their frustrations or retreat from others to think.

PROGRAM

This is a health farm, not a spa. The New Age philosophy emphasizes the interrelationship of the mind, the body and the spirit. Elza suggests that guests tell themselves, "I am going to reserve a week of my life just for me. Although I don't know fully how my body works, I know I haven't always listened to it or done the best things for it. Despite the abuse I've given it, it has served me well. Now I am going to stop giving it stress, stop abusing it, and just for one week I am going to find out what it can really do for me if I give it some rest and just let it do its own thing." By "give it some rest" she is talking about fasting, a main focus of the New Life program, and the effect it has on the spirit as well as the body.

"It is my conviction," says Elza, "that there is no way to true health without going through the pain. Fasting opens the door to the subconscious so that the negative thoughts and feelings can come out, and once they come out I can look at them, accept them and forgive myself for them."

Elza explains in the orientation that some people experience a physical and emotional crisis several days into a fast in which all the feelings that have been quashed by food—anger, jealousy, despair and grief—come pouring out, causing acute anxiety. What makes New Age a special place is that Graeme and Elza stand ready and willing to help support and lead a guest through this period by their warm presence, even if it happens during the night.

Elza talks throughout the week about psychological blocks and negative thinking that often result in being overweight, and she applies that to personal relationships as well. She describes many women as preferring a "carbohydrate man," by which she means a man who flatters, giving attention and gifts, and makes a woman feel "high," then (after he is loved), moves on quickly, leaving a woman's ego to come crashing down just as her blood sugar level would fall suddenly after eating too much of a simple carbohydrate food like candy. She feels if you are healthy emotionally and physically, you will not be drawn in by such persons. One assumes this advice goes for men as well.

Since 80 percent of the guests at New Age are there to fast, which often makes people feel tired or sleepy, the daily program is not especially rigorous.

At 9:30 A.M. each guest weighs in and has "breakfast" (juice or water for fasters). At 10:00 one is expected to perform "detoxification," a polite term for taking an enema. The Graydons insist that any fasting guest who stays longer than three days must take a daily enema or "internal cleansing." If you are a little sketchy on this procedure, don't worry, since it is carefully but completely addressed in the orientation session, including how to hook the enema bag into the mysterious wire hanger you found in the bathroom. The staff is not without humor about the subject. When Elza says "We don't serve coffee—in the *usual* way," with a demure smile, she is referring to the coffee enema, which many guests swear is a major reason for the healthy energy they feel by the end of the week.

Late each morning guests can take a whirlpool bath or sauna, then at noon an exercise class is offered for stretching and toning.

After "lunch" Graeme usually leads a vigorous hour walk through the forest. Most guests follow this with a sauna or take the relaxing yoga class offered at 4:30, which ends with rhythmic chanting. After dinner "spiritual nutrition" is offered consisting of sessions on astrology, meditation, herbal medicine or proper nutrition.

One of these programs, "Elza's meditation," is held in the exercise room on the upper floor of the barn. The only light is provided by flickering candles. After a quiet period, Elza speaks about self-acceptance, how to tune into the love and energy of others and how to share your real self with the world. Following this inspirational talk, guests meditate quietly, then embrace one another and file quietly down the stairs and back to their rooms.

FOOD AND DIET

Although most guests come to New Age to fast, there are several diet options available. For the iron-willed there is the water fast, recommended for short-term therapy—three or four days only. More popular is the fresh juice fast, which allows approximately 350 calories from fruit or vegetable juices. For those who can't see themselves fasting there is the Spartan diet (400 to 500 calories, no dairy products), the Lite diet (600 to 650 calories, fruits, vegetables, grains, eggs) and, for those who need some animal protein, the Pro-Lite diet, which is the Lite diet plus fish or chicken. Red meat is not served at New Age.

For guests who are not dieting, the gourmet plan is available, which is all natural foods with no chemicals added, and usually includes vegetables, chicken, fish and natural desserts. Calories vary on this plan. Whatever plan you decide on, choose carefully because guests are not allowed to switch from a fast to a solid diet during their stay. If anyone begins to feel weak or headachy, medications such as aspirin are not available; herb tea is offered instead.

HEALTH AND BEAUTY SERVICES

The range of services here is wide: Swedish massage, facials, manicures and pedicures, hair treatments, skin peels, aromatherapy and paraffin waxing are offered. The Quickslim body wrap is also available; it involves rubbing a gel (made from seaweed and sea salt) on the body, which generates heat and reduces the fatty tissue most people know as cellulite. Special "toning tapes" are then wrapped around the body to hold in the heat and provide compression on areas you want to reduce.

The process leaves you with a sense of exhilaration, reportedly because the bloodstream now has a new source of energy derived from the material that was stored in the intercellular tissue spaces.

Beauty and health treatments can be scheduled in the morning or afternoon. There is an extra charge for all treatments.

OTHER PLEASURES

The major pleasure at New Age is the breathtaking setting, with 130 acres of fields, mountains and forest available for exploring. The bracingly fresh air, the smell of newly mown hay and the occasional glimpses of wild animals are a real delight, especially for the urban guest.

WHAT TO BRING

Outdoor clothes that fit the season are a must, since you will be taking long walks. Jeans, slacks, shirts, sweaters and jackets are needed for most seasons, as are good walking shoes. A bathing suit and cap and a beach coverup will come in handy. You may bring your own enema bag or buy one at the desk. Remember to tuck a washcloth into your luggage.

HOW TO GET THERE

From New York City you can take a Shortline bus to Liberty, New York, then take a cab to Neversink. If you are driving, take the New York State Thruway north to Exit 16 at Harriman; take Route 17 west to Exit 100 at Liberty; turn left and go one block to a traffic light, then turn left again onto Route 52 west; follow Route 52 for one mile and make a sharp right to the village of Neversink. The New Age sign and private drive are on the left opposite the Neversink Firehouse. From New Jersey, take Route 17 north and then Route 17 west to Exit 100 at Liberty, then proceed as above.

SUMMARY

New Age Health Farm is no place for shirkers, for the dietary program is strict and serious. However, more than 50 percent of the guests are repeaters, and they are convinced that the New Age program, based on the nutritional philosophy of eminent naturopathic doctor Paavo Airola, gives them an unusual vitality and energy. Weight loss is often dramatic; a pound a day is common on the juice fast, and many guests come several times a year to tune up and slim down.

The crowd is as eclectic as one will encounter at any spa. Because of the fairly low price, young office workers, nurses and teachers are frequent guests, but you'll also meet affluent businessmen, high fashion models and well-off older women. Some of the guests are committed to a health food regimen all year long, but many come to detoxify their systems from the habits of a usual hectic urban lifestyle.

Elza and Graeme Graydon are warm and humane with guests, lending a stability and dignity to what is for some a total reversal in eating behavior and personal habits.

You will either love this place or leave early! Most who do stay reap substantial health benefits.

FACT SUMMARY

NAME: New Age Health Farm

MAILING ADDRESS: Neversink, NY 12765

TELEPHONE: (914) 985-2221

ACCOMMODATIONS: Clean, pleasant rooms in buildings separate from farmhouse

FEE: Depending on accommodation:
   Daily: Single, from $65 to $79 per person, per day
          Double, from $43 to $53 per person, per day

   Weekend: Single, from $144 to $167 per person,
             per day
   (Fri.-Sun.) Double, from $96 to $112 per person,
             per day

   Weekly: Single, from $351 to $446 per person
   (7 days) Double, from $234 to $297 per person

   Accommodations range from simplicity (cheapest), country charm (moderate) to our best (best).

MAXIMUM NUMBER OF GUESTS: 70

MAXIMUM NUMBER OF STAFF: 30

SEASON: Year-round

AMBIANCE: Warm, no-nonsense, health conscious in natural setting

GENDER AND AGE RESTRICTIONS: Adults over 16; coed

DIET: Light and gourmet diet, water fasts, juice fasts

FACILITIES: Hot tub, swimming pool, exercise room, acres of woods for walking, cozy farmhouse

PROGRAM: Holistic health, yoga, meditation, self-awareness seminars

SPECIAL FEATURES: Swiss doctor available by consultation to prescribe an exercise/diet plan for your life

LOCAL ATTRACTIONS: Beautiful scenery

New Life Health Spa

What makes any spa special is an essential guiding spirit, someone who is part guru, part coach and part zealot who can convince, cajole or startle preoccupied guests into taking better care of themselves. Jimmy LeSage of New Life is the perfect prototype of this species. A dynamo with nonstop energy and unflagging enthusiasm, he hovers with earnest interest over every aspect of the New Life program, from cautioning guests against muscle strain in yoga class to exhorting them to read the label on any food product they are about to buy. His imprint can be seen in the deliciously prepared natural food meals (he is a former professional cook), the crisp sheets (he is also a former hotel manager) and in his concern for guests' psyches (he's been rolfed—a psychophysical body massage experience known to heal emotional troubles). This holistic health retreat is based on the philosophy that a healthy body creates a healthy mental attitude. Good nutrition based on whole foods, proper exercise and the development of a positive attitude are the basis of the program.

Jimmy LeSage has found a perfect setting for his retreat at the Liftline Lodge on Stratton Mountain in the Green Mountains of Vermont. Stratton Mountain, which is a popular ski area in the winter, is sprinkled with Bavarian-type chalets and lodges, of which the Liftline Lodge is a picturesque example. The spa program begins in April of each year and runs until mid-September.

The New Life Health Spa plan is designed to both fine tune and tone your whole system with early morning walks in the mountain air, yoga, slimnastics, aerobic dance and a variety of body movement activities. Interspersed are massages, facials, soaks in the wooden hot tub and time in the herb-infused sauna to help your body deal with the unaccustomed exercise without strain.

ACCOMMODATIONS

Rooms are located in the two-story Liftline Ski Lodge; each has two double beds, dressers and simple but pleasant country decor accented with lots of wood.

Each room has a private, modern bath with shower, and a telephone.

FACILITIES

The lodge is of charming alpine design. Boxes of geraniums and wood trim grace a huge front porch, which wraps around the lodge.

You enter a lounge filled with comfortable soft furniture. Downstairs are the massage rooms, California hot tub and sauna. The dining room is a small but cheerful room on the second floor, where tea and decaffeinated coffee are available all day and evening. The main exercise gym, equipped with gymnastic equipment, is located downstairs.

The second exercise room is a few yards away in another building near the small but pleasant outdoor swimming pool.

PROGRAM

Guests arrive Sunday evening and get acquainted by playing a "toss the glove" name game in the lounge with Jimmy. The group is usually fifteen to twenty guests so that you are soon familiar with everyone by name. The daily schedule is passed out, and guests are reminded to fill out the health questionnaire they received on arrival, which is designed to make them more aware of their own health habits and personal goals rather than for any evaluation purposes.

Wake-up is at 7:30 A.M. so that the brisk walk can begin at

7:50. This twenty-minute hike is taken along maple- and pine-shaded back roads up and down rolling hills in the cool, quiet morning.

After breakfast, the first class of the day begins, yoga.

Jimmy LeSage is a devotee of Sivananda yoga, and believes in starting and ending each day's exercise schedule with yogic movements. He thinks bodies need the gentle stretch of yoga postures to prepare muscles for the day ahead, and that in the afternoon yoga promotes relaxation and helps with fatigue.

Yoga neophytes shouldn't feel intimidated, because Jimmy starts from the beginning with simple postures, but yoga aficionados will not be bored either, since he moves along at a fair clip, introducing a number of new postures at each session. At the end of the week, guests will have completed a basic course in yoga.

After yoga, you're ready for slimnastics, a rigorous but friendly workout led by an energetic mother-daughter team of gymnasts. There is a definite advantage to having two instructors per class as Nina and Garet Holmes demonstrate.

One of these pert ladies leads the exercise at the front of the room while the other "floats" among the group, repositioning a leg here or a back alignment there. The exercises are basically stretching and dynamic body movements. Body conditioning is stressed through the use of light weights, vertical bars, and ropes, in order to build muscle tone and flexibility.

Both yoga and slimnastics are given twice each morning so that you can concentrate on one or the other if you choose. From either class you can move on to the more strenuous exercise sessions involving aerobic dance. The purpose is to get your heart rate up for a sustained period followed by a cool-down and relaxation exercises.

After lunch, Jimmy leads a vigorous walk to ward off any ideas of nap taking.

The program is arranged so that strenuous exercise is done in the morning. This leaves the afternoon free for "major activity," which translates into time for tennis—the John Newcombe Tennis Center is a short walk—horseback riding, swimming, or taking a planned hike with Jimmy to a hidden waterfall. If you have your own transportation and have something less vigorous in mind, you can hop into a car and take the short trip to the picturesque town of Manchester, which is a quintessential New England village complete with interesting shops.

Every Wednesday Jimmy arranges a trip to a local country health food store where he strides up and down the aisles with his charges, pointing out sugar and additives on labels. He is not a purist or a nut, but he feels people should know what they're buying and makes the point that even in a health food store not everything is healthful. He recommends raw whole foods and makes suggestions for creative and tasty changes in your diet using these foods at home.

The afternoons are also a time to fit in the health treatments such as a massage or an herbal facial.

At 4:15 a relaxing stretch or yoga class is offered. The exercise schedule is generally quite flexible, so check the daily program passed out at breakfast to keep updated.

The day ends with a 5:30-to-6:30 period set aside for visits to the hot tub or sauna to soothe any kinks your muscles may have developed during the day.

Every evening after dinner there is a program on some aspect of the healthy life as Jimmy LeSage and his staff see it. The first evening the New Life philosophy is explained, the program for the week is discussed and LeSage answers questions on the diet and exercise plan. Other evening programs include a beauty talk on makeup, skin care and accessories; a nutrition lecture by Jimmy on the modified Pritikin diet used at the spa; a film and discussion on rolfing; and a lecture on stress and how to deal with it when you return to the "real world."

The staff are all young and enthusiastic devotees of the New Life program, and they rotate jobs from food shopping to serving meals to leading walks. A good index of how mentally healthy a spa is for guests is the nature of relationships among staff who work together. Here, the feeling is of energized harmony; the staff functions as a family, with common goals and interests. Any question or problem from a guest gets prompt and concerned attention.

FOOD AND DIET

As you might expect from a former professional cook, Jimmy LeSage knows food. While he believes everyone should enjoy what he eats, he cautions followers against the standard American diet, which, according to the American Heart Association, contains 40 percent fat. He has developed his diet philosophy around a modification of the Pritikin diet, which is a low-fat, high-complex-carbohydrate plan with lots of fruits and vegetables. Although he feels that both the average American diet and Pritikin's program are extreme, he thinks that one can find a middle ground, somewhere between the two, tailored to individual needs. All natural, low-sodium foods and chicken, fish, and vegetables are stressed.

Breakfast could be papaya juice and whole-wheat French toast, cantaloupe with blueberry muffin or boysenberry juice and assorted cereals and blueberries.

Lunch is usually the simplest meal of the day: assorted fruit with cottage cheese, chicken curry salad, a pita bread sandwich stuffed with a spicy tofu mixture or a chef's salad.

Dinner, which is always quite welcome (partly because it isn't served until 7:00 P.M.!) is the most creative meal of the day. Take, for example, the choice of taboulie and cold cherry soup for an appetizer, veal cacciatore or lentil loaf for a main dish and palatschinkin (a rich-tasting pastry) or tropical fruit for dessert. At breakfast you choose a dinner menu, so you never have to eat something you can't stand or go hungry. If either dinner option is not appealing or if you are on a special diet, the staff will prepare something you can eat. It's best to let them know your special dietary needs when you make your reservation. The complete day's meals, including a fruit served in the afternoon, make up only 600 to 800 calories. Vitamin supplements are provided twice a day to replace potassium and calcium the body loses during exercise. That's not all the body loses; most guests register about a five-pound weight loss for the week.

Before you leave you will receive a complete list of recipes, a cooking demonstration and a take-home diet plan.

HEALTH AND BEAUTY SERVICES

The program includes two massages per week for each guest. Natural massage oils such as lemon or almond oil are used. Technique is a combination of Swedish strokes and delicate Japanese acupressure. Facials are also offered, in which steam from herb-infused water and a variety of natural preparations such as honey or lemon are used, depending on your skin type.

OTHER PLEASURES

Hiking in these beautiful mountains will take your breath away; the staff will give you maps and suggestions of where to hike and occasionally will come along.

The John Newcombe Tennis Center offers clinics for all levels of tennis player as well as time on its courts for a small fee. For golfers, the Stratton Mountain Country Club offers spectacular views and some interesting challenges.

Stratton Lake nearby is a good place for a day sail; rentals are available.

Stratton Mountain, although not as busy socially in the summer as it is during ski season, nevertheless offers good jazz, rock and country music some evenings in the lounges of several of the lodges, a short walk from the Liftline Lodge. It's not unusual for LeSage to organize guests for an evening at the local disco or summer theater.

WHAT TO BRING

Sturdy well-broken-in hiking shoes are a must, as well as jogging shoes.

Leotards and tights for women or loose shorts and T-shirts for men are needed for exercise, and bring a bathing suit or two for swimming and pool exercise.

Almost any time of year mornings and evenings are cool, so bring warm-up suits, sweaters and a jacket plus warm pants for hiking. For dinner, pants and shirts or sweaters are fine. Men wear pants and shirts or sweaters for meals also. It's a good idea to bring rain gear just in case. A blanket or mat or large towel is handy to have for yoga, and if you plan to golf or play tennis and prefer your own equipment to rentals, bring it along.

HOW TO GET THERE

Stratton Mountain is approximately four hours from New York City (via Routes 91 and 30) and three hours from Boston (via Routes 88, 9 and 30) by car. You can also take a Greyhound bus from the New York City Port Authority terminal to Manchester, then ask to be picked up there by a staffer and driven to Liftline Lodge (there is a small fee for this service). You can also fly into Rutland, rent a car and drive to Stratton; it is considered too far for staff pick-up. The two flights a day between Rutland and New York City (La Guardia) are not necessarily at convenient times, however, so plan ahead.

If skiing is your idea of exercise, write and ask for a brochure on special ski fitness weeks held in January and February.

These combine a moderate diet (1,000 calories); conditioning exercises and sauna; and hot tub and massage treatments.

SUMMARY

This is a well-planned, no-nonsense approach to good mental and physical fitness. In the seven days of the New Life program you will see real improvement in how you look and feel. There are no gimmicks here, just sound nutrition and a well-balanced exercise program. The low fee makes it one of spadoms best bargains, a fact not lost on several guests who stay two to three weeks for the price of a single week at a more expensive spa resort.

FACT SUMMARY

NAME: New Life Health Spa

MAILING ADDRESS: Summer—Liftline Lodge, Stratton Mountain, VT 05155; winter—E & M Associates, 667 Madison Ave., NY 10021

TELEPHONE: Summer—(802) 297-2600, winter—(212) 755-7220; toll-free (800) 223-9832

TRANSPORTATION: Spa picks up guests in Manchester

ACCOMMODATIONS: Lodge rooms in chalet hotel

FEE: 1 week—single, $555; double, $525 per person

MAXIMUM NUMBER OF GUESTS: 25

MAXIMUM NUMBER OF STAFF: 12

SEASON: Late April to mid-September

AMBIANCE: Casual, ski resort turns into summer health retreat

GENDER AND AGE RESTRICTIONS: Men and women over 16

DIET: Modified Pritikin—high in carbohydrates, low in fat, protein and salt; choice of vegetarian, can include chicken and fish; 600 to 800 calories

FACILITIES: Gym, hot tub, swimming pool, saunas, tennis center, 18-hole golf course, massage room, some beauty services, horseback riding, hiking

PROGRAM: Individually planned program with reeducation in health, nutrition and physical activity; body-mind awareness; classes in yoga, slimnastics, aerobics, body conditioning

SPECIAL FEATURES: Evening lectures on nutrition, meditation, rolfing

LOCAL ATTRACTIONS: Sailing on Stratton Lake, town of Manchester

NORTHERN PINES

The squirrels, chipmunks and deer of Raymond, Maine, may be among the healthiest animals in the northeastern United States. Until recently these forest folk made periodic visits to sample the flat beds of sprouts grown on wooden shelves outside the kitchen of Northern Pines health retreat. The staff of this unique summer resort had to develop a hard heart and move the half-dozen varieties of sprouts to the screened porch of the main lodge to protect one of the primary staples of the Northern Pines diet.

Situated on a fifty-acre pine-covered hillside that slopes to a sparkling three-mile lake, the massive two-level lodge melts into the pine, spruce and oak forest that surrounds it. "Simple," "back-to-basics," "rustic," these words all describe Northern Pines, from the bumpy unpaved dirt road that serves as a connection to the outside world, to the tiny, quiet log cabins sans plumbing and electricity.

Originally built in the thirties as a vacation camp for single business and college women, the self-help health retreat created by its owners Pat and Marlee Coughland and directed under the careful guidance of massage therapist and holistic health student, Kenneth Cadigan, seems to flourish in its new role.

Viewed by its founders as a "reeducation retreat" with emphasis on diet, massage, self-help and fasting, Northern Pines follows the philosophy and nutritional practices of Paavo Airola, a world-renowned naturopathic doctor and nutritionist. A physician closer to home, Dr. Margaret Millard, a holistic practitioner and herbalist, acts as a consultant to the six-person staff.

The retreat has a private half-mile waterfront on Crescent Lake with a cream-colored sandy beach. There is an antique wooden pier for sunning and boating, plus an equally ancient deep-water diving platform for long, quiet swims in the quartz-clear water. Tiny pine-dotted coves and inlets around the lake boast numerous private homes and summer cottages.

There is nothing elitist about Northern Pines. Its summer camp atmosphere and its attentive, warm staff are a tonic for the guest who is looking for a real no-frills retreat. There is a feeling of pioneering here, so be prepared for the rugged setting that awaits you. You'll be required to wash your own towels and sheets and to maintain your own room and communal bath.

Guests at the spa tend to be plain, down-to-earth folk. No yoga experts or vegetarian zealots here. A recent week combined three attractive thirtyish American Airlines flight attendants, an author, a teacher, a New York model and a slightly overweight, preppie executive. All acknowledged that it took them two or three days to adjust to the dramatic change of diet and philosophy advocated by Northern Pines. But what followed was a time of almost euphoric peace in this caring atmosphere free of pretensions and competition. Leave your Adidas and velour warm-ups at home along with your ego.

ACCOMMODATIONS

Northern Pines houses twenty-five guests at a time in two types of lodging. Very rustic log cottages, many cantilevered on stilts near the water, sleep two or three on thin-mattressed cots. Screened glassless windows and the absence of electricity, heat or plumbing takes some getting used to for the average guest, but the silence, fresh air and feeling of freedom make up for the lack of modern conveniences. Two of the six cabins, Fireside and Deep Woods, have double beds and quaint stone fireplaces. The communal bathroom/shower for the log cabins is less than fifty feet up the hill and through the woods to the main lodge. It is equpped with electric outlets, hot water, mirrors and shelves for cosmetics.

Hillside, a pineboard two-story structure, is the newest guest quarters, equipped with modern bathrooms and electricity for the less hardy souls. Built around a central living room with a tiny wood stove, Hillside has a spacious open-air deck and an appealing view. The four guest rooms in this building are furnished in plain country furniture found at farm auctions. The emphasis is definitely on simplicity. Large stone crocks full of wild flowers are a nice touch. However, some guests voiced a quiet wish that the staff would do less flower picking and more bathroom cleaning.

No television, radios or phones are in evidence at Northern Pines. An elaborate stereo system and a wide range of contemporary and classical music is available in the main lodge. One pay phone for outgoing calls is located on a porch of the lower level of the lodge. Incoming calls are a little tricky; the pay phone rings, but since it is not in a central location, it sometimes goes unanswered.

FACILITIES

The view of the lake from the generous front porch of the sixty-foot-long lodge is spectacular and is interrupted only by an occasional towering spruce or hemlock. The lodge, divided by a mammoth stone fireplace open on two sides, serves as the social core of this natural health center. The central dining room with adjoining kitchen is flanked by a room of equal dimension that serves as a library, meditation room and lecture area for evening classes. The lodge is built into a hill and the lower floor houses several guest rooms (used primarily in the early and late summer when the nights are nippy), some staff quarters and a communal bathroom.

Homey touches are an aged upright piano for community sings and a handcrafted cradle suspended from the ceiling timbers that is filled with antique lace pillows.

The wooden hot tub adjacent to the lodge is located on a tiny rise overlooking the spring-fed Crescent Lake, and is used primarily at night, with guests and staff alternating between the 105-degree water of the redwood tub and the cool lake. (Bathing suits are optional and are worn or not by general consensus of guests.)

There are several canoes and a small sailboat made available to guests for exploring the lake. A mammoth white hammock strung between two giant oaks near the shore actually sways out over the sandy-bottomed lake when set in motion.

There are many tranquil and colorful nature trails on which joggers, bikers and hikers sight deer, rabbits and an occasional moose in one of the flowering meadows.

An extensive health-oriented library provides books, pamphlets and tapes that can be signed out and taken to an old oak rocker on the sunny screened porch, or to giant wooden lawn furniture on an outdoor deck.

PROGRAM

If you like informality, Northern Pines will definitely appeal to you. The personal noncompetitive program is geared to the individual needs of each guest with a schedule that is revised daily. You will register with the help of a staff member who will then get you settled in your room, introduce you to other guests and take you on a tour of the facilities.

If you haven't completed the health questionnaire that was mailed to you, you can do that after settling in; you will also be given several pages of information to read on running, warm-up exercises, other health-oriented topics and the Northern Pines diet.

The only "formality" at Northern Pines is the lovely tradition of grace before each meal, with songs and thoughtful psalms or quotes chosen by guests and staff. This "grace" is usually secular, as are the posters and clippings reflecting health and love which adorn the walls of the lodge.

Morning at Northern Pines begins at 7:20 with the ringing of a giant triangle. Thirty minutes later guests gather in a clearing behind the kitchen for warm-up exercises, then an hour's walk or jog through the piney forests, followed by a half-hour cooldown in the lake or a swing in the hammock. Breakfast follows (around 9:00).

After breakfast there is usually a lecture on natural health. From this point in the day you are on your own. You can read, swim, sit in the hot tub, hike or have a massage or special treatment by prearrangement (see Health and Beauty Services).

Unlike most other spas, Northern Pines does not have a structured program per se. The morning hike and a 4:30 yoga class are the only constants during the day.

A 6:00 P.M. dinner is followed by evening programs that change daily. Focusing on health, nutrition or skin care, the organized discussion usually leads to informal chats by the fire, group singing or an impromptu evening swim, followed by a quiet, starlit walk to bed.

Since the number of guests is kept small, staff is always available for private consultation should a guest have a question on fasting or one of the health and beauty treatments such as polarity therapy, reflexology or any aspect of the Northern Pines philosophy. An herbalist comes once a week for herb-identification walks and a lecture on how to incorporate various herbs into your life.

Books on all of these subjects and more are available in the library; ask a staff member to recommend one if a topic especially interests you.

With an emphasis on blending the benefits of conventional medicines, Oriental medicine, folk remedies, exercise and nutrition, Northern Pines teaches a person how to take responsibility for his or her own health through preventive actions. Not geared to health extremists, the program attempts to provide the average person with the means to improve his or her health by example, diet reeducation and regular exercise programs. Stress-reduction techniques are also emphasized, such as deep body tissue massage, yoga and meditation.

The meal plan helps guests eliminate salt, white sugar, white flour, caffeine, red meat and preservatives from their diet. The staff suggests that guests alternate between active exercises, such as jogging, and more relaxing pursuits like yoga, for best results.

FOOD AND DIET

The diet here is based on a regimen developed by Paavo Airola, which combines seeds, nuts and grains, vegetables and fruits, complemented with milk, cold press vegetable oils and what are termed "special protection foods" such as brewer's yeast, kelp and wheat germ.

The Airola diet dictates that (1) excessive use of protein is to be avoided, (2) liquids are not to be taken during meals or for one hour afterward and (3) raw fruits and raw vegetables are not eaten at the same meal. Therefore, meals are vegetarian and emphasize raw foods, with sprouts and juices making up a total of 80 percent of the daily diet.

Fasting is encouraged at Northern Pines but is by no means mandatory. Liquid fasts, with fruit and vegetable juices along with spring water, and the recommended utilization of colonics are considered an excellent way to purify and rejuvenate the body.

Before fasting at Northern Pines, a participant must eat a totally raw diet for seventy-two hours. One recent guest began the raw food regimen before she arrived to assist the fasting process. She lost seventeen pounds in less than ten days.

The food is of good quality, but there's not much variety. Breakfast for nonfasters is usually a beautifully prepared fresh fruit salad in the warm weather, or if the thermometer drops, hot whole-grain cereals. The fruit salads are accompanied by a separate sauce of pureed fruits with grated coconut and apricot kernels for added crunch.

Lunch is always a giant salad of sprouts or vegetables with a variety of dressings. Complementing the salad is sometimes a seed loaf of sesame and sunflower pâté or perhaps a flavorful Middle Eastern eggplant dish served with whole-wheat pita.

The final meal of the day might be a West African stew made primarily of cooked pureed yams with mushrooms, green pepper and broccoli. The stew sometimes makes a return performance served with small unpeeled boiled potatoes with a smidgen of unsalted butter. Apparently even health resorts have leftovers!

At Northern Pines, guests are encouraged to participate in meal preparation. One evening a week a food preparation class is held in the kitchen.

In keeping with the Airola food plan, liquids are not permitted with meals, and for anyone who enjoys water, milk or a hot beverage with meals, the lack of one takes some adjustment. There are no drinking glasses in guest rooms or bathrooms and getting an (unauthorized) drink of the pure unchlorinated mineral water that flows from the tap is a little frustrating. Although various herb teas such as laurel grass, hibiscus and rose hips are present in the kitchen, the process of access to them is unclear. The diet recommends fresh-squeezed juices periodically, but they were also hard to get for the staff seemed nonchalant about providing them.

HEALTH AND BEAUTY SERVICES

A very limited number of beauty services are offered at Northern Pines. If you are looking for pampering and beauty treatments, this is not the place to be. All Northern Pines "beauty services" are viewed as healing and prevention arts. There is no schedule as such for these treatments. A chart is posted in the dining room daily describing the staff's various offerings and each guest makes arrangements for that day or evening by scheduling directly with the appropriate staff person. These beauty and health services are all extra, with charges averaging $10 per half hour.

Skin care and facial demonstrations are held once every week in the common room of the main lodge. At least one member of the staff provides facials using natural ingredients such as avocado and French clay. Instruction on dry brushing, a technique for cleansing and stimulating body skin, is also an evening option. For shiny hair be sure to take a hair treatment that combines hot oil application and scalp massage. Other treatments include integrative massage in which Swedish and Japanese techniques are offered, along with deep muscle work.

Reflexology, a massage system that charts and applies manual pressure to parts of the feet and hands that correspond to specific body parts, is popular. Polarity, a form of body therapy that is similar to massage but uses pressure on meridian or pressure points to release "energy blocks" in the body and restore balance, is also popular.

Another interesting treatment is iridology: a practitioner looks into your eyes and notes the patterns and color of the iris. These observations are then interpreted, and you are given a rundown on the state of your general health, what effect your diet is having on your health and the condition of your colon. One young woman who had this done was told that although her eyes appeared hazel they really were naturally blue, but that her diet high in refined flours and sugars had affected her colon in an unhealthy way, which was reflected in her iris color. This sounded strange to many guests, but everyone listened politely then went off for a healthy soak in the hot tub.

OTHER PLEASURES

For fishermen, Northern Pines offers endless promise. Crescent Lake and the many small freshwater lakes, like Sebago Lake, abound in bass and white perch. Numerous tiny streams that wind through the hills are good for trout fishing. There is also good salmon and smelt fishing within driving distance.

The Portland waterfront offers ocean fishing less than forty-five minutes from Northern Pines. The old port has several sightseeing cruises, is a center for aspiring sailors and is the site of Gulf of Maine Aquarium.

Everyone eats fresh Maine lobster at least once during a visit to this part of the country. Northern Pines's guests are no exception and the staff is well aware that there are numerous excellent lobster restaurants nearby. Some are rather lavish, while others are very temporary, built of striped canvas, wood frames and screening and erected only for the season. The majority are open "early spring till late fall."

All of Maine is famous for barn sales, yard sales and antique auctions. The prices are terrific and the selection is amazing. If you're driving, limit your luggage and save room in the car for a treasure or two. If used merchandise is not for you, the many factory outlets from various shoe and clothing manufacturers located in Maine offer some great bargains.

There is a summer theater within walking distance of the resort. A canoe ride down the Teriney River at dusk can result in a glimpse of deer and moose grazing among the delicate water flowers while lazy turtles snap at brilliantly colored dragonflies.

WHAT TO BRING

Don't bring anything that would be ruined by a healthy application of pine sap or grass stain. You'll want to be outside walking through the woods, sitting on pine needles under a gracious spruce or flopped comfortably in the elderly wooden lawn chairs. Loose, nonrestricting clothing is important to your comfort.

Dig out those old sweat shirts from college and that favorite heavy sweater with the worn elbows; even the paint-splattered jeans are all perfect for Northern Pines. Dark colors are best as they won't show the dirt.

Jogging T-shirts and shorts and a minimum of two bathing suits are important. Rubber-soled shoes are also a good idea plus plenty of socks. Don't forget a poncho or waterproof windbreaker for rainy days.

Several towels and a flashlight are essential. No towels are provided and you will need them continuously for the lake, the hot tub and for bathroom walks.

Ask for the suggested clothing and supplies list furnished by Northern Pines. If your stay is longer than three days, bring enough clothing to last because the laundry facilities are sparse.

Dark green cotton T-shirts with a nifty Northern Pines logo

are available along with books exploring fasting, iridology and nutrition. Meditation tapes, healing salves, various vitamins and supplements and sprout bags are also for sale.

HOW TO GET THERE

Bus, plane or auto will all get you to Northern Pines. Automobile travel is the most direct and the staff will send you a hand-drawn map with very specific folksy direction tips.

If you are flying into Portland, Maine, you can be picked up by the Northern Pines van, which is scheduled twice daily on Sunday for $10 or at off times of the day for slightly more.

Van pick-ups are also available from the bus station from Grey, Maine.

Flying into Boston and renting a car to drive the remaining 125 miles is more than worth the time invested. The scenic ride past quaint villages, fishing ports and the coast help prepare one's mind for the serenity of Northern Pines.

SUMMARY

Northern Pines is a great place for you if you are adventurous, flexible, appreciate the natural life and have a good sense of humor. It is the most rustic spa we visited, but the warm, unpretentious staff and the beautiful surroundings certainly have their charms. If you can't get in touch with your innermost self here, you're just not trying.

FACT SUMMARY

NAME: Northern Pines

MAILING ADDRESS: P.O. Box 279-P, Route 85, Raymond, ME 04071

TELEPHONE: (207) 665-7624

TRANSPORTATION: Northern Pines van will pick up at Portland airport or Grey bus station for a fee

ACCOMMODATIONS: Very rustic log cabins with communal bath facilities and no electricity; two modern guest rooms with electricity and shared bathrooms

FEE: 1 week—$315, per person shared log cabin accommodations; $350 per person shared modern lodge accommodations

MAXIMUM NUMBER OF GUESTS: 25

MAXIMUM NUMBER OF STAFF: 10

SEASON: May through September

AMBIANCE: Summer camp atmosphere, very serene and stress-free

GENDER AND AGE RESTRICTIONS: None

DIET: Restrictive vegetarian meals with emphasis on raw fruit, raw vegetables and natural whole food based on Paavo Airola diet, supervised fasting

FACILITIES: Beach and dock facilities, boating, sailing and canoeing; hot tub; Samadhi isolation tank (equipment in which the body is suspended in an enclosed tank for total relaxation); hiking trails

PROGRAM: Very permissive with much self-direction; educational retreat for weight loss or healthful stress-free vacation, reflexology, polarity therapy

SPECIAL FEATURES: Lakeside setting on 50 acres of pine forest

LOCAL ATTRACTIONS: Ocean fishing, fresh lobster restaurants, Portland Old Port, Gulf of Maine Aquarium, factory outlets for shopping

Other Spas

Holliday's
Nantucket House

This is a small homey retreat with a sound nutritional program. An exercise program emphasizes walking the picturesque streets of Nantucket. Behavior modification is emphasized.

FACT SUMMARY

MAILING ADDRESS: 2 East York Street, P. O. Box 165, Nantucket, MA 02554

TELEPHONE: (617) 228-9450

TRAVEL DIRECTIONS: Fly into Nantucket, or drive to Hyannis and take ferry to Nantucket

TRANSPORTATION: Spa staff will pick up at airport or ferry by prearrangement

ACCOMMODATIONS: 2 double rooms, 1 cottage for two

FEE: 1 week—single, $375; double, $300 per person (includes meals, instruction and lodging)

MAXIMUM NUMBER OF GUESTS: 6

MAXIMUM NUMBER OF STAFF: 3

SEASON: May to October

AMBIANCE: Small, intimate house; caters to individual needs

GENDER AND AGE RESTRICTIONS: None

DIET: Low calorie, poultry, fish, fruits and vegetables, diet individually planned

FACILITIES: Exercise area for aerobic dance class, tennis courts nearby, bicycles

PROGRAM: Behavior modification approach to extra-eating habits

SPECIAL FEATURES: Nature tours, bicycle tours of island

LOCAL ATTRACTIONS: Shops, museums, colonial architecture and cobblestone streets in Nantucket, which was an eighteenth-century whaling center; beach, horseback riding, fishing and tennis nearby; Nantucket has band concerts, theater

Englewood Cliffs Spa

Englewood Cliffs Spa of Englewood Cliffs, New Jersey, is a short drive from New York City. It provides an informal medically owned and operated health and weight-reduction center for a major Eastern market. For women only, Englewood Cliffs offers many personalized services including nutritional counseling, fitness guidance and evaluation and a wide variety of exercise classes and beauty services.

FACT SUMMARY

MAILING ADDRESS: 619 Palisade Avenue, Englewood Cliffs, NJ 07632

TELEPHONE: (201) 568-5502

TRAVEL DIRECTIONS: At George Washington Bridge, connect to Palisades Parkway north, first exit, 1, is Palisades; go through light; spa is 2 blocks beyond light on right.

TRANSPORTATION: Limo service by spa with prearrangement

ACCOMMODATIONS: Homey-style rooms in main building or dorm-style in adjoining building

FEE: Private, $95 to $98 per day; dormitory, $48 to $55 per day; 1 week (7 nights)—private, $585; dormitory, $310

MAXIMUM NUMBER OF GUESTS: 90

MAXIMUM NUMBER OF STAFF: 40

SEASON: Year-round

AMBIANCE: Self-contained medically controlled facility, very informal

GENDER AND AGE RESTRICTIONS: Women only, age 20 to 70

DIET: Balanced low-calorie meals—700 to 1,000 calories per day

FACILITIES: Skin care center, beauty salon, solarium, outdoor pool, exercise room, dining room

PROGRAM: Personalized exercise plan for stay and at home, behavior modification daily lectures, nutritional consultations

SPECIAL FEATURES: Medical supervision

LOCAL ATTRACTIONS: 20 minutes from midtown Manhattan

Turnwood
Organic Gardens

Turnwood Organic Gardens is located in a rural valley of the Catskill Forest Preserve in New York State. It takes a holistic view toward health and also practices chemical-free farming. The Turnwood program basically consists of fasting and instruction on natural hygiene principles. Smoking, alcoholic beverages and drugs are not permitted. They suggest that you consult your physician prior to participation in the program if you are under treatment or on medication. A one-week minimum stay is required. Space limitations require reservations prior to registering for the program.

FACT SUMMARY

MAILING ADDRESS: Star Route, Livingston Manor, NY 12758

TELEPHONE: (914) 439-5702

TRAVEL DIRECTIONS: Catskill Forest Preserve 2½ hours northwest of New York City, Exit 96 off route 17

TRANSPORTATION: Shortline bus transportation from New York City's Port Authority terminal to Livingston Manor, then cab to Turnwood

ACCOMMODATIONS: The 130-year-old renovated farmhouse has rooms with two or three beds, limited private rooms, no private bathrooms

FEE: $225 (water fast) to $266 (juice fast) per week

MAXIMUM NUMBER OF GUESTS: 15

MAXIMUM NUMBER OF STAFF: 5

SEASON: May to November

AMBIANCE: Peaceful, natural, homelike, individual attention

GENDER AND AGE RESTRICTIONS: None

DIET: Choice of 1 regimen—pure vegetable juice fast, pure fruit juice fast, or water fast, all fasts are broken 2 or 3 days before leaving; no fish, meat or eggs

FACILITIES: Nearby lake swimming, boating, horseback riding, hiking and sunbathing

PROGRAM: Based on natural hygiene principles with individual instruction and supervision; classes are offered in hatha-yoga and/or exercise; lectures on health-related topics are also given; massages and colonics available

SPECIAL FEATURES: Formal meditation hall with instruction and daily practice, reading and record library

LOCAL ATTRACTIONS: Zen monastery in area, Little Pond State Park, great antiquing, craft centers in area

Seton Inn Spa

Seton Inn Spa is on ten acres of land in a stand of giant pine trees in Lakewood, New Jersey. The spa is directed toward a program of weight control through fasting, physical rehabilitation and relaxation. A low-calorie menu is offered. Exercise, daily hikes, group sessions, workshops and individual consultation with a certified psychotherapist are also offered.

FACT SUMMARY

MAILING ADDRESS: 510 Hope Road, Lakewood, NJ 08701

TELEPHONE: (212) 962-4360 or (201) 363-7733

TRANSPORTATION: Bus from Port Authority terminal in Manhattan every half hour to Lakewood; bus from Philadelphia Union bus terminal; bus or limo from Newark airport

ACCOMMODATIONS: Double occupancy, single occupancy (if available)

FEE: Double with private bath, $294 per person, per week; double, near bath, $274 per person, per week; for those on a 7-day fasting program there is a reward of a 10 percent discount if you make it to 5 days

MAXIMUM NUMBER OF GUESTS: 40

MAXIMUM NUMBER OF STAFF: 25

SEASON: Year-round

AMBIANCE: Informal, casual, natural setting

GENDER AND AGE RESTRICTIONS: None

DIET: High protein, low calorie, low carbohydrate, low fat, no salt or sugar, not a vegetable-type diet; total fasting programs available; specially designed diets also available

FACILITIES: Sauna, whirlpool, bicycling (bicycle provided), outdoor pool, golf and tennis facilities nearby, solarium

PROGRAM: Weight control, physical rehabilitation, relaxation, exercise classes

SPECIAL FEATURES: Group and personal counseling

LOCAL ATTRACTIONS: Rockefeller estate, antique shops, Gould estate, 20 minutes from ocean

Pawling Health Manor

Pawling Health Manor is a year-round, natural health retreat located one hundred miles north of New York City. The environment is very informal and geared for fasting and health reeducation, featuring exercise, natural food, fresh air and sunshine, daily lectures and food demonstrations. The minimum stay is one week.

FACT SUMMARY

MAILING ADDRESS: P.O. Box 401, Hyde Park, NY 12538

TELEPHONE: (914) 889-4141

TRAVEL DIRECTIONS: Take New York Thruway and get off at Exit 18, proceed to Mid-Hudson Bridge, follow signs reading Hyde Park, Route 9N; fly to Kennedy or La Guardia and take Hudson Valley Airporter limo

ACCOMMODATIONS: Restored Georgian mansion plus shared lodging in two other buildings

FEE: 1 week—single, $485; double, $418 per person

MAXIMUM NUMBER OF GUESTS: 62

MAXIMUM NUMBER OF STAFF: 30

SEASON: Year-round

AMBIANCE: No-frills weight-reducing retreat

GENDER AND AGE RESTRICTIONS: Adults over 16; coed

DIET: 4-day water fast is used when possible; fresh fruits and vegetables break the fast; low-calorie vegetarian menu also

FACILITIES: Swimming pool, nature trails, solarium for nude sun-bathing, gym, massages and manicures available

PROGRAM: Daily lectures and food demonstrations designed to teach healthier eating habits and how to maintain weight loss at home; exercise not required

SPECIAL FEATURES: Supervised fasting

LOCAL ATTRACTIONS: Franklin D. Roosevelt home and library, Vanderbilt and Astor estates, Vassar and Bard colleges, antique shopping

HRH Body and Mind Center

HRH stands for health, relaxation and hair. The concept behind HRH programs is that beauty is a reflection of a person's inner self. Programs are based on an overall outline of development of mind and body (relaxation for the inner self and health for the body). Along with the weekend programs, HRH also offers various one-day programs during the week. The Body and Mind Center is located in a nineteenth-century home in Pound Ridge, New York, remodeled to reflect the HRH concept by incorporating Far Eastern accents.

FACT SUMMARY

MAILING ADDRESS: Scotts Corner, Pound Ridge, NY 10576

TELEPHONE: (914) 764-8161

TRAVEL DIRECTIONS: Approximately 1 hour from New York City, along the Connecticut state line

TRANSPORTATION: HRH provides transportation to and from train station

ACCOMMODATIONS: Japanese-style sleeping accommodations (futons) on upper level of the HRH Center, partitioned by shoji screens

FEE: Fasting weekend (2 days and 2 nights) with 2 massages included, $250; Day of Total Beauty, $110 per person

MAXIMUM NUMBER OF GUESTS: 10

MAXIMUM NUMBER OF STAFF: 25

SEASON: Year-round

AMBIANCE: Relaxed, private, peaceful, nineteenth-century house; Far Eastern serenity

GENDER AND AGE RESTRICTIONS: Women only for weekend programs

DIET: Fasting weekend—distilled water or apple juice; fast is broken with a piece of fruit

FACILITIES: Whirlpool, sauna, steam rooms, massage, full-service beauty salon, nearby swimming

PROGRAM: Fasting weekend includes exercise and stress-reduction classes, discussion groups on nutrition and beauty, nature walks and use of facilities, plus 2 therapeutic massages

SPECIAL FEATURES: Nutritional counseling, hypnotherapy,

astroanalysis/numerology, shiatsu massage, reflexology; ornate Japanese gardens

LOCAL ATTRACTIONS: Cross-country skiing, Pound Ridge Indian reservation

Poco Lodge

Poco Lodge is a dieting and fasting resort located in the Pocono Mountains of Pennsylvania. Food at Poco Lodge is served only at specified times and is served and eaten only in the main building. (Anyone bringing food onto the premises is asked to leave.) An exercise program is also offered six days a week. There are various other activities such as lectures and discussions. Group trips to various points of interest in the Poconos area are also made available.

FACT SUMMARY

MAILING ADDRESS: P.O. Box 56R, Minisink Hills, PA 18341

TELEPHONE: (717) 424-2200

TRAVEL DIRECTIONS: 1¾ hours from the George Washington Bridge or the Lincoln Tunnel

TRANSPORTATION: Bus, train and limo service are available from New York City and Philadelphia

ACCOMMODATIONS: All rooms are arranged for double occupancy; however, limited single and triple arrangements are available with advance notice

FEE: Varies depending on occupancy and length of stay, there is a 2-night minimum stay policy; rates range from $65 per person for triple occupancy for 2 nights to $360 for single occupancy for 7 nights

MAXIMUM NUMBER OF GUESTS: 36

MAXIMUM NUMBER OF STAFF: 12

SEASON: Mid-April to Mid-October

AMBIANCE: Relaxed, friendly

GENDER AND AGE RESTRICTIONS: None; however, children not on a diet or on the fasting program can only eat off the lodge grounds

DIET: Foods for those on the dieting program include melons, cottage cheese, hard-boiled eggs, salad, fresh vegetable juice, orange juice, lemon juice, coffee, tea, and mineral water

FACILITIES: Swimming pool, tennis courts, badminton, volleyball

PROGRAM: An exercise program that includes yoga, isometrics and calisthenics is offered 6 days a week; formal and informal discussions are held on fasting and dieting, and guest speakers are also presented

SPECIAL FEATURES: Setting in Pocono Mountains

LOCAL ATTRACTIONS: Tocks Island National Recreation Area, Pocono International Raceway, reptile farm, summer stock theater

Green Mountain at Fox Run

Green Mountain at Fox Run is a weight-management community for women in the Green Mountains of Vermont. The program is presented in either four-, eight- or twelve-week sessions and consists of overall instruction in exercise and nutrition with a commitment to the long-term management of obesity.

FACT SUMMARY

MAILING ADDRESS: P. O. Box 164, Fox Lane, Ludlow, VT 05149

TELEPHONE: (802) 228-8885

TRAVEL DIRECTIONS: From New York City, go north on Route 95 to north 91, Exit 6 in Vermont (Route 103 north) into Ludlow; spa is 1½ miles beyond the town of Ludlow

TRANSPORTATION: Bus from New York, Boston and Montreal; spa pick-up and return on opening and closing days of sessions

ACCOMMODATIONS: Room in the lodge: 2 double beds; view of mountain

FEE: 4-week session—single, $2,750 or $2,650 for bilevel room; double, $2,500 per person; 4-person duplex, $2,350 per person

MAXIMUM NUMBER OF GUESTS: 60

MAXIMUM NUMBER OF STAFF: 25

SEASON: Year-round

AMBIANCE: No-nonsense program in beautiful surroundings

GENDER AND AGE RESTRICTIONS: Women between 18 and 65

DIET: 1,000 to 1,200 calories, well-balanced meals, with attention to low sodium, fat and cholesterol

FACILITIES: Swimming pool, exercise rooms, bicycles, hiking trails, tennis courts, skiing, skating

PROGRAM: Serious program of exercise and nutrition education

SPECIAL FEATURES: Small group interaction on obesity and quality lifestyle repatterning, incorporation of physical activity in lifestyle

LOCAL ATTRACTIONS: Mountain climbing, hiking trails, summer stock theater

Kleines Baden

Kleines Baden (meaning "little spa") is located in a secluded woods on the shores of Bomoseen Lake in Vermont. The program centers around fasting, exercise and the nutritional philosophy of Paavo Airola. Light diets consisting of natural foods are offered as an alternative to fasting. Smoking is not permitted at Kleines Baden.

FACT SUMMARY

MAILING ADDRESS: P. O. Box 90, Lake Bomoseen, VT 05732

TELEPHONE: (802) 468-5581

TRAVEL DIRECTIONS: Fly to Albany airport, take Route 87 to Exit

20, take 149 to Fort Ann to U.S. Route 4; cross Vermont border, take Exit 4 (left), 3 miles to the spa

TRANSPORTATION: Bus service to Rutland, Vermont, and from all points via Greyhound or Vermont Transit Lines, taxi service to hotel; spa will pick up guests by prearrangement

ACCOMMODATIONS: Deluxe—large motel rooms overlooking the golf course; country casual—smaller rooms located in the spa overlooking the lake; dorm style—bed roll in spa

FEE: Varies; 3 days—$60 to $180 per person, depending on program, accommodation and diet

MAXIMUM NUMBER OF GUESTS: 10 for each program

MAXIMUM NUMBER OF STAFF: 3

SEASON: Mid-May to mid-October

AMBIANCE: Country setting located directly on Bomoseen Lake

GENDER AND AGE RESTRICTIONS: Adults over 18; coed

DIET: Vegetarian menus, eggs and milk; juice fasts

FACILITIES: 9-hole golf course, sauna; private beach; large grounds

PROGRAM: Features a special juice fasting program; beginning and intermediate yoga; a vegetarian vacation—all including group discussions, exercise, sauna, etc.

SPECIAL FEATURES: Individual attention in all programs, will work with any guest who wishes to work out a lifetime eating plan tailored to his or her personal lifestyle

LOCAL ATTRACTIONS: Slate and marble quarries; lake tours; many small, quaint shops located in small towns around the area; scenic country roads

MEXICO

Featured Spas

Rancho La Puerta

Your first glimpse of Rancho La Puerta, coming over the hill on the highway, is of a native village set in a valley, surrounded on two sides by warm green-brown hills. Tiny brick and terracotta tile buildings stand amid waving silver gray eucalyptus and bright green olive trees.

"The Ranch," as it is known by its fans, was opened more than forty years ago by Edward Szekely, a European naturalist and philosopher, and his American bride of seventeen, Deborah.

This coed natural health retreat, located thirty-five miles south of San Diego, became the model for Deborah Szekely's superelegant Golden Door Spa seventy miles to the north in Escondido, California.

The gentle, natural setting encourages the do-it-yourself feeling that prevails. Everyone uses The Ranch in his or her own way—some to meet people, some to escape people, some for weight loss, some for toning and firming, some to get away to work quietly on a project, some to forget work ever existed; but *all* come so that they can rejoin the real world relaxed and reenergized.

The Ranch has a simple, noncontrived atmosphere. There is nothing faddish or complex in either the exercise program or the diet; and, as a result, it's simple to carry both plans home and fit them into your daily routine.

ACCOMMODATIONS

There is a wide range of accommodations available, ranging from the economy of the modest casitas, a bit spartan for some, to the rustic luxury of the larger haciendas, with living rooms, fireplaces and kitchenettes.

The beamed-ceiling cottages, surrounded by bricked walks,

flowers and olive tress, are always clean, private and cozy. All are furnished in Mexican furniture and rugs; each is unique.

The most modern accommodations are the newly constructed villas. They are large and airy, with two bedrooms, and they are furnished in pleasing modern furniture with Mexican crafts adding a decorative touch.

There are no televisions, radios or phones in the rooms. It is possible to place and receive phone calls at the registration office.

If you plan to go alone and wish to save money by sharing accommodations, the staff will try to arrange this for you.

FACILITIES

The Ranch encourages individuality. From accommodations to exercise classes to beauty services, the choice is yours. No one structures your day but you.

This is a vast place. The eighty-plus buildings are located on only a fraction of the entire 150 acres. The gyms, dining rooms, recreation center, exercise pavilions and beauty service areas are centrally located and are connected by a series of winding paths among manicured landscapes. The guest cottages are all a short walk from the public buildings, and even the most sedentary soul will log a few miles going to meals, the pools or massages.

Several outdoor exercise pavilions dot the landscape. These open-air ramadas have charming thatched roofs, thickly padded floors and a terrific view of The Ranch from any angle. In addition, there are several gyms for rainy days and early morning classes. The only problem with these is the full wall of mirrors that reflect every bulge in the clear morning light.

The Ranch offers two large swimming pools in the central complex, one heated and used primarily for water exercise classes, and another, unheated, for hardier souls. In addition there are a pool, whirlpool and sauna in the new villa area. A whirlpool jet-therapy pool is located next to the unheated pool and is wonderful for soothing overextended muscles.

A newly designed twenty-exercise station parcourse takes advantage of the inherent natural beauty and terrain of The Ranch; here you can swing, lift, bend and sit up, enjoying a different (and spectacular) view at every move. Incorporated in the parcourse is a running track, the center of which holds gnarled but growing and producing grapevines.

Six tennis courts, a putting green and volleyball and basket-ball courts complete the athletic offerings.

The Ranch is the place to bring all those best sellers you have never found time to read; however, if your luggage does not include written material, do not despair. The professor's library of more than 6,000 books is still intact and has been added to over the years. Any interest is reflected in this collection, from ancient history to witchcraft, from organic gardening to con-temporary poetry.

After dinner there is always an interesting selection of activi-ties, including speakers who present films, art and handicraft instruction, travelogues and lectures. Many of the speakers are best-selling authors. (On one visit Harold Bloomfield, coauthor of *How to Survive the Loss of a Love*, spoke.) You may have come to The Ranch to relax, but you may leave having learned how to quilt a vest, paint an American Indian pot or folk dance.

The number of men using the spa has steadily increased over the years. Some come with their wives, but there is an increas-ing number who come alone to diet, rest or recuperate. The Ranch has also just started couples' weeks. Check for special dates on these.

During the summer months and Christmas vacations, more families, including children, are in evidence (fourteen is the recommended minimum age). To go from hamburgers and television to papaya and yoga does not seem to stunt their growth.

PROGRAM

If you like doing things for yourself and hate regimentation, then The Ranch is the place for you. At registration, you'll be given a daily schedule that lists moderate and vigorous exer-cise classes, and you'll be left alone to decide your schedule.

This is not to suggest you can't have guidance if you want it. Hostesses, most of whom are former guests, are available at registration and throughout each day for direction and sugges-tions.

Every hour, there is a choice of at least two classes that are held outside, under shaded pavilions where the valley breezes cool even the most energetic participants.

You might begin with the early morning "moderate" hike, followed by limbering and stretching, then a jazz dance exer-cise class or a body awareness class. Jazzex, a vigorous dance routine session, or a supervised tour through the parcourse are usually offered before lunch.

At 2:00 P.M. another group of classes begins, including pool exercises, body conditioning, ballet-barre calisthenics or scientific stretch and posture. A favorite class, the last scheduled session of the day, is yoga.

The direction, speed and quality of each class depends entirely on the instructor; all are excellent and take their work seriously, but several are special favorites to frequent guests. Their approach to exercise is intelligent, enthusiastic and supportive. Each day the instructors rotate and seeking your favorite is difficult, since the assignments are not announced.

Other athletic choices are tennis lessons with a tennis pro, putting greens, lap swimming or weightlifting. Though not reflected in the daily schedule, they are available any time. Check with the desk.

FOOD AND DIET

The Rancho La Puerta diet has always been vegetarian; lacto-ovo to be specific. A lacto-ovo-vegetarian diet includes milk, milk products and eggs, supplemented with nuts, grains, seeds and beans for protein. Fish is served every three or four days. Breakfast and lunch are served buffet style and dinner is a more formal family-style arrangement.

Low in sodium and cholesterol, the menu includes plenty of fruits and vegetables, which add bulk to the diet and help reduce the hungry feeling experienced on many diets. One thousand calories per day is the target of guests on The Ranch diet.

Hot cereals, fruit, cottage cheese and scrambled eggs mixed with various vegetables are the usual breakfast fare. The famous Tecate Bread (not on the diet) is served toasted in the morning. If you like your food spicy, use their famous salsa, a mélange of fresh tomatoes, onions, serrano peppers and cilantro chopped to a lovely consistency that can be used on everything from cottage cheese to eggs. Lunch is usually a fruit or vegetable salad, and dinners feature meatless main dishes, such as lentil loaf.

The Virtue-Making Diet, a liquid fast, is offered once a week. Some guests (obviously lacking in virtue) have continually steered clear of the almond milk, gazpacho drink and thimbleful of sunflower seeds, but many swear by this twenty-four-hour fast and insist that it speeds the weight loss.

Those who can't endure another vegetarian meal can "go over the wall," by cab, to downtown Tecate, a small, charming border town. There, several restaurants will cater to Ranch guests with broiled chicken and salad, or waiters will turn their heads and supply guacamole, tacos or lobster.

HEALTH AND BEAUTY SERVICES

The elaborate newly constructed women's beauty treatment facility is an architectural delight. High windows, colorful Mexican glass and natural stone complement the stucco and heavy-beamed construction. Light streams in and contributes to a feeling of dignity and serenity as you go about having treatments that make both your skin and psyche content. The men's treatments are the same but offered in a more modest, older building. All services are provided by local Mexican women, many of whom have been with The Ranch for years.

The beauty treatments are all extra but inexpensive compared to other spas, running from $8 to $10 a treatment.

Massages, facials, scalp treatments and herbal wraps use natural oils and hypoallergenic Golden Door cosmetics. The beauty shop offers manicures, very thorough pedicures and all hair services. If you choose a scalp treatment, schedule a shampoo and set for the following day. The water pressure on The Ranch is not always the best, and to remove the oil takes some work. Pack a scarf to cover your oil-saturated head since staff members recommend that you keep the oil application on for at least one day for best results. It's worth the trouble. There are real benefits from the oiling, heat cap and scalp massage; it always seems to make the hair follicles leap to attention!

The herbal wrap is always a point of dispute among guests. You either love it or you hate it. Experiencing this European concept, guests recline on low beds and are wrapped, mummy style, in cotton sheets dipped in herb-infused hot water. You then lie quietly in this condition for twenty minutes. Those suffering from claustrophobia should ask to keep their arms outside the wrap.

Used as a diuretic, muscle relaxer and tension reducer, the herbal wrap also helps shed a layer of dry skin. The peace and relaxation that results from being totally warm, wet and quiet produces a real feeling of serenity, and those who can stand the confinement float out of the room after the treatment feeling like Cleopatra rising from a bed of lotus.

A massage after the herbal wrap feels terrific, especially if you are feeling any muscle soreness; you will then be ready for a nap by the pool.

Schedule your beauty services as soon as you arrive—before you eat or swim or unpack, or even glance at your room. The treatments fill up quickly (usually on the day of registration), and the earlier you register the better chance you have of getting the times you want for that massage or pedicure.

OTHER PLEASURES

Each trip to The Ranch reveals another dimension of this unique resort: a quiet conversation with a new friend, perhaps, while swinging in a Mexican hammock in the shade of a grape arbor, or a nap in the private elevated wooden structures designed for nude sunbathing.

In the summer months, at midday, a man appears, dispensing shaved ice covered with fresh fruit concentrates.

Another special pleasure is climbing the mountain trail just before dawn to watch the sun come up from a perfectly quiet peak.

WHAT TO BRING

The dress at The Ranch is quite informal, although this can mean anything from a plush Oscar de la Renta jogging suit to a pair of K mart jogging shorts and a T-shirt.

Leotards and tights are essential for all seasons, and you'll need a few terry-cloth warm-ups (jackets and pants) to wear over your leotards and tights for morning exercises. These can be shed as the day and your body warm up. Warm-ups or sweat shirt and pants combinations are worn at breakfast and lunch. Informal sportswear is fine for dinner and all evening activities.

In the warm months, some women slip a loose skirt over their leotards and tights for meals. The evenings can be somewhat cool and it's a good idea to pack a light sweater. Men wear T-shirts and shorts for all activities and warm-up trousers with T-shirts for meals.

Eastern friends sometimes have difficulty understanding

that Mexico really does have seasons. Seasons certainly prevail at The Ranch, open year-round, and though the changes are subtle, be prepared for cold mornings—not scraping ice off your windshield mornings, but the kind that will require hats and gloves with warm-up suits for early morning mountain hikes. Going to northwestern Mexico in December does not always mean white tennis shorts and halter tops. Heavy sweaters and socks are needed in the winter months.

Bathing suits and a terry coverup for trips to the whirlpool, saunas and even beauty services is a nice idea. During the summer months, shorts are a necessity.

Anything that has been forgotten (from sunglasses to running shorts) can usually be found in the Mexican shop, called Maya, on The Ranch grounds.

HOW TO GET THERE

It is best to take a plane to San Diego, where The Ranch's van will pick you up by prearrangement. It is wise to get a visa or have an active passport, in case you are checked on your return to the United States.

Reservations are a must, and planning several months ahead is essential. If for some reason the van does not arrive at the appointed time, you can tell the driver of any cab you are a Rancho La Puerta guest and he will take you to the Mexican border, which is about an hour's drive. The American taxi must stop at the border; there you are on your own to engage a Mexican taxi to take you the remaining few miles to the ranch. Neither taxi will charge you anything—they will be paid by The Ranch.

SUMMARY

Rancho La Puerta is a favorite of young professional people or anyone who is busy and interested in feeling more fit. It draws guests from all over the United States, many from Chicago and New York City. Nearly everyone there is fairly fit to begin with, but a wide range of classes is offered for people on any fitness level.

Guests need to supply their own discipline because there is no coddling here; independent types will love the ability to create their own daily schedule from many choices of activities.

The Ranch is a large spa and can handle more than one hundred guests. The grounds are so vast and so well laid out, however, that you never feel crowded. The setting is exhilarating yet serene; the staff dedicated and gracious.

FACT SUMMARY

NAME: Rancho La Puerta

MAILING ADDRESS: Tecate, CA 92080

TELEPHONE: (714) 478-5341

TRANSPORTATION: Spa van will pick up in San Diego at airport

ACCOMMODATIONS: Single, double, triple, some with wood-burning fireplaces, many with private patios; cozy, rustic; several family accommodations

FEE: 7-day plan—double, $600 per person; beauty services extra

MAXIMUM NUMBER OF GUESTS: 110

MAXIMUM NUMBER OF STAFF: 100

SEASON: Year-round

AMBIANCE: Relaxed, unpretentious rustic atmosphere, on 150 acres of rolling countryside in dry climate

GENDER AND AGE RESTRICTIONS: Coed; children under 14 not encouraged

DIET: Vegetarian with eggs and cheese; fresh fish twice weekly; buffet-style service; dinner is family style on an honor system; 24-hour optional fast; 800- to 1,000-calorie plans

FACILITIES: Indoor and outdoor gyms, 3 outdoor pools, 2 whirlpools, 3 saunas, 6 tennis courts, putting greens, hiking trails, 2-mile fitness parcourse, massage rooms, new beauty center for facials, massages, herbal wraps

PROGRAM: For active outdoor people, moderate to vigorous, permissive; classes in yoga, jazz exercise, body awareness, calisthenics, pool exercise, body conditioning and stretch and posture

SPECIAL FEATURES: Evening lectures on reflexology, travel, etc., craft classes, movies

244

LOCAL ATTRACTIONS: Tecate, a Mexican border town for shopping; San Diego offers a zoo, Sea World, The San Diego Wild Animal Park and Balboa Park

Ixtapan Health and Beauty Institute

Evidently Mexican emperors had bad days just like the rest of us; and when the best-known emperor of all, Montezuma, had a particularly dismal period after a battle with unfriendly Indians during the sixteenth century, he would gather up his entourage and soldiers and they would trek over the mountains to a beautiful lush valley where warm springs flowed and flowers bloomed in profusion. Here they would rest and recuperate until they revived themselves.

Over the next two hundred years the word spread and the area now known as Ixtapan de Sal became famous for its healing waters. In 1850 the first bathhouse was constructed by (surprise) an Italian, and it functioned until 1910, when it closed because of the revolution.

The resort was revived in 1930 and later a new owner expanded it into a resort extravaganza of lakes, pools, islands and fountains. Both Mexicans and Americans are attracted to this spa to "take the waters" and tone up in the programs Ixtapan offers for men and women.

ACCOMMODATIONS

You can stay either in the hotel or in one of the fifty-eight private chalets located throughout the grounds. The hotel rooms vary from a simple room with bath to more elaborate suites with two bedrooms, two baths and a terrace. Decor is hotel modern, with imitation wood paneling and flowered bedspreads. The chalets are a little roomier, but decorated in a similar way.

FACILITIES

As you enter the hotel grounds you will notice the quiet—no cars are allowed—enhancing the Garden of Eden atmosphere provided by the palm trees and the colorful, meticulously kept beds of flowers. Here is a courtyard that has a blue and white carriage at its center, surrounded by pots of flowers, and beyond it are several of the fountains for which Ixtapan is famous.

If you have trouble remembering Mexican history, Ixtapan offers a painless refresher course in a unique fashion. There are more than 15 fountains with 150 mosaic murals that tell the story of Mexican history and popular legend. Obviously these are no ordinary fountains; they are three-dimensional constructions that would dazzle Disney.

In one, entitled "In Quest of a Country," the fountain includes three large rapids and several small ones, where the water drops for 130 feet then runs a 500-foot course that passes several bridges, tunnels and monoliths, depicting the hardships and obstacles encountered by the Aztecs during their long journey in quest of a country.

Set apart from the hotel grounds, in the Parque de las Lagos, are thirteen lakes, each flowing into the next. Some are for swimming, some for boating and some simply for scenery. Thirty acres of perfectly tended gardens surround the lakes, and a water toboggan slide snakes its way for 500 feet through part of the grounds. There are also tennis courts, a golf course, miniature golf and a children's playground in this area. Just when you think you can't stand another picturesque vista, you'll notice the stream that winds its way under clumps of palms, charming footbridges crossing it at convenient points.

Near the Parque de las Lagos and just outside the main resort grounds is the heart of Ixtapan, its *balneario*, or bathhouse. It's hard to see at first, as the front of the *balneario* is unassuming and covered with lush vines. Through its doors guests find two large mineral pools (one indoor and one outside) filled with the sulphurous waters, which give the area a musty odor. The Roman baths are also in this building.

Inside the hotel itself, the decor reminds one of Miami Beach hotels of twenty years ago; flocked wallpaper and figured carpets set the tone. There are all the usual amenities you expect from a large hotel plus a few extras: it has a movie theater, library, several large sitting rooms, two restaurants and a cocktail lounge, solarium and a discotheque.

On the fifth floor of the hotel are the facilities especially for spa guests: exercise rooms, a gymnasium, and facial and massage rooms. Guest room accommodations are also on this floor.

PROGRAM

The spa program begins on Monday morning and runs until Saturday noon. It starts with a medical check-up with the resident physician; then a staff member meets with you to design your program of diet, exercise and beauty treatments.

On a typical day, breakfast is served in bed at 8:15 A.M. At 9:00 you will join other spa-goers for a fifty-minute class in rhythmic gymnastics in the sunlit gymnasium. Nothing too strenuous happens in this class; it's mostly aimed at limbering up unused muscles. At 10:00 A.M. a pool class is held in one of Ixtapan's mineral water swimming pools.

At 10:45 a consommé break refreshes you for the taxing experience of having a massage, which follows at 11:15 A.M. At noon a Supernumectron, or cellulite, massage treatment is scheduled followed by lunch at 1:00 P.M. Following the civilized Mexican custom of having a siesta at midday, you are on your own until 3:00 P.M. so that you can sunbathe, nap, go for a walk or simply rest. At 3:00 it's time for a fascinating facial using a fresh fruit or vegetable pack such as apple, butter and honey, spinach juice or avocado. This is followed by a daily hair treatment such as a vitamin or oil pack, and a nail treatment for both hands and feet.

After a quick juice break, it's time for a mineral bath in one of the Roman pools. For this you wrap yourself in a robe and walk over to the *balneario*, going through the door and past the large mineral pools to a long hallway that ends at a reception area studded with Art Deco statuary.

An attendant takes you to a private room with the name of a famous French femme fatale such as Madame du Barry or Madame Pompadour on the door. The room is designed with glistening tile, gilded mirrors and marble columns. You disrobe and sink into the marble tub, which is fast being filled with opaque water. After a good soak you will be grateful for the freshly made single bed in the anteroom so that you can rest and gather strength before returning to your room to dress for dinner.

There are many other activities available for the energetic guest. Horseback riding is available free to spa guests, and once a day a train on a small-gauge track takes guests on a tour around the grounds. An old-fashioned horse-drawn carriage is available once at a set time each day as well. Reservations must be made for these in advance at the front desk.

FOOD AND DIET

The food plan is based on 800 calories per day. The philosophy here is to detoxify the body by eliminating excessive amounts of red meat and carbohydrates from the diet.

Meals make extensive use of fresh fruits and vegetables, chicken and fish. Salt is used, but sugar is avoided.

Breakfast is usually fruit and toast in your room; lunch is often a salad, broiled fish, a vegetable and fruit. (It is perfectly safe to eat fresh fruits and vegetables in Ixtapan de Sal.) Dinner is usually a salad, a simple chicken or fish entree and fruit for dessert. You can choose to eat your spa meal in the spa dining room or the larger hotel dining room. A 500-calorie diet is also available; check with the doctor on your arrival and he will advise you whether it is a good idea for you personally.

HEALTH AND BEAUTY SERVICES

Beauty services include hair and scalp treatments, steam baths, body massages, facials and mineral baths; all are included in the spa fee. All beauty services are given in the fifth-floor spa area. The massages are excellent, and the facials use a natural line of products made in France.

OTHER PLEASURES

On Saturday and Sunday all guests go off the diet plan and eat in the hotel dining room. The spa director schedules an optional trip to Taxco for Saturday, where you can get good buys on authentic crafts of the region. A multilingual guide goes with each group so you will not have a problem with language.

Closer to the spa, the picturesque town of Ixtapan is a small, clean village built around a *mercado* (market) and a stately Catholic church. Stores are closed during the week but open on Thursday to cater to weekend resort guests.

Several times a week in the evening pageants and dance performances are presented by staff dressed in colorful Mexican costumes. The setting for these folklore ballet extravaganzas is often one of the remarkable fountains backed by a mosaic tile mural. The night is filled with live Mexican music.

You see groups of energetic costumed dancers against the flood-lit historical mural as they dance in and out of the spray of the fountains. It is a sight you should not miss.

The spa also offers free movies every night in the theater on the grounds. On weekends they have dancing in the nightclub, Leotica.

WHAT TO BRING

Robes, slippers and exercise suits are provided. Bring a bathing suit and leotards for the exercise program.

In the public areas, resort wear is acceptable; pants or shorts and tops are fine. Bring a dress or dressy pants outfit for the evening.

Men will need shorts and T-shirts for exercise, slacks and sports shirts for day and a sports jacket for dinner and evening programs.

HOW TO GET THERE

Ixtapan de Sal is southwest of Mexico City. Fly into Mexico City and rent a car (or take the spa limousine from the Ixtapan building on Paseo de la Reforma, Mexico City, at 9:00 A.M. any day) to Ixtapan de Sal. The spa is about an hour's drive via Route 55, on mountain roads that pass the towering volcano at Toluca. When you make your spa reservation be sure to make a limousine reservation at the same time if you plan to take advantage of this service.

SUMMARY

Ixtapan Health and Beauty Institute is a jewel of a resort, known as Mexico's finest mineral springs retreat. Although deep enough into the country to be truly Mexican in flavor, visitors from the States will be happy to know all the staff members speak English, and that, in fact, most guests are fellow Americans. The spa attracts an older affluent group during the week, with younger guests arriving for weekends.

This is a supremely romantic setting—a nice place to retreat with a special friend. The staff is professional and gracious, and the reasonable price makes it a good winter spa choice, even counting the airfare.

FACT SUMMARY

NAME: Ixtapan Health and Beauty Institute

MAILING ADDRESS: Hotel Ixtapan, Paseo de la Reforma, 132, Mexico City 6, D.F., Mexico

TELEPHONE: (905) 535-7622 or 535-2553

TRANSPORTATION: Spa limo will pick up in Mexico City at Ixtapan building

ACCOMMODATIONS: Hotel rooms or private chalets

FEE: $42.50 to $62.50 per person, per day, double (American plan)

MAXIMUM NUMBER OF GUESTS: Hotel, 500; spa, 50

MAXIMUM NUMBER OF STAFF: Hotel, 250; spa, 20

SEASON: Year-round

AMBIANCE: An extravaganza of lakes, pools and fountains

GENDER AND AGE RESTRICTIONS: None

DIET: 800 calories a day; fresh fruit, vegetables, chicken, fish

FACILITIES: *Balneario*, several hot pools, private mineral baths, acres of gardens, lakes, horseback riding, exercise rooms, sauna, steam, nightclub, movie theater

PROGRAM: Variety of exercise classes including rhythmic gymnastics, walking, water exercise, massages, facials, hair treatments

SPECIAL FEATURES: Mariachi bands, horse-drawn buggy, staff dance performances

LOCAL ATTRACTIONS: Shopping in Taxco for silver, museums and Indian market at Toluca, murals and fountains on the hotel grounds

Other Spas

Rio Caliente

This is a meditation and yoga retreat near Guadalajara, Mexico, featuring hot pools and waterfalls in a secluded jungle setting. Natural foods are served. Special week-long yoga workshops are offered several times a year.

FACT SUMMARY

MAILING ADDRESS: (For reservations) 1307 South Buena Vista, Pacific Grove, CA 93950

TELEPHONE: (408) 646-9375

TRAVEL DIRECTIONS: Maps and directions on request at time of reservations

TRANSPORTATION: Fly into Guadalajara, rent car to drive to Rio Caliente

ACCOMMODATIONS: Comfortable single and double rooms with shower or bathtub, U.S. electrical current

FEE: Single, $41 per day; double, $35 per person, per day (price includes all spa facilities plus meals; tuition for special sessions range from $395 to $495 for each 8-day seminar)

MAXIMUM NUMBER OF GUESTS: 50

MAXIMUM NUMBER OF STAFF: 20

SEASON: Year-round excluding May and June

AMBIANCE: Relaxing atmosphere in a simple, comfortable and informal facility

GENDER AND AGE RESTRICTIONS: Adults over 16; coed

DIET: Vegetarian meals served buffet style, fruits and vegetables grown organically in spa's gardens or nearby orchards and farms—tropical fruits such as mango, papaya, pineapple and zapote abound; soups, casseroles, cheese, fresh vegetable and fruit juices, eggs, homemade breads, etc.

FACILITIES: Hot baths, swimming pool, volcanic steam room, horseback riding, hiking, 104-degree waterfall, body massage, herbal wraps, manicures and pedicures

PROGRAM: Daily yoga and pool exercise classes; guided hikes

SPECIAL FEATURES: Top-name instructors in the health, awareness and spiritual fields present a total of 4 hours of class instruction each day

LOCAL ATTRACTIONS: Located in the center of one of Mexico's-largest national forests; daily sight-seeing trips to Guadalajara and the surrounding points of interest

Hotel Spa
San Jose Purua

The Hotel Spa San Jose Purua is located 115 miles from Mexico City in the picturesque Tarascan Indian country in Michoacán. Surrounded by mountains, the hotel is located in a valley that offers a semitropical climate year-round and a natural spring of thermal water. There is no diet plan, but all food is fresh and well prepared.

FACT SUMMARY

MAILING ADDRESS: P. O. Box 46, Zitácuaro, Michoacán, Mexico

TELEPHONE: 3-14-55 Zitácuaro, Michoacán; Special number 3-15-44

TRAVEL DIRECTIONS: Kilometer 182, Road 15, Jungapeo, Michoacán

TRANSPORTATION: Daily limo service to spa, leaving from Hotel

Purua-Hidalgo in Mexico City, located on Colon 27 and Paseo de la Reforma, telephone 585-43-44, $40 per person, round trip

ACCOMMODATIONS: Hotel-like rooms, many with balconies; also chalets

FEE: Depending on accommodations: Single, $72 to $87 per person; double, $51 to $66 per person (plus 10 percent tax)

MAXIMUM NUMBER OF GUESTS: 500

MAXIMUM NUMBER OF STAFF: 300

SEASON: Year-round

AMBIANCE: Lovely gardens, close to river, tropical vegetation surrounded by mountains

GENDER AND AGE RESTRICTIONS: None

DIET: Mexican and international cuisine; most food grown on the spa's nearby ranch

FACILITIES: Swimming pools, facial massages, movies, bars, thermal water, baths, body massages, mini-golf, horseback riding, games, tennis

PROGRAM: Very informal, no organized exercise program; hiking, swimming, golf, horseback riding and tennis, at guest's own pace

SPECIAL FEATURES: Thermal water baths from a natural spring

LOCAL ATTRACTIONS: Morelia, the state capital of Michoacán; Lake Pátzcuaro; archaeological diggings in San Felipe de las Alzate.

CANADA

The Harrison

It was a cold winter day in 1858 when gold prospectors left the British Columbia interior to seek fresh provisions. Making their way in an Indian canoe down the deep and icy Harrison Lake, the miners decided to make camp for the night on the lake's heavily wooded bank.

Just as they were about to land, one of the men lost his balance and was pitched into the dark water. As his companions peered over the bow in horror, what would have been a fatal tragedy in most of Harrison's icy waters ended in a happy surprise for the miner. "It's warm!" he cried. "The water's warm!"

It certainly was. And is. The natural mineral hot springs that bubble up near the sleepy village of Harrison Hot Springs on the southern shore of the lake still maintain a constant 165 degrees Fahrenheit.

In 1885 the first hotel, the St. Alice, was built at the site of the springs. After it was destroyed by fire in 1920, a new hotel opened in 1926 as the Harrison Hot Springs Hotel, now shortened to the Harrison. This venerable British Columbia institution has been operating continually ever since, on 700 acres of densely wooded grounds.

The natural setting is more stunning than any scene in a Nelson Eddy–Jeanette MacDonald movie. The startling blue of the lake stretches as far as your eye can see, surrounded by lush primeval-looking forests on the ragged shoreline and framed by high blue-gray ranges of the Cascade mountains, known also as the Coast Mountains.

The hotel sits right on the edge of the lake. Sailboats and yachts at the dock create a double reflected image in the clear mirrored surface of the lake. The air is incredibly fresh and pine-scented. The hotel grounds stretch back from the lake's edge, and include flower gardens, picturesque walking bridges and streams that run down to feed the lake.

This area is the home of the legendary Sasquatch, or Big Foot, which was originally "sighted" only two miles away in 1927. The resort is quite safe and secure from the world, although you might sneak a look over your shoulder from time to time if you hear any heavy shuffling behind you when you're out walking in the woods.

Though not in every sense a health and fitness resort as we

know them in the United States—it has no structured exercise or dietary program—the Harrison, very much like a European health spa, focuses on "taking the waters" with the whole family in a beautiful natural setting.

Years ago the main clientele of the Harrison was, as one local wit put it, "the nearly dead and the newly wed," who sought peace and solitude equally, but for presumably widely divergent reasons.

In the last ten years, however, the crowd has become more varied and now includes young singles and couples, and families with children of all ages, many of whom have been coming for an annual holiday for thirty years. One thing returning guests can count on is seeing familiar faces. Of the 300-plus members on the staff, almost half have been with the resort more than five years and many are twenty-and thirty-year veterans. Naturally they come to know and remember guests from year to year. Delightful rolling accents and the can-do attitude of the Scottish, British and Canadian staff make the place more amiable than most hotels its size. When asked if it was possible to make a small change in schedule, the moustachioed assistant manager smacked his hand smartly on the counter and said, "*Anything's* possible at the *Harrison*, mum."

ACCOMMODATIONS

There is wide variety in room accommodations, both in cost and decor. The rooms and suites in the original main hotel have a slightly Victorian flavor, with dark wood reproduction furniture (usually including a bed, chest and a small writing desk) and etchings in quaint groups over the bed. Curtains and bedspreads are done in soft blues and greens—in general the sort of ambiance one would find in a favorite aunt's guest room. Each room has its own bath. A two-story lodge building near the main hotel offers similar rooms, but rates are cheaper, presumably to make up for the twenty-foot walk from the hotel proper.

The six-story tower offers rooms and suites that are a little larger, decorated in pleasant hotel modern. Most of these rooms have balconies that look out on the lake. There are no televisions in the rooms so that guests can better remove themselves from the real world. There is, however, piped-in muzak, so be sure to turn the switch to "off" before retiring or you will be awakened by what sounds like moonlighting members of the Mormon Tabernacle Choir in an exercise in audio banality. There are also great dressing areas in these rooms, ample closets and telephones.

For those who like more rustic accommodations, there are one- and two-bedroom bungalows with pine-paneled interiors and comfortable furniture. They are arranged on the grounds between flower beds and shaded by tall Scotch pines and red maples.

FACILITIES

The Harrison is a vaguely pleasing hodgepodge of architectural styles.

The original red brick main hotel section with its slightly Norman flavor is now flanked by a modern tower and west wing and a separate cozy lodge building. A group of simple but appealing wood bungalows sit behind the main hotel.

Furniture is somewhat ordinary "hotel eclectic" and is neither in period nor modern design; this is not an elegant hotel in decor, but then it's not depressing either—"comfortable" is probably the best word for it.

If you are staying in the main hotel, you may be surprised when the elevator door opens at the ground-floor level to reveal assorted guests in their bathrobes and slippers, a look of pleasant anticipation on their faces. They are not on their way to the health pavilion for a dip in the hot mineral pools. The pavilion is an attractive round stone structure lit by a high central skylight and made curiously ceremonial by the native carved totem poles and stone carvings around its walls.

The centerpiece is a twenty-foot round pool filled with the sulphurous waters for which the place is famous. The temperature in this "hot pool" is kept at 104 degrees.

A few feet away is a crescent-shaped "warm" pool maintained at a slightly cooler 95 degrees; and for the hardy souls who want to complete the cycle, there is a large "cold" pool outdoors a few steps from the pavilion (it can seem like miles!).

One section of the curved pavilion wall is solid windows, which give a sort of CinemaScopic view of the lush green forest that edges the property. It's particularly satisfying to sit in the hot pool and watch the rain, which, when it comes, is usually not a timid sprinkle but that vigorous, no-holds-barred downpour that the Pacific Northwest is famous for and which makes anyone safe inside feel very snug indeed.

The enormous main hotel is connected to the newer wings by what seems like miles of corridors that lead up and down to various floor levels, and which sometimes turn abruptly to lead to another wing. One of these leads to the Copper Room, which is in every sense the heart of the resort. It is a huge high-ceilinged dining room with copper-lined walls and fixtures and furniture covered in soft grays and tans.

All meals are served here and in the evening a band plays for dancing on the enormous dance floor in the center of the room. Closer to the lobby is a large, comfortable cocktail lounge that offers upbeat live "easy listening" entertainment until the early morning, when more than one guest often gets the brilliant idea of taking a dip in the hot pool and goes trudging off with a determined look in the direction of the health pavilion.

In the upper lobby a huge stone fireplace is the focal point for groups of cozy chairs and sofas. At four o'clock every day the silver tea service appears and afternoon tea is served simply but generously with homemade cookies, banana-nut bread and plenty of strong dark tea.

There is the requisite gift and sundries shop off the lower lobby near the check-in desk, which offers good British china and a remarkable selection of books from D. H. Lawrence to Judith Krantz along with the usual necessities. Across the hall is a fashion boutique that features expensive and elegant clothes, mostly for women, although there are a few casual wool sweaters for men. Whatever you buy, keep in mind that the American dollar buys more in Canada (the rate of exchange is 16 percent, which means that $1 American equals $1.16 in Canadian money), so remember things will cost somewhat less than the first glance at the price tag tells you.

For the evening when you are feeling a need for something a little more rowdy and convivial than the elegant Copper Room, you can step across the parking lot to the Good Queen Bess Pub, which is thoroughly Tudor in flavor and attracts younger guests as well as local types.

PROGRAM

Although there is no structured exercise program at the Harrison, there are plenty of options from which you can build your own fitness schedule if you are serious about it and can use self-discipline.

Miles of well-marked paths surround the lake; one leads past the original hot springs, which steam constantly. Walkers or joggers can also explore the village of Harrison Hot Springs with its small shops, simple wooden houses and surprising variety of ethnic restaurants. Bikes can be rented at the hotel for a jaunt to the local provincial parks or a visit to neighboring lakes.

There are tennis courts located on the grounds, and the old curling rink has been rebuilt as a pickle ball court on which one can play a game with a wooden racket that has holes in it. When you get over feeling silly swatting the air with it, the game is easy to learn. A nine-hole championship golf course is also nearby; it is well designed with many challenging holes.

If you still need vigorous exercise, you can swim laps in the heated outdoor pool or climb up the nearby mountain. Twice a week the mail boat stops at the Harrison and you can ride along as it chugs up the lake to deliveries along its perimeter. The boat's captain, Jack Sterling, used to tow logs down the lake to the mills, and he knows lots of entertaining stories about the history of the lake and its neighbors, including the Indian population at the north end of the lake. The trip takes about six hours.

If solitary activities on the lake are more your style, you can rent a motor boat or sailboat and go fishing for rainbow trout or spring salmon. The even more adventurous can rent equipment for windsurfing.

After exercise, you can always trot over to the health pavilion and sink with relief into the warm or hot pools. Surprisingly, it's a very sociable location and you are likely to meet people there who will later become your good friends.

During the summer and on holidays, a lively program of activities is planned for children. Sand castle contests, boat rides, crafts and nature outings are offered under the competent supervision of a college-aged director.

This comes as a real boon to single parents. One single father, who had custody of his children for a few weeks out of the year, remembers being terrified of what to do with them on their first custody visit. His answer was to bring them to the Harrison; during part of the day they were entertained and met new friends in the children's program, and there was still plenty they could do together as a family throughout the day and evening. "It really took the strain off that first few days," he said with obvious relief. Children are not the only ones to be "organized." Everyone booked into a single room at the Harrison over a holiday weekend receives a discreet invitation to join a table of "single-roomers" for drinks and a festive dinner at a special table.

The best program of all is found nightly in the Copper Room. A band, known as "Charlie and Mary's Band," has been playing in the Copper Room for thirty years, and to sit and watch people of all ages and descriptions dance to this antique foursome (*two* saxophones, a piano and drums) is to marvel at the variety suggested by the term "romance."

A typical evening we spent was no exception: near us was a slick cosmopolitan couple alternating between affecting bored sophistication and exchanging yearning glances with each other. Farther out on the dance floor a couple in their sixties, she in a proper black dress, hair in a tidy bun, and he wearing a plaid suit, red suspenders, and tennis shoes, danced with practiced grace. In between were innocent-looking young couples (possible honeymooners) and crowds of respectable middle-aged couples delighting in the romantic music and their recent lessons from Arthur Murray.

Dancing to "Charlie and Mary" is an emotional touchstone critical to a successful stay, as the management has learned the hard way. Now, to prevent irate customers, the reservation staff always warn people when Charlie and Mary will be on vacation. Needless to say reservations dip during those periods.

FOOD AND DIET

The food is good here, but don't expect to diet on the selection offered. People come here more to indulge than deny themselves.

Breakfast and lunch are what you might expect in any large resort hotel; quality food is served, but the menu is standard and lacks imagination. Eggs, hash or pancakes for breakfast, sandwiches and a daily special for lunch are about the limit.

Dinner at the Copper Room is, however, another matter. From the maître d' to the menu, the place is definitely first class. Linens, silver, china and crystal are combined to create an elegant understated effect and the service, in the French style, is professional but never showy or bombastic. An example of this is the story the staff tells about Ivan, a perennial favorite waiter who, upon observing that a flambé pan had fallen to the floor in full torch, setting fire to the carpet, immediately flipped the pan over and nonchalantly returned to serving the salad course as he discreetly stamped out the flames with one foot.

You can start a meal with smoked salmon, escargot or pâté, move on to a salad and then choose from entrees such as prime rib or fresh salmon. Everything is à la carte. The wine selection is excellent, with wines from France, California, New Zealand and even Washington State to choose from. There are plenty of rich desserts from the Harrison's bakery and you can finish with cheese cake, Bavarian cake or parfaits.

HEALTH AND BEAUTY SERVICES

Good Swedish-type massage is offered for men and women in the health pavilion, and individual small Roman pools are provided for those who want to enjoy the sulphured waters in privacy. There is also a beauty salon on the premises, providing the usual resort hair and nail care. Fees for beauty and health services are separate but can be charged to your room.

OTHER PLEASURES

Special weekends are planned throughout the year. The Bavarian Fun Fest is a sort of Oktoberfest in December complete with lederhosen-clad staff *und die Fräulein*. There are costume prizes for these theme weekends and many guests dress up to get in the spirit. In January, the Robbie Burns Weekend features Scottish food, bagpipes and the whisper of tartans and tweeds brushing by in the halls. Valentine weekend is, as you might guess, also a favorite. Within an hour or so of the Harrison are a children's farm and museum, beautiful public gardens, the Hemlock Valley ski area and a tram ride over Hell's Gate, an incredibly deep canyon through which the Fraser River churns and roars. This is where two million sockeye salmon pass each year on their way to inland spawning grounds, where you can visit fish hatcheries.

WHAT TO BRING

You'll need outdoor clothes—jeans, hiking shoes, warm sweaters and jackets for cool evenings are a must. Bring rain gear too, as it rains a lot in this area at the most surprising moments.

For hotel wear, dress is informal in the public rooms and cocktail lounge but you will need more formal wear in the elegant Copper Room in the evenings. Short or long dresses are appropriate, jackets and ties for men. Since the pools are coed you'll need a swimsuit or two.

HOW TO GET THERE

You can fly into Vancouver, rent a car and drive the four-lane Trans Canada Highway (Highway 1) through rich, mountain-rimmed pasture lands dotted with large green barns. Take the Agassiz-Harrison turnoff beyond Chilliwack. The trip is about 129 kilometers or 80 miles from downtown Vancouver. It is also possible to take the scenic Sasquatch Drive (Highway 7) on the north side of the Fraser River to Harrison Hot Springs.

If you love trains you might want to take the Canadian Pacific Railway (C P Rail) to Agassiz, then taxi to the hotel. If money is no object, charter a seaplane wherever you choose; the Harrison offers seaplane landing facilities right in front of the hotel for anyone who enjoys making a dramatic entrance.

SUMMARY

The Harrison is a good place to escape from urban internal and external pressures. A couple of any age can retreat comfortably here, and children are welcomed and well cared for. Although it's not likely you'll lose weight here, you can certainly expect to return to the real world rested and relaxed simply from the terrific natural setting and marvelous cleansing fresh air. There is enough access to a variety of sports and activities so that family members can all feel happily entertained, and the staff members really extend themselves, since they fully expect to see you return. Since so many guests do, it's clear the Harrison does something right.

FACT SUMMARY

NAME: The Harrison

MAILING ADDRESS: Harrison Hot Springs, British Columbia, Canada

TELEPHONE: (604) 796-2244

ACCOMMODATIONS: Rooms and suites in main hotel, cottages, simple rooms in lodge

FEE: Hotel room rates range from $50 to $110 per night, depending on accommodations, which includes use of all facilities. (This is in Canadian dollars.)

MAXIMUM NUMBER OF GUESTS: 500

MAXIMUM NUMBER OF STAFF: 300

SEASON: Year-round

AMBIANCE: Self-contained resort in lake and mountain setting—family vacation spot

GENDER AND AGE RESTRICTIONS: None

DIET: No special diet available

FACILITIES: Health pavilion, hot mineral pools, Roman baths, whirlpools, massages, elegant dining room, boutique, pub, cocktail lounge, beauty salon

PROGRAM: Seasonal programs at holidays; many sports available

SPECIAL FEATURES: 2 hot mineral (sulphur) pools, water skiing, golf, curling, skating, seaplane landing

LOCAL ATTRACTIONS: Hemlock Valley ski area, salmon hatcheries, tram ride over Hell's Gate canyon

THE WEST
INDIES

The Deepdene Health
and Beauty Studios

The Deepdene Health and Beauty Studios are located on Harrington Sound, five minutes from Hamilton, one of the picture-perfect villages of Bermuda. This English-managed spa has offered an almost endless number of European health and beauty treatments for women long before they were popularized in the rest of North America.

FACT SUMMARY

MAILING ADDRESS: c/o Bersalon Company, P. O. Box 235, Flatts, Smiths Parish 3, Bermuda

TELEPHONE: (809) 292-8570

TRAVEL DIRECTIONS: Fly into Bermuda airport; transportation available to spa by taxi and coach, or else airport limos available with prior arrangement

ACCOMMODATIONS: At Palmetto Bay Hotel, Smiths Parish; Coral Island Hotel, Smiths Parish—both of these facilities are within easy walking distance of Deepdene Studios; also at Pink Beach Cottage Colony and Castle Harbour Hotel, Golf and Tennis Club, both 10 minutes away by taxi

FEE: The rate for a 7-day, 6-night stay is as follows: *Program No. 1 "Slimming in Luxury"*—single, $991.00; double, $721.00 per person; *Program No. 2 "Health and Beauty"*—single, $1040.00; double, $770.00 per person. All guests stay in the Palmetto Bay Hotel. All beauty and spa plans may be reserved without evening meals. Deduct $5.00 per person daily. Add 5 percent hotel tax to hotel room rate. Gratuities for hotel staff are added to the above rates for your convenience at a rate of $4.50 per person per day on MAP and $3.50 per day on the Bermuda plan (breakfast only). Gratuities for spa staff will also be added—Plan No. 1, $60.20; Plan No. 2, $68.40.

MAXIMUM NUMBER OF GUESTS: 15

MAXIMUM NUMBER OF STAFF: 16

SEASON: Year-round

AMBIANCE: Old manor house, garden setting, with European-trained beauty therapists, hairstylists and health instructors

GENDER AND AGE RESTRICTIONS: Women only

DIET: No special diet menus at accommodations, dietary counseling is included in the program

FACILITIES: Sauna and whirlpool; dancercise, yoga, exercise, jazz and tap-dancing classes; manual and mechanical massage; therapeutic paraffin wax baths; infrared massage; European hairstyling salon

PROGRAM: Tailored to your needs based on the following two programs—Slimming in Luxury and Health and Beauty; both stress exercise and massage; Health and Beauty option includes more beauty services

SPECIAL FEATURES: Cathiodermie facials; successful "inch loss" program

LOCAL ATTRACTIONS: International shopping facilities, historic buildings, beautiful beaches, taxi tours, nearby golf, tennis, swimming, water sports

GLOSSARY
AND
INDEX

Glossary

Acupressure A light massage in which pressure is applied by the fingers to "energy points" or "meridians" in the body to release muscle tension.

Aerobic exercise Vigorous exercise that raises the pulse rate sufficiently to strengthen the heart. Special aerobic activities are aerobic dancing, jogging, jumping rope and swimming.

Aromatherapy Oils from plants and flowers, such as rosemary, lavender, eucalyptus or pine are massaged into the skin in order to treat specific skin problems.

Balneology The science of the application of mineral waters for their healing powers.

Behavior modification The application of principles of learning to change personal habits, including careful repetition of the desired behaviors.

Biofeedback A technique by which one can learn conscious control of biological processes by means of monitoring one's physical responses. This is usually accomplished by placing an electronic sensing device on the skin; changes in temperature and chemistry of the skin's surface then reflect internal changes. Through this method one can learn to control physical functions formerly thought to be involuntary, such as blood pressure, pulse rate, digestion and deep muscle tension.

Calipers A device to measure skin fold, determining the percent of fat in the body.

Cathartic A laxative; usually from a natural or organic compound.

Collagen The main organic constituent in animal connective tissue and bone, produced in gelatin form by boiling. An important ingredient in many natural cosmetics.

Colonic irrigation A water enema high in the colon.

Fango therapy A vitamin-enriched volcanic mud coating

or pack applied to a localized area for athletic injuries, strained ligaments or arthritic pain.

Fasting Abstinence from food or drink or both. Fasts vary from simply water to juices, nuts and seeds.

Herbal wrap Hot wet linens infused with herbs are wrapped around the body, then covered with a plastic sheet to retain the heat. A cool compress is applied to the forehead. Purpose of the treatment is to eliminate toxins through the skin and promote muscle relaxation.

Herbology The study of herbs for therapeutic use.

Holistic health Health care that focuses on integration of mental, physical, emotional and spiritual aspects of a person.

Holistic nutrition A nutritional philosophy based on the concept that food is a natural medicine and that the body only needs whole foods to remain healthy.

Homeopathy A healing system based on the premise that a remedy can cure a disease if it produces symptoms similar to those of the disease in a healthy organism.

Hydrotherapy Treatment of a condition with externally applied water; examples are whirlpool and mineral baths.

Inhalation room A wood-paneled room filled with hot vapors, often augmented with eucalyptus oil, inhaled to relieve respiratory congestion.

Iridology A science by which a doctor or practitioner can tell, from the markings or signs in the iris of the eye, the condition of various organs in the body.

Kinesiology A system to restore the structural, mental and chemical balance of the body through testing and strengthening weak muscles, stimulation of meridian points and diet.

Kneipp cure A variety of hydrotherapy treatments developed in the nineteenth century by Father Sebastian Kneipp; the best known is the herbal wrap.

Massage Manipulation of skin, muscle and joints (usually by hand) to relax muscle spasm, relieve tension, improve circulation, hasten elimination of wastes. It also stretches connective tissue and improves circulation.

Mineral waters Water (any temperature) containing mineral salts or gases.

Naturopathy A system of healing that seeks to promote health by the use of natural agents.

Pedicure A manicure of the feet that includes soaking feet in warm soapy water and removing dry skin with a pumice stone or a special razor, includes also a foot and leg massage and concludes with polishing of the nails.

Polarity therapy Balancing the energy in the body by gentle massage, meditation, proper attitude, exercise and diet supervised by a polarity practitioner.

Rebirthing An extension of yogic breathing technique that allows total relaxation and clearing of the mind of nonsupportive thought patterns. Sometimes includes reliving the birth experience.

Reflexology A massage of the feet where pressure points that correspond to certain organs are stimulated on different parts of the foot. The purpose is to "clear impurities" by stimulating circulation to these organs and reducing stress.

Rolfing A technique for reordering the body so that major segments (head, shoulders, palms, legs) are pulled to lengthen the body and allow for balance between the left and right sides of the body. Involves deep pressure, is thought to have psychological benefits as well as physical.

Salt rub or salt glow A treatment involving warm almond or avocado oil, which is blended with sea salt and applied to the body to remove dead skin. The mixture is left on for several minutes for skin to absorb oils, then is rinsed off using soap and a natural sponge.

Sauna A wood-lined room heated with dry heat from 160 to 210 degrees Fahrenheit. Levels of wooden benches are provided for reclining. Usually entered in the nude (remove jewelry), always follow with a cool shower. The purpose is to cleanse the body by sweating out impurities.

Scotch hose An invigorating shower that tones circulation by contracting then dilating capillaries as water from multiple nozzles is turned quickly from hot to cold to hot for several seconds at a time.

Skin mask or masque A preparation usually applied to the face and neck to stimulate local circulation, tone, cleanse and tighten pores and remove dry skin. Ingredients are varied to accommodate specific needs of one's skin type and condition.

Steam room A ceramic-tiled room heated with steam at temperatures from 110 to 180 degrees Fahrenheit. The purpose is to soften skin, cleanse pores, calm the nervous system and soothe tension.

Tai chi Traditional Oriental discipline intended to unite body and mind through carefully practiced movements that take on aspects of meditation.

Thalassotherapy Use of seawater and sea air to treat a disease; living near the sea, bathing in the water and breathing sea air. Also includes use of seawater, seaweed or sea algae in water treatments.

Waxing Warm wax (usually honeycomb wax) or cloth dipped in wax is applied to various parts of the body, including legs, arms, upper lip or brow for removal of unwanted hair. Just as the wax dries the strip is pulled quickly and hair is removed all the way to the roots. Results last for three to six weeks. Can be painful for delicate areas.

Yoga An Oriental discipline based on controlled deep breathing and ritualistic movements or postures that require both physical and mental concentration. Results include physical toning and tension reduction.

Index